Beyond the Good Death

Beyond the Good Death

THE ANTHROPOLOGY OF MODERN DYING

James W. Green

University of Pennsylvania Press

Philadelphia

Published by
University of Pennsylvania Press
Philadelphia, Pennsylvania 19104-4112

Printed in the United States of America on acid-free paper

10   9   8   7   6   5   4   3   2   1

A Cataloging-in-Publication record is available from the Library of Congress

ISBN: 978-0-8122-4042-9

CONTENTS

1 GETTING DEAD

ON A NOVEMBER EVENING IN 1998, a national television audience watched Thomas Youk die at his home in Waterford, Michigan. He did not expect millions to witness his death, but his attending physician thought it was a good idea. Youk actually died several months before the broadcast, but what the audience saw that night on the CBS show *60 Minutes* was not a studio recreation but raw footage of his last breath. At fifty-two, he suffered from amyotrophic lateral sclerosis (ALS), also called Lou Gehrig's disease, in which nerve cells slowly die and muscles atrophy until the heart no longer receives signals from the brain and stops. Like many ALS victims, Youk was lucid but had so little muscular control he feared he would die from choking on his saliva. He and his family were desperate and so contacted a Michigan pathologist with a reputation for assisting in cases like his. Dr. Jack Kevorkian agreed to help.

With over 130 assisted suicides to his credit, Kevorkian was at the height of his notoriety as "Dr. Death." Flaunting that, he brought his videotape of Youk's death to CBS, offering it to Mike Wallace for use on his program. Wallace agreed, and on November 22, Kevorkian narrated the video and explained why he wanted it shown nationally. "Either I go or they go," he said of the prosecutors who for years tried to get homicide convictions from reluctant juries. But Kevorkian's challenge to the courts in the Youk case was different. Previously, Kevorkian's clients activated his "suicide machine" themselves, turning a knob or pulling a handle to start the flow of fatal chemicals. But Youk was paralyzed and could not do that, so Kevorkian personally injected the lethal solution into his client's right arm, which in medicine would be called active euthanasia. Youk died quietly in less than a minute. Weeks later, no arrest had been made, despite the video evidence of what appeared to be a homicide. Kevorkian joked with Wallace about that, asking if the police needed fingerprints. Apparently not. Soon he was arrested, tried for manslaughter, and convicted. A resident of the Lakeland Correctional Facility in southern Michigan, Kevorkian was released in 2007, at age eighty.

Youk's story, and Kevorkian's part in it, is notable beyond the details of his death. Tom's wife said she was relieved that his suffering was finally over, satisfied and appreciative of what Kevorkian had done for them both. A brother described a family at the "end of our rope," with no other options, and fully supportive of Kevorkian's help. The CBS program also featured a Chicago physician, appearing as a professional counterbalance to Kevorkian, who commented in shocked tones how sad it all was, saying that much more could have been done to help Youk in his desperation. Yet Wallace himself did not seem interested in exploring one of the obvious themes of this story—the gap between the Youk family's frustrations and the physician's assurances that help is available for those who ask. Nor did he pursue the question of whether Youk's death qualified as a "good" one, a controversial idea debated in the medical literature and well known to the lay public through popular media over several decades. And beyond his dismay at Kevorkian's enthusiasm for his peculiar cause, Wallace seemed uninterested in why this medical gadfly was a hero to some. That is unfortunate because many 60 Minutes viewers may have had questions about how well the health care system works for people like Youk, what qualifies as a "good death" in an ethical or a religious sense, and how others make hard decisions for themselves and family members when the prospect of a painful death seems unavoidable.

While death is a natural event, in the sense that cells die off and body systems fail, Youk's experience was shaped by medical, demographic, and cultural trends that are new. They include the demographics of mortality, with more of us living longer and dying later from chronic rather than acute diseases; new medical technologies that prolong life but raise questions about its quality, while dying bodies are kept alive with powerful medications and machines; movements within medicine challenging heroic life-prolonging measures and the traditional view that death is the profession's enemy; an emerging international system of organ "harvesting" and transplantation; the institutionalization of hospice and palliative care as newer medical specialties; objections to commercial body handling and disposal and the rise of so-called designer deaths, including ecologically friendly ways of disposing of remains;

the marginalizing of religion and religious authorities and their replacement by secular grief counselors deploying the rhetoric of psychology rather than theology; spontaneous memorialization at the sites of traffic accidents and national calamities; virtual cemeteries on the Internet and on-demand streaming of videotaped funerals; and ballot box rebellions, successful so far only in Oregon, seeking to legalize physician-assisted suicide. In addition, the most catered-to generation in American history, the baby boomers, are confronting the mortality of their elderly parents and beginning to recognize their own temporal limitations. This new cultural context presents death as less hidden, less explicitly religious, and more individualized.

Not too long ago, things were different. The parents and grandparents of today's baby boomers did not talk much about death, and when they did it was in a polite, euphemistic, hushed manner. No one died—they "passed away." Children were usually excluded from those conversations to "protect" them from unpleasantness. The newly bereaved were thought to need more privacy than the rest of us, and what they did in their grief was tightly contained within a closed circle of family members guided by a minister or priest. Nor was death openly discussed with the dying—certainly not by the family and rarely by doctors. Glaser and Strauss (1965) wrote of the decorum of death-bed visitations that typified the 1950s and 1960s. Verbal games of mutual pretense and closed awareness were required of the living as well as the dying; deceit was thought to be a kindness. Some of that has changed, partly due to the polemics of Jessica Mitford (1963), who lampooned the stodgy, occasionally unethical practices of the funeral trade. But more credit goes to Dr. Elisabeth Kübler-Ross (1969), who gave professionals and the public a new language for speaking about death. In plain prose, she redefined death as the last great opportunity for "growth," a time of personal transformation, even triumph. If we talked more about death, she said, it would become less fearful for everyone. Communication was the key. Her famous five steps of dying, "the way of optimum growth and creative living" (1975: 163), became a mantra in American popular culture, although after an initial enthusiasm, they faded from the nursing, pastoral, and social service journals. Promoting the possibility of a "good death," even a heroic one, as replacement for the rhetoric of denial was Kübler-Ross's remarkable achievement. Contemporary popular efforts such as those of Webb (1997) and a host of self-help writers are indebted to Kübler-Ross's perseverance with an idea that was iconoclastic and not universally appreciated when she first proposed it.[1]

Kübler-Ross's approach was the solution to a problem that engaged other critics as well. Anthropologist Geoffrey Gorer (1965), in his classic study of

British death practices, was interested in rituals of mourning, or rather their absence, among men and women of all classes in the UK, a situation he compared to the Victorian banishment of sex from public discussion a century earlier. The same kind of prudery that distanced Victorians from their "natural sexuality," as he called it, now separated moderns from the healthy effects of public mourning, thereby generating a contemporary "pornography of death." Based on extensive interviews, he determined that for many in the UK death had become essentially a private, rather than social, experience. Grief was self-focused, rarely shared with friends, and emotionally constrained out of fear of embarrassing oneself and others. And just like Victorian sex, mourning was hidden, little discussed, and kept from the children. "The natural processes of corruption and decay have become [in the modern view] disgusting. . . . Our great-grandparents were told that babies were found under gooseberry bushes or cabbages; our children are likely to be told that those who have passed on (fie! on the gross Anglo-Saxon monosyllable) are changed into flowers, or lie at rest in lovely gardens. The ugly facts are relentlessly hidden; the art of the embalmers is an art of complete denial" (1965: 196).

Writing about the same time but from a more psychodynamic perspective, Ernest Becker, also an anthropologist, advanced his own thesis about the denial of death. There exists in all of us, he claimed, an innate terror of death, but its beneficent effect is that it is also the mainspring of all human cultures and creativity. *The Denial of Death* (1973) won Becker a Pulitzer Prize for exploring what he called the depth psychology of heroism. We strive to be heroic because that is the only reasonable response to the terrible truth of mortality. We imagine ourselves living in service to a god or laboring to leave a legacy of meritorious works, all in the vain hope that it will open a doorway onto salvation. "It doesn't matter whether the cultural hero-system is frankly magical, religious, and primitive or secular, scientific, and civilized. It is still a mythical hero-system in which people serve in order to earn a feeling of primary value, of cosmic specialness, of ultimate usefulness to creation, of unshakable meaning" (5). But at their best, these heroic endeavors produce only a "vital lie" that temporarily distracts from our fatal predicament. Apparently, Becker himself was not dismayed by this, attracted as he was to the Danish theologian Søren Kierkegaard and his image of the "knight of faith," that rare soul who acknowledges and lives the "creative illusion" without assurances of a more permanent place in the cosmos. Becker concluded, "The most that any one of us can seem to do is to fashion something—an object or ourselves—and drop it into the confusion, make an offering of it, so to speak, to the life force" (285).

As discouraging as this argument seems, Becker made it with an unforgiving logic, and he does have contemporary followers. Pyszczynski, Greenburg, and Solomon (1999) have put some of his claims to an empirical test with what they call "terror management theory." They propose that human belief systems evolved from our hominid ancestors' discovery of their mortality, and that "cultural worldviews" evolved to help us manage the anxiety that discovery generated. Cultures do this by creating the illusion that each of us is a valuable member of society, and through the psychological mechanism of self-esteem, death is conveniently, if only temporarily, denied. A culture assures us we have a continuing place in the cosmos and that our projects are literally of undying importance. Thus we beat the drums loudly, drowning out the prospect that death is the catastrophic end of everything we have worked so hard for.

The success of this line of argument depends, however, on a willingness to interpret a vast amount of historical and cultural experience using a single causal variable, Becker's fear of death, to explain the last four million years of human evolution. For some, that kind of reductionism is not immediately convincing. Do we delight in a sunset or the taste of morning coffee only to distract ourselves from thoughts of death? Do we care about friends, family, and who runs the country because we see in that the refraction of a cosmic agenda? Could mythopoetic beliefs about the origins of the universe be satisfying only because they ease a mortal dread and not, as Claude Lévi-Strauss once observed, simply because myths are good to think? The denial of death, where it can be demonstrated to exist, may be more a feature of the historical trajectory of a specific culture than anything innate in human nature.

The influential French historian Philippe Ariès (1974, 1981) produced his own variant of the death-denial thesis, a historical alternative to Becker's more psychological one. Ariès proposed the idea of the "tame death," said by him to typify the Middle Ages of Europe and to contrast with the "forbidden" or "invisible" style he says predominates now. In those past times, a tame (really, "tamed") death began with some kind of clear forewarning, usually physical symptoms, which initiated "a ritual moment" of preparation for dying. First, the ailing person expressed sorrow that his or her life was coming to an end, followed by an expected display of generosity, pardons, and forgiveness given all around. To die unburdened of old grievances sped the soul toward its final reward in paradise. Family, friends, servants, children, neighbors, and even enemies gathered at the bedside for these exchanges, which ended with the dying commending them all to God's good care. Food, drink, music, and even games were part of this highly social, choreographed event, interspersed with earnest prayers for a comfortable dying and requests for heavenly pardons. Thematically, the emphasis was on the soul's future, the health and continuity of the family, and the hope of communication with the spiritual world beyond this life. When the bedside ceremonies were completed, everyone waited patiently for death to occur, now tamed because it came under ritual (and God's) control. At the end, a priest performed absolutions, evoking the authority of the church on behalf of the departed and the bereaved. The entire sequence, which could take days, was organized by the dying person and the family and was understood to be a public occasion that brought the wider community into the home and to the bedside. Decorum and ritual propriety guided the process, everyone knowing exactly what was to be done, and that it would be both memorable and instructive if done well. In Ariès's view, all this ritual and display took the nasty sting out of dying. "Familiar simplicity is one of the two essential characteristics of this death. The other is its public aspect, which is to last until the end of the nineteenth century. The dying person must be the center of a group of people" (1981: 18).

Ariès's tamed deaths were scripted in a genre of small books and pamphlets called *ars moriendi*, copies of which circulated widely among the literate and well-to-do and which described in detail the etiquette of proper dying. An early example is William Caxton's *The Arte & Crafte to Know Well to Dye*, which he says he translated "oute of Frenshe in to Englysshe" in 1490 (Atkinson 1992). It opens, "Here begynneth a lityll treatise shorte and abredged spekynge on the arte & crafte to knowe well to dye," and it continues with sections on planning the well-managed and well-mannered death, temptations faced by the dying and how they can be resisted, questions for leading "the seke persone" to affirm his or her Christian faith, and examples of prayers one can use. All this prescribed activity is to take place at the bedside, preferably in a crowded room filled with onlookers, as the dying person is interrogated by a priest on his or her beliefs and hopes for the afterlife. When correctly and fully done, Caxton says, the confessions, prayers, and pardons model a "studyous exhortacyon" and create an enthusiasm so spirited that "yf it were possyble all, an hole cyte oughte renne hastely to a persone that deyeth," just to behold a good performance (1992: 31). No doubt, some people did run hastily to the bedside, since any death was a dramatic community event, a chance to witness a soul's departure to an eternal place populated with "archangelles" and "cherubyns" as well as "patryarkes" and many "vyrgynes and the wydowes" too. Both this life and the hereafter were connected, were intensely social places, and, according to the authors of the many circulating examples of the ars moriendi, were combined in a natural and reasonable state of affairs.

In contrast to the public nature and stylized rhetoric of the tame death, modern deaths seem "invisible," and Ariès makes clear his disdain for that. In a long chapter entitled "Death Denied," he describes, as did Becker, "the lie," a reluctance to speak openly about what happens as we die: "everyone becomes an accomplice to a lie born of this moment which later grows to such proportions that death is driven into secrecy" (1981: 562). Unlike their remote ancestors, modern people avoid the obvious when they are with the dying. At the bedside, they talk not of the soul but about the weather or grandchildren, as though nothing special were happening. Gathered in a terminal ward, family and friends are reduced to onlookers who come to "pay respects" and "show support" but are not sure what to say or how long to stay. The bedchamber, once a small theater of piety, is now a private retreat where physicians replace religious functionaries and hushed discussions of vital signs substitute for affirmations of religious faith. The sights and odors of death are banished, privacy curtains and powerful cleaning agents supplanting public confessions and incense. Even funerals, says Ariès, are "very discrete," semi-private events where "the indecency of mourning" (Gorer's phrase) is concealed and visible control of strong feelings is taken as a sign of "strength."

In this characterization, is Ariès an old-fashioned romantic yearning for an imagined past? Even if his description of medieval practices is historically accurate, does that mean the customs of the present are, by contrast, a denial? Sociologist Allan Kellehear (1996) suspects not, arguing that all forms of the death-denial hypothesis rest on several assumptions that may not hold. First, "denial" refers to a psychological state, and when used to describe social practices it anthropomorphizes something that more correctly should be thought of as behavioral and the product of a specific historical trajectory. The "fear of death" argument, so strongly held by Freud and his followers, may be more situational than anything innate. Longtime death researcher Robert Kastenbaum (2004) is clear also on this point, that "acceptance" or "denial" is due to a variety of factors, mostly social, and they include the circumstances of a specific case, the range of culturally appropriate responses, and individual needs to compartmentalize strong feelings in order to get through an immediate crisis. It is true that sequestration of the dying has become a common practice and that many doctors are unprepared to talk about death openly with patients and families. But for them that may be a matter of professional training, bureaucratic expediency, and institutional agendas, not a generalized human tendency to "deny" death. Finally, many people in the West have cut themselves off from the guiding religious narratives that inspired their ancestors, from the scripts so well represented in the old ars moriendi, and they look now to the authority of medicine and secular professionals instead for guidance on coping with the end of life. But that does not mean they have lost sight of death's radical inconvenience, or that they do not think or talk about it in ways illustrative of their time and place. Just in the last few decades a newer set of models, appropriate to the times, has appeared.

UPDATING THE SCRIPT LINES

Ariès's notion of the tame death, and particularly its secular companion, the "good death," came into prominence partly as a reaction to the twentieth century's medicalization and commercialization of life's end. "Good death" imagery and the hopeful narrative style associated with it became popular because they were ways of thinking about death that were personalized and positive. The expression "good death" entered the public realm through a number of sources: in a genre of published illness narratives or "pathobiographies" generated by AIDS, cancer, and other chronic diseases; through illness-and-struggle confessionals featured on talk shows and in advice columns; in the proliferation of grief specialists—"bereavement counselors"—and their workshops and seminars; and in popular books about death, grief, angels, and out-of-body experiences, their titles aimed with increasing precision at niche markets as varied as those who suffer from pet loss, a gay partner's death, sibling suicide, or loss of a child. Some titles in this genre have achieved national best-seller status. Betty Eadie's *Embraced by the Light* (1992) and Mitch Albom's *Tuesdays with Morrie* (1997) are two notable examples.

Implicit in all this publishing, promotion, advising, and inspired healing is the voice of Kübler-Ross, who as a grandmotherly physician and psychiatrist wrote *On Death and Dying* (1969) and its sequel *Death: The Final Stage of Growth* (1975) for professional and popular audiences. For her, the important issue was less denial than lack of familiarity: "death has become a dreaded and unspeakable issue to be avoided by every means possible," while "other societies have learned to cope better with the reality of death than we seem to have done" (1975: 5). Echoing the moral intent of the old ars moriendi, she writes that death is always hard to accept. "But if we can learn to view death from a different perspective, to reintroduce it into our lives so that it comes not as a dreaded stranger but as an expected companion to our life, then we can learn to live our lives with meaning—with full appreciation of our finiteness, of the limits of our time here" (6). Death brought back into life as an "expected companion" can teach older truths that have been forgotten and that physicians ignore altogether. She cites as a precedent her own experience when, as a child growing up in Austria, she witnessed the death of a local farmer. What she describes matches closely Caxton's injunctions on the "arte and crafte" of dying well. The man chose to die at home, quietly arranged his affairs with his daughters in private bedside consultations, and then had his relatives and friends in for goodbyes. Kübler-Ross and her siblings were invited to help with the preparations, and they were there for the mourning and body viewing in the house the farmer had built himself. "In that country today," she writes, "there is still no make-believe slumber-room, no embalming, no false makeup to pretend sleep" (1969: 19). Death there is real. But not real scary.

Much like an anthropologist, Kübler-Ross went to the dying themselves to learn what death had to teach. For more than two years she interviewed terminal patients, collecting stories and observing what happened to them in their final months and days, and these visits led to her well-known stage theory of dying. She felt that at the end of their lives many people had similar experiences but—she was clear on this—there was no lockstep or idealized process that anyone had to go through in order to die well. That interpretation came later, among some professionals and in the wider public, as her stages became better known and were misconstrued as a how-to recipe for achieving a last, grand "growth experience." Kübler-Ross herself saw the stages as ever-shifting events that, under the best circumstances, lead to reconciliation with the inevitable and a sense of completeness or "closure." Dying, she believed, was a last opportunity to achieve that state, perhaps the only kind of triumph over death that is possible.

Her stages of death are not complicated, and she observes that each person will travel through them in their own way. The first is denial, accompanied by a profound sense of isolation; not an unreasonable response to the shock of being told one has a disease that is fatal. This stage is short and usually traumatic, often filled with doubts about the accuracy of the diagnosis, hopes for a better "second opinion," and ruminations of the "why me?" and "why now?" sort. But few of her patients remained there long. "Depending very much on how a patient is told, how much time he has to gradually acknowledge the inevitable happening, and how he has been prepared throughout life to cope with stressful situations, he will gradually drop his denial and use less radical defense mechanisms" (1969: 55). Following denials, most patients move into a phase of anger and resentment. For many, this stage is the most difficult part of dying. Nor is their anger irrational. Many do not expect to die, at least not yet, and they have projects to finish and interests to pursue. Death is not on schedule, something especially difficult for those who have been active throughout their lives and accustomed to managing their affairs. Time is suddenly in short supply, and the sense of desperation that that arouses leads to another stage, bargaining for a reprieve. By offering good behavior in exchange for a delay, some patients hope to cut a deal with God. Promises are made to right old wrongs, change former attitudes, or do good works if, by a miracle, more time is granted. But that too is a brief phase, for it exposes how few resources are left, and it leads, understandably, to depression and hopelessness. But Kübler-Ross thinks the depression can be a good thing; it opens the possibility of "preparatory grief that the terminally ill patient has to undergo in order to prepare himself for his final separation from this world" (98). A sensitive nurse, social worker, or pastor can help the distressed individual work toward a sense of finality and separation by encouraging, for example, plans to distribute important possessions and decisions which will effect the well-being of survivors. A feeling of partial control can come from that. "We are always impressed by how quickly a patient's depression is lifted when these vital issues are taken care of" (1969: 98). This final stage of completing unfinished business, then, is a time neither for vague, sunny reassurances nor for ignoring the obvious. What the dying need are opportunities to acknowledge that while life is near its end they can still make decisions about issues that matter. That, says Kübler-Ross, makes the individual's "final acceptance much easier, and he will be grateful to those who can sit with him during this stage of depression without constantly telling him not to be sad" (1969: 99). Acceptance, the last stage, is our grand finale.[2]

This model of a systematic, gentle, peaceful resolve into death is one modern ars moriendi, and it has had a powerful impact. Others may talk of death denial, but among "the families and friends of dying people her stage theory gave a tangible script for dying and death that in many ways assisted them to make sense of their interactions and behaviours, and gave them some guidance in ways of responding" (Hart, Sainsbury, and Short 1998: 68). Kübler-Ross provided a formula for talking about death openly and humanely that was, at the same time, a critique of a public etiquette of avoidance and embarrassment and the medical establishment's reliance on technology for "managing" terminal patients and their families. Yet in its simplicity and dependence on anecdote, the model raised questions. Does it work with everyone? Are its proposed stages a human universal, normative only for the (apparently) middle-class white people she interviewed, or just one of many routes to a comfortable and comforting end? Is it applicable to deaths other than the slow, lingering ones we associate with cancer and other chronic diseases? Are the model's stages the result of social expectation, particularly the expectations of hospital and hospice staff, that people die a "good" death according to formula whatever their cultural background or traditions?

> The good death concept was embraced by health caregivers as they struggled to fashion the experiences and lives of their patients toward this ideal. . . . Death was defined by healthgivers as "good" if there was awareness, acceptance and a preparation for death, and a peaceful, dignified dying. The good death was epitomised by the nurses' comfort with events and interactions. Bad deaths were characterized as a lack of acceptance of death by patients and patients' families, or a failure to actively pursue fulfillment of living until the final stages of dying. These bad death scenarios were seen as problematic. . . . Thus the lives of dying people were shaped by caregivers to fit the good death hospice philosophy and expectations. (Hart, Sainsbury, and Short 1998: 70)

If this critique is true, then the rhetoric of "good death" and "death denial" may be more a matter of powerful institutional agendas for the efficient management of dying people than of individual patient preferences. Where death is seen as a "failure" despite the best in contemporary medical skill, technology, and service, patients who acknowledge they are dying and work to achieve a state of acceptance do their part in turning medical failure into heartfelt triumph. Critics have claimed, however, that Kübler-Ross and her followers promoted fantasy deaths, a so-called happy death movement, pathologizing those who fail to follow their one-size-fits-all agenda. One critic, Lyn Lofland, remarked that "in modern social orders, dying scripts—if they can be said to exist at all—tend to be individualistic, varied, emergent and uncodified" (1978: 49). In a chaotic democracy of idiosyncratic dying, any professional agenda of good dying as therapy is an imposition, yet it is one that has been elevated to the status of an American entitlement. Why does that happen and what is its appeal? Historian David Morgan (1998), whose interest is religious imagery, comments on the potency of imaginary devices, pictorial and ideological, and why they are a piece of human experience. "The cultural work that popular images perform is often a mediating one, serving to bolster one world against another, to police the boundaries of the familiar, or to suture the gaps that appear as the fabric of the world wears thin" (1998: 9–10). Death is a prime staging ground for such cultural productions, for exercising the imagination, precisely because "the world wears thin" when our grip on it is failing. To appreciate that insight, I look briefly at three newer script lines, modern versions of the ars moriendi, that explicitly function as explanatory and teaching devices of the kind Morgan has in mind. They have all but superseded Kübler-Ross's five-stage model and are more than a counterpoint to the theatrics of Kevorkian with his suffering patients.[3]

HOW A HOLY MAN DIES

When Joseph Cardinal Bernardin, archbishop of the Catholic Church of Chicago, died of pancreatic cancer on November 14, 1996, it did not go unnoticed. He was on the cover of *Newsweek* (November 25, 1996) under the headline, "The Art of Dying Well." The *New York Times Magazine* of December 1 declared, "He freely announced that he had terminal cancer and conducted his life in a way that was a model of how to meet death." While keeping a busy schedule of administrative work, he offered pastoral care to others who were terminally ill and still had the energy to write a memoir of his dying experiences. *The Gift of Peace* (1997), much of it done in longhand, invited "those who read this book to walk with me the final miles of my life's journey." As if to heighten the public visibility of his dying, in a single month he traveled to the White House to receive the Medal of Freedom from the president, delivered a major address at Georgetown University, received another medal from the Archdiocese of Boston, and then "left for Rome to report personally to Pope John Paul II about my health" (1997: 139). Along with the book, a 57-minute video was produced, tracing his rise from near poverty in an Italian immigrant family to his position as one of the most prominent and occasionally controversial Catholic archbishops in the country. Presenting a familiar American trajectory of rags to spiritual riches, the video revels in the public character of his death, from his mingling with the great to the affectionate crowds along the funeral procession route. His memory is perpetuated in the Cardinal Bernardin Cancer Center at Loyola University and in the Bernardin Center in Chicago, which promotes ecumenicalism and Catholic-Jewish dialogue. The high visibility of Bernardin's last year of life ended with a public vigil outside his home the day before he died, the press announcing that he "slipped away peacefully" at 7:33 a.m. on a wintry Chicago morning, and a cathedral funeral reminiscent of the last rites of kings and popes, all a model of contemporary dying that could fairly be described as "beatific."

That a cardinal's death would be shaped by his religious interests and language is expected. What is of interest here is how they were combined to create a singular public message about dying well, a lesson to the faithful and to nonbelievers alike. Always a teacher and exemplar, Bernardin was explicit about his mission. After the first rounds of chemotheraphy, he said that he had discovered a new ministry, spending more of his time with the sick and dying. "Even if they are not committed to any specific religion, men and women everywhere have a deep desire to come into contact with the transcendent. Members of the clergy can facilitate this through the simple goodness they show in being with their people. The things people are naturally attracted to and remember most are small acts of concern and thoughtfulness. Years later, that is what they tell you about their priests and other clergy" (1997: 89–90). It was the way Bernardin understood his "small acts" that gave his approach to dying its explicitly sacred character. He saw himself as a priest first, a patient second, and in his priestly role he became the "good shepherd" to a new constituency, other people dying of cancer. "Those in this community see things differently. . . . it becomes easier to separate the essential from the peripheral" (93). He imagined life as a journey, a motif that appeared often in both his public appearances and his book. The journey is "a three-act play that I now believe constitutes my spiritual pilgrimage over the past three years" (30). As with any pilgrimage, a journey is both a goal and a practice, and Bernardin's was to recast his dying as a "cause." Causes were familiar to him. An activist cleric, he opposed abortion and the death penalty. He worked hard to build trust with the Jewish community and spoke often on the evil of anti-Semitism. He advocated economic justice and economic reforms that were sometimes controversial. Finding in cancer another cause was a logical ending for a long life of energetic ministry.

Activist though he was, the idea of surrender to his medical circumstance also came from a religious orientation. He recalled how difficult that was, his cancer "giving rise to a certain kind of loneliness, an inability to see clearly how things are unfolding, an inability to see that, ultimately, all things will work for our good, and that we are, indeed, not alone" (1997: 46). He then adds a point very different from the model of dying I will discuss next: how hard it is to surrender to whatever awaits. As a religious counselor he wants to be a "fixer" of other people's pain but discovers that simply being present with them, just as his theology envisions a god who is present, is enough. The practice of presence, he says, "unlocks the mystery of suffering" and grants freedom, "the freedom to let go, to surrender ourselves" and place ourselves in trust to an agency larger than we can understand. "It's in the act of abandonment that we experience redemption, that we find life, peace, and joy in the midst of physical, emotional, and spiritual suffering" (48–49). He is emphatic about this, that to win you have to lose, to find freedom you must submit; to gain peace requires enduring turmoil, even to the point of seeing death "not as an enemy or a threat but as a friend." Throughout, Bernardin's messages are laced with paradoxes, cast in recognizably Christian language and imagery. His metanarrative of an ultimate Presence, beyond human comprehension, guides his "good shepherd" imagery and understanding of suffering and resurrection. That theme was repeated at his funeral by a fellow priest and eulogist who concluded, "we all knew, those of us who were close to him, and those on the far edges of the city, that we have been privileged to live in a time when a holy man was the Archbishop of Chicago." Barnardin's video and book are a modern hagiography to religious, even saintly, dying. In a culture singularly devoted to planning, striving and achievement, he is completely at ease telling the rest of us that submission is the better choice.

HOW AN EVERYMAN DIES

Not a holy man but probably close to it in the minds of millions, Professor Morrie Schwartz exemplified in his dying a very different style. Schwartz is well known for his book *Morrie: In His Own Words* (1996), for his role in Mitch Albom's best-selling *Tuesdays with Morrie* (1997), and for three appearances on Ted Koppel's *Nightline*, the last taped at his home just before he died. He was also the subject of a 1999 television movie, which featured Jack Lemmon as Morrie and was produced by Oprah Winfrey's film company. Albom's book was on the *New York Times* best-seller list for well over three years, becoming a giant of the "inspirational" genre. With a top-selling book, a movie, and dozens of Web sites, Morrie's death, like Bernardin's, was a modern media event.

In the late 1970s, Albom was an undergraduate at Brandeis University and, after graduation and a bit of drifting, worked as a sports columnist for a Detroit newspaper. Almost twenty years later, he caught his old sociology professor one evening on ABC's *Nightline* explaining to a national audience what it was like to die with ALS. Koppel introduced the guest by asking, "Who is Morrie Schwartz and why, by the end of the night, are so many of you going to care about him?" Overwhelmed by nostalgia, Albom sought out Morrie ("coach," he called him) and thus began a series of regular visits to the latter's home in a Boston suburb. These were always on Tuesdays, and from the Tuesday conversations came the book, the movie, and Morrie's fame as a contemporary teacher about dying.

In the intimacy of its style and the hopefulness of its message, *Tuesdays with Morrie* belongs to a confessional, inspirational genre of American letters long popular with readers and publishers. That literary tradition goes back to at least 1852, and the teary, highly romanticized deathbed scene with Little

Eva and her panicky father in Harriet Beecher Stowe's *Uncle Tom's Cabin*. Like Eva, who glimpsed the eternal as she hovered at the margin of life, Morrie too is on to a greater wisdom—about friends, the value of family, human love— which he conveys through Koppel and Albom to a sympathetic audience. After their first meeting, Albom was not sure he really wanted to see Morrie again. Life for him was all work, hustle, and deadline-driven newspapering, and he worried that his favorite professor would be disappointed with how his former student had turned out. But Morrie was still the kindly, humble teacher Albom remembered, and while Morrie's dying did not seem overtly beatific, it was nevertheless quietly brave and ennobling. The son of Jewish immigrants from Russia, Morrie was not particularly observant of his parent's faith. He rarely spoke of God and seemed uninterested in transcendent places, emphasizing instead themes that Kübler-Ross would recognize: our potential for personal growth even to the end, reconciliation with others and, at the last, with ourselves. Through these images, Morrie died his good death, foregrounding the primacy of the compassionate self and fidelity to a lifetime of learning and caring.

Imparting personal wisdom is the central trope of Albom's story about his teacher, each chapter presented as a little seminar lesson. The book has all the expected features of a university class—a syllabus, the first-session orientation, attendance taking, chapter titles as lecture topics for the Tuesday meetings, a concluding lecture, and graduation day. Each chapter is short, only a few pages, and like a good lecture it is just long enough to survey the topic, make several key points, and lead the reader to reflect on what it all means. In his chapter on the fear of aging, Morrie is asked how he manages to remain positive despite the debilitating losses he is experiencing. That question opens the way for a series of minilessons. Morrie says he does not mind being dependent because that is how we came into the world, held and rocked by our mothers, and most of us never get enough of that kind of touch as adults. He chastises those who pretend they can always be youthful; the life of the young is full of doubting and unhappiness, and no one should want to live that way permanently. "If you stayed at twenty-two, you'd always be as ignorant as you were at twenty-two. Aging is not just decay, you know. It's growth. It's more than the negative that you're going to die, it's also the positive that you understand you're going to die, and that you live a better life because of it" (1997: 118). Morrie had his youth once, and, in a sense, he still does.

> The truth is, part of me is every age. I'm a three-year-old, I'm a five-year old, I'm a thirty-seven year old, I'm a fifty-year old. I've been through all of them, and I know what it's like. I delight in being a child when it's appropriate to be

a child. I delight in being a wise old man when its appropriate to be a wise old man. Think of all I can be! I am every age, up to my own. Do you understand? (120–21)

Always the teacher, each Tuesday, Morrie offers a homily on family, emotions, regrets, money, marriage, and love, presented graciously with an affecting wonderment.

Morrie's teachings clearly had their effect on Albom and, probably, on his huge viewing and reading public. One of the little subthemes of the book is Mitch's inability to cry, to let emotions show as tears. Morrie repeatedly urges him to try, without feeling any shame for it. I will not give away whether or not he succeeded with his former student, but he did with Koppel. The ABC film crew had arrived for their third taping at a time when Morrie had little energy left. The two men had come to like each other and toward the end of the interview the camera zoomed in on Morrie as Koppel asked if he had any final words for the *Nightline* audience. As Albom tells it: " 'Be compassionate,' Morrie whispered. 'And take responsibility for each other' . . . . He took a breath, then added his mantra: 'Love each other or die' . . . . Koppel was near tears. 'You done good.' 'You think so?' Morrie rolled his eyes toward the ceiling. 'I'm bargaining with Him up there now. I'm asking Him, Do I get to be one of the angels?'" (1997: 163).

Morrie's final lesson summarized what he felt was the lasting importance of the life he lived. He wanted to be cremated, the ashes buried on a particular hillside overlooking a cemetery duck pond, a good place, he said, for Albom to visit and talk. Morrie assured him he would be listening. How did he think that could happen? "As long as we can love each other, and remember the feeling of love we had, we can die without ever really going away. All the love you created is still there. All the memories are still there. You live on—in the hearts of everyone you have touched and nurtured while you were here. . . . Death ends a life, not a relationship" (174). Morrie was not greatly interested in otherworldly visions of "Him up there" or heavenly repose somewhere else. Memory, specifically the memory of love and a life of wisdom, was his concern, and in that vision, memory replaced the supernatural as the site of our immortality.

Despite profound differences on the nature of survivability, Bernardin's and Morrie's views on dying overlap in an interesting way. The archbishop invoked the biblical image of a heavy burden, "Take my yoke upon your shoulders and learn from me" (Matthew 11:29), and prayed a prayer of submission: "not my will, but Thine be done." Morrie, always eclectic, was interested in Buddhism and Christianity as well as Judaism and preferred nature imagery for making his point. At the beginning of the chapter entitled "We Say Good-bye," Morrie tells Albom a little story about a wave headed for a crash against the shore. The wave is fearful that its doom is near until it is reminded (by another wave) that "You're not a wave, you're part of the ocean." "Part of the ocean," Morrie sighs, "part of the ocean" (190). Invoking the natural world, he too is ready to submit to whatever waits.

HOW THE REST OF US MAY DIE

Bernardin is the saintly "good shepherd" to his flock of followers, Morrie an Everyman, a plainspoken, decent person who dies unpretentiously and modestly. Heartwarming he is, but neither his nor the bishop's quiet grace is the theme of a third contemporary script line for dying. In the medical model, dying is about heroic struggle and control. While we know death eventually wins, with much hope and a little savvy we may be able to manage the timing and manner of our exit. The determination to be in control, to win small, temporary victories along the way, and to be in charge up to the last drives this model. It was featured in an acclaimed PBS series hosted by Bill Moyers and titled, accurately, *On Our Own Terms*. First aired on September 10, 2000, the entire program is six hours long and was broadcast nationally in four segments of ninety minutes each. Purchasers of the video package got additional material through a program called "Eyes Wide Open," which included extensive bibliographies and an impressive thirty-page discussion guide that could be downloaded from a PBS site. In addition to the program, there were plans to promote grassroots discussion, activism, and a death education movement that would be more comprehensive than anything in the past. The project was underwritten by some of the largest and most prestigious names in American philanthropy, and those who viewed all six hours had a remarkably intense experience. Subtitled "Moyers on Dying," the series showed him again as one of television's premier public intellectuals and cultural commentators.

The style of the four programs is similar. The viewer is introduced to a topic—living with a prognosis of death; palliative care; making hard choices; end of life services—followed by individuals stories of family struggles, failures, and quiet heroism. Moyers is present in each, compassionately interviewing the dying, their caregivers, and medical professionals. What is clear in his intense engagement with these people is that the well-managed death, the "good death" of so much public rhetoric, is unlikely from the start. Says one dying man, an articulate middle aged pediatrician with cancer, you feel you have been "locked in" by an enemy pilot who has you in his sights; you are already "dead meat." His issue is not "dying well" but, as he frankly puts it, learning how to "get dead." The struggle is not for a peaceable end but for finding something to say, anything at all, about what dying means. As individual stories are told, the ambiguities and frustrations of "getting dead" are the grim lesson.

In the introduction to the third program in the series, "A Death of One's Own," Moyers says dying well is a matter of controlling how we die, how we take charge of our final days.[4] Death is about well considered choices and not, in the manner of Kevorkian, voting it up or down. One episode features Jim, a Louisiana veterinarian and horse breeder who has ALS. He has been told he may live five years, and he says a good death for him would be to simply "go to sleep." But as medical and caretaking expenses climb and as his ability to manage everyday tasks declines, his wife and sole caregiver is overwhelmed by their burdens. Simply going to sleep is not going to happen soon, and in one difficult scene, Jim, his wife, and their doctor are in intense conversation about getting help with a proposed suicide. As a licensed vet, Jim can get medications to end his life, but he needs help because his wife is reluctant to administer them and he is physically unable to do so. The doctor, obviously a caring man, refuses this request, citing the better option of hospice care, his unwillingness to participate in an illegal act, and a strong Southern ethos against suicide. But talk of suicide continues at home. Jim complains repeatedly that the system is "unfair" because it is bankrupting the family and forcing his wife to help him end his life when she is not emotionally able to do so. At the end, he does not "go to sleep," nor does he use veterinary medicines to induce a fatal coma. His choice, the last bit of control he has, is to refuse food and water. He will starve himself to death.

A similar medical dilemma confronts Kitty, an Oregon woman dying of ovarian cancer. She lives in a state where assisted suicide is legal but infrequent. With only a few months to live, she too says controlling the time and circumstances of dying is what she wants, adding that she will know when the time for that is right. Legal drugs for inducing death will be at hand, and Kitty's adult daughters have agreed to the plan. So has a physician, her second, because the first is willing to provide palliative care but has moral objections to suicide. The two doctors work in the same suite of offices, and on camera they talk about their patient's request. They obviously respect one another but have quite different ideas about what a doctor should or should not do. But as with Jim, Kitty's hopes for a controlled death are frustrated. She is persuaded to delay taking a fatal dose so that a traveling family member can be at the bedside when she dies. When he arrives it is too late; Kitty can no longer swallow, and the prescribed barbiturates, which by law must be self-administered, are useless. The daughter who asked for the delay feels guilty and ruefully speculates that her mother's death was more difficult than it should have been; death was not the controlled experience Kitty had wanted.

In Moyers's programs, only a few of his subjects die as they planned. One man's victory is no more than dying sitting up because he insists he will not let death catch him lying down. A woman with a large, caring family dies the peaceful home death she wanted because she has the best that family and medical support can offer. But most do not get what they want, even though the medical staff and hospice workers are compassionate people, doing all they can for their patients. In these four programs, the image of the good death, let alone a "better death," is barely sustained. Each is different, each unpredictable and disrupted in some way, and only a few occur as hoped. Good deaths elude even the most meticulous planning.

Moyers, as he usually does, takes on hard issues, here the frustrations of medicalized dying. Unlike Bernardin's confessional presentation, he offers no transcendent goals to frame the PBS presentation. Control "on our own terms" is the theme. And unlike Morrie, none of Moyers's subjects muses on camera of eternal verities. When a show on a topic like this is broadcast to a national audience, one would expect the occasional expositor of a higher wisdom—a grief counselor or a philosophically minded physician—and there are some. But what they offer is modest, or at least modestly offered, and perhaps in that they are more truthful to the realities of death than either Bernadin's hagiography or Albom's mass-appeal story. Thomas Lynch, a best-selling essayist and small town funeral director, makes a cameo appearance and observes that all the dying really want is "witness" so that at the end they can go knowing that those they love also love them. Reciprocated love, he says, is "the big item." There need not be anything particularly transcendent or heroic in that, only ordinary people willing to sit with the dying in the way ordinary people had always done in times past.

Despite the modesty of Lynch's suggestion, there is nevertheless something heroic going on. Morrie became a genuine folk hero for millions of Americans, as did Bernardin and, in their own way, some of the patients in Moyers's documentary. They all faced up to their deaths, clear-eyed and without pretense or denial, openly struggling with the immensity of their pain and knowledge of their fate. They methodically sorted out personal affairs so others would not have to later. More than that, they allowed the rest of us to hear their narratives through mass readership and national television. Sociologist Clive Seale argues that such is the contemporary style, "the traditional emphasis on courage in the face of external danger now becomes courage to explore and express the dying self in a drama of inner adventure" (1995: 599). Self-revelation and an unashamed articulation of inner adventure with medical staff, family, friends, and an unseen public—those are the elements of a newer heroic style. Moyers is explicit that the people who consented to his gentle prying and the daunting presence of film crews agreed that the bother was worth it if their story benefited others. While the national media routinely report the deaths of celebrities and military figures in heroic terms, Albom and Moyers showed that heroism is possible with ordinary folk as well, Ariès and Becker notwithstanding.

There is something else here as well. Seale suggests that heroism, as it has conventionally been understood, is male. "While everyday life is routine, repetitive and mundane, the heroic is filled with self-defining moments in which adversity is overcome by acts of courage and sacrifice" (1995: 598–99). We see this all the time on the sports pages, in war reporting and in "human interest" stories. But shifting the venue for drama from the external world of action to the inner world of private experience, as Bernardin and Morrie do, "converts traditional masculine heroism to a specifically female (and indeed feminist) heroics. . . . involving emotional expression and self-sacrifice. . . . The inner adventures of self-exploration, and the depiction of emotional labour as sacrificial, contribute to a late modern heroic script, which has been powerfully underwritten by some feminist ideals, relayed via both professionals and the media" (599). Suddenly, heroism looks more interesting, more varied, and more widely distributed than it otherwise had.

MODELS THAT TEACH

How might we interpret these three models of contemporary dying, each saying something different about the manner in which many of us will come to our end? One way is to think of them as instances of modern mythology that, like all mythic systems, offer instruction on large existential questions. Myths and symbols, says Clifford Geertz (1973: 216), "provide a template or blueprint for the organization of social and psychological processes"; they are "extrapersonal mechanisms for the perception, understanding, judgment and manipulation of the world." Like all myths, the narratives of Bernardin, Morrie, and Moyers are edited, simplified, idealized reconstructions of otherwise chaotic and threatening events in the lives of their subjects. They simplify not to deceive but to generate a coherent, meaningful story line for the edification of their audience. They offer prototypical images against which we as spectators can compare our own expectations. Thus, Bernardin draws on traditional religious categories to make sense of what is happening to his body and his life. His small, temporary triumphs over the disease and his cheerful determination to continue with priestly duties are recognizable features of the "suffering servant" imagery central to his Catholic faith. Viewers need not share his religious commitment to find in the story something useful for coping with their own anxieties.

Second, like all myths, these media narratives rely on a specialized language. While Bernardin's is the language of his church and theology, Morrie's is that of psychology, particularly the discourse of recent self-help movements with their focus on personal growth and meaningful human relationships. Albom mentions briefly Morrie's attraction to nature, another modern motif that is important to some, but the dying professor is more concerned with a few basic, humanistic values: love, caring, open self-disclosure, and a legacy of cherished memories. His stock of images would be familiar to many Americans who grew up the in 1960s and 1970s and who rejected traditional theological language for that of growth, spiritual wholeness, and therapeutic self-regard. By contrast, Moyer's subjects speak of pain, timing, control, and management, issues laced with the terminology of medicine, palliative care, legal encumbrance, and bureaucratic power. They recite lists of prescriptions, medical procedures they have endured, a newfound knowledge of human anatomy, and technical names for the stages of their diseases. Theirs is neither the language of sacred sacrifice nor of self-discovery but of a sustained struggle to leave this world on their own terms if they can. While some may have spoken religiously or psychotherapeutically when off camera, that is not the narrative line, the mythic present, that Moyers shows the rest of us.

Finally, these mythlike stories invest specific times, places, and events with special, enduring significance. That is not difficult to see with Bernardin. He understands his dying as a way of participating in the gruesome death of the founder of his religion roughly two thousand years ago, and that participation enables him to make sense of his own death as a mystery and even a victory.[5] Morrie is far more modest. Less interested in eternal bliss, he asks for burial in a bucolic setting where he wants Albom to drop by and resume their conversation. He promises to be listening. That said, it seems a good possibility that for Albom as well as devoted readers, Morrie's hillside grave will become a sacred site, a potential shrine for pilgrimage and private contemplation. There is ample precedent for that if one thinks of the Vietnam Memorial or the burial sites of film stars and music celebrities. More prosaic, Moyers's subjects tell of different "special" settings altogether: hospital rooms, doctors' offices—and home, the place they most want to die. Indeed, the idea of "dying with dignity" is almost synonymous with dying at home, surrounded by family and friends in reenactment of Ariès's tame death. In a touching and quietly dramatic scene in Moyers's second program, a middle-aged woman with ovarian cancer is at her end, lying in the hushed bedroom of her comfortable suburban home. The film crew has a camera set up in the darkened hallway as family members quietly go in and out. But all we see is the bedroom door slightly ajar, a sliver of light streaming through. The camera lingers on the stark image of the door with its thin halo of light, and the soundtrack is silent, allowing viewers a moment to imagine the reverential scene within. The message is clear. Home is where everything ends and there is nothing else to say.

Dying as participation in God's cosmic process, as a last chance for personal growth, and as an embattled departure on terms of our choosing are three distinctive constructions of dying, prototypical script lines that have enormous persuasiveness in a pluralistic, mediacentric culture no longer dominated by a master religious narrative. Each story is "mythic," not because it is untrue but because it is a construction built from culturally specific discourses, standardized images, and distinctive values associated with the times and spaces of dying. Each is convincing because it vouches for a larger truth implicitly understood, the possibility of an integrated self even as body and selfhood are disintegrating.

In addition to their mythic status, there is something else these three models share. Despite their distinctive story lines, each is a contemporary manifestation of some older, surprisingly durable ideas in Western death and mortuary practice. These latter may not be obvious, but they are there, implicit in contemporary experience. How in an anthropological sense could we characterize them?

AS IT WAS IN THE BEGINNING

Death is a human universal and so too, it seems, are stories about its origins. However fanciful or speculative, they are important because as mythopoetic statements they deal with the known, the unknown, and, more importantly, the unknowable (Sproul 1979). As narratives, they are "true" not because they pretend to historical specificity, as literalists would have it, but because they concern themselves with existential realities that are problematic. Think, for example, of Adam and Eve's short-lived frolic in Eden. There are those for whom that was an actual event and that, had a good journalist been there, he or she would have reported it exactly as stated in the biblical text. For others, the same story is an elliptical, poetic way of talking about human nature and our predilection to error. Viewed as a wisdom narrative, it addresses some of the big "Why?" questions, including why death came into the world. The fact that origin stories occur so widely in human societies, persisting even in highly technocratic ones like our own, argues that they remain meaningful to people in some sense. One does not have to be a "believer." Simply knowing something of the stock ideas and images the stories put in circulation is enough.

The foundational story, the origin myth of Western civilization is, of course, that in Genesis, the first book of the Jewish Torah and the Christian Bible. The fateful events described there were originally part of an ancient oral tradition that most certainly included multiple versions of the things that went on in a utopian garden inhabited by the first human beings (Kugel 1997). Eventually these narratives were compiled, reworked, and standardized by scribes, "redactors" in the language of biblical scholarship, to form the texts now considered sacred in Judaism, Christianity, and Islam. The story is familiar even to those with little or no interest in formal religion because it is part of the folklore of the Western and Middle Eastern worlds. Death was the consequence of humanity's "fall" from a prior state of innocence and goodness, a tragedy brought about by a fast-talking snake, a willful first woman, and a gullible first man. The woman unwisely took what the snake offered and urged it on her hapless partner. Suddenly, the two were aware of their nakedness, less here a matter of nudity than exposure, "unprotectedness" perhaps, to their moral and mortal condition. The consequence was eviction from their earthly paradise, he condemned to live and die by the sweat of agricultural labor, she to know the agonies of childbirth. The snake was not spared either, sentenced to permanently slither in the dirt at risk of becoming roadkill. And just to be sure they did not return to the nest, "great winged creatures" and a fiery sword were installed at Eden's gate to keep them out and guarantee their knowledge of death. Forever.

What is distinctive about Genesis, perhaps making it unique among the world's origin accounts, is its insistence that evil and death came into the world solely through human intention, by an act that was deliberately transgressive. Christianity's first and most vigorous popularizer, Paul of Tarsus, was authoritative on this point in a familiar biblical verse: "Well then; it was through one man that sin came into the world, and through sin death, and thus death has spread through the whole human race because everyone has sinned" (Romans 5:12). Commenting on that passage nearly three centuries later, Augustine solidified the linkage of a first or "original" sin with death, making it a central dogma of the nascent Church. "The entire human race that was to pass through woman into offspring was contained in the first man when that married couple received the divine sentence condemning them to punishment, and humanity produced what humanity became, not what it was when created, but when, having sinned, it was punished" (quoted in Pagels 1988: 108–9). Our mortality is tied to a specific primordial act of colossal disobedience. Having committed that folly, the offending couple could not undo it, and, consequently, neither can we, at least not without special effort.

The moral of that ancient story, an alleged human need for redemption and "salvation," is normally the bailiwick of theologians, historians, and religious commentators, but it has been taken up by anthropologist Marshall Sahlins (1996) as well. He sees it as a critical piece of the enduring folk wisdom or "native anthropology" of the historically Christianized cultures of the Middle East, Europe, and post-Columbian America. In his argument, the story is part of a very long running cultural ethos as well as a religious ideology. The Genesis image of the Fall locates the origin of the knowledge of death in a crime of willful defiance for which we have been out of sorts with ourselves and the creator deity ever since, an unhappy condition still expressed in a number of common images and metaphors. We live, for example, with bodies irredeemably bifurcated into "higher" and "lower" components of spirit and flesh, the two in an uneasy alliance of conflicting aspirations and desires. The loss of wholeness (from an original holy-ness) is a condition not only of the body but of human relationships as well. In the post-Edenic world, scarcity, greed, deception, inequalities, and the path of least resistance infect even the most altruistic deeds. Motives are always suspect, open to doubt, and often double edged, and the consequences of human behavior are often enough unintended, hurtful, and less than pleasing to the deity who created life. Living is a struggle between what we know is good for us and what we prefer in spite of it, between body and soul, self and neighbor, good and evil. Sahlins argues that this peculiar ideological construction sets the cultures of the West apart. "The idea of a war between self and society within every human breast, the eternal conflict of the flesh against the spirit, is our peculiar Adamic heritage" (1996: 403).[6]

The philosophical and practical subtleties of this ethos have preoccupied Christianized cultures for two millennia, from the western Church of late antiquity to the contemporary democracies of Europe and North America. The pleasure-pain principle, the apparent selfishness of human personality, the animality implicit in sex, a fear that power and coercion may be necessary evils of living, and a suspicion that there is something ennobling in suffering, most admirably expressed in martyrdom, are well-known themes. They derive from a view that human nature is untrustworthy enough that we have permanent need for something external—God, government, maybe the neighbors —to save us from our worst instincts. Sahlins notes that "This kind of self-contempt does not appear to be a general preoccupation of humanity" (1996: 396), although it has been of commanding interest to those who see Adam and Eve as their spiritual if not biological ancestors.

There has been, of course, a relaxing of some of these ideas in recent decades, particularly as they relate to the senses and physical experience, and we are less inclined now to apologize for the indulgence of small pleasures than were Americans of earlier generations. But an older, religiously inspired impulse to find something that will save us from our deficiencies keeps resurfacing in new and creative ways. Contemporary examples of modern moral repair include five-, seven-, and twelve-step programs of all kinds, dietary fads, personal fitness programs, save-the-earth crusades, born-again piety, pilgrimages to exotic sites of spirituality, motivational and leadership seminars, and fascination with spiritual entrepreneurs from Deepak Chopra to Billy Graham. These and countless other instances exemplify the salvationist hope that we should at least try to manage what ails us, even if we cannot conquer our failings altogether. Death is a most fertile site for engaging that struggle; cloning, cryonics, and organ transplantation are just a few of the technologies employed by those who hope to beat the game. Although secular maneuvers, they are inspired by imaginings of cosmic consequence, of salvation somewhere somehow.

My argument is that in multiple ways the imagery of an enduring salvationist ethos survives as Western "canonic memory" (Welker 2000), however far from the ancient languages and landscape of Genesis we may think we have come.[7] It is embedded in a wide range of expressive forms. On occasion Sahlins has used the term "mythopraxis" to suggest that such myths are active presences, shaping the story lines of the present in almost infinitely malleable ways. "The final form of cosmic myth is current event" (Sahlins quoted in Kuper 1999: 175), people being agents of their own mythologies. Discussing the practical and moral problems associated with death, Margaret Lock (2002) suggests something similar. Any culture's historic story lines are an "endless series of self-reflecting regressions . . . a fluid, contestable entity comprising sets of practice, ideas, imagination, and discourse, much of it barely available to consciousness" (2002: 46). As culture-bearing symbol-dependent creatures, we are daily perpetrators of received traditions whose ultimate origins we do not need to know or even care about. Their availability as resource, as a stock of ideas, images, and practices, is all that counts, the deaths of Bernadine, Morrie, Jim, and Kitty serving as exemplary retellings of "cosmic myth as current event." In the matter of death, human ingenuity in manipulating those imaginative resources is at its best.

VERNACULAR VARIATIONS

Ideas such as "mythopraxis" and "salvationist ethos" are useful as framing devices, and they are important to how I understand contemporary ways of dying. But more is needed to make a connection between these large abstractions and the immediate, lived experience of ordinary people. There is, after all, a social landscape where these big ideas play out as lively, localized expressions of belief and practice, where salvationist themes are recognizable in seemingly secular contexts. We can begin with some numbers.

Pollster George Gallup says 84 percent of Americans believe in God; 94 percent think they have a fair or better chance of getting into heaven; and, interestingly, those "more orthodox in their beliefs and more faithful in their churchgoing, differ little from other Americans on a number of non-Christian beliefs such as astrology, reincarnation, ghosts and channeling" (Gallup and Lindsay 1999: 40). Recent scholars of contemporary religion including Roof (1993), Stark and Bainbridge (1985), and Stark and Finke (2000) have described just how unconventional some of our religious interests are, while the literary critic Harold Bloom has remarked that "The United States of America is a religion-mad country" (1992: 37). It would be better, Bloom says, to stop trying to make distinctions between the secular and sacred because religious imagery is no longer contained by that distinction. From manger displays in shopping malls to ET's resurrection and starry ascension in the closing sequence of Spielberg's film, secular/sacred is a moot distinction. David Lyon (2000) opens his illuminating account of "religion in postmodern times" with a description of a Sunday morning family values crusade held, of all places, at Disneyland. "Jesus in Disneyland. A bizarre sounding collaboration. Or is it?" (1). Not really, because "much religious activity—often relating to orthodox belief—goes on outside conventional settings of churches and, for that matter, mosques and synagogues," and this expansion of pietistic expression into unexpected arenas is "central to religion in postmodern times" (xii).

And if religiosity invades the secular, symbolic traffic flows the other way too. The studio sets of many televangelists look much like those of Jay Leno, David Letterman, and Johnny Carson before that. Christian rock, once an oxymoron and confined to church basements for small audiences of true believers, came to commercial success as it morphed into a subgenre of pop music (Romanowski 2000). The interiors of suburban megachurches look like theaters, not cathedrals, and many function as full-service social centers for their membership. A do-it-yourself morality, a style Ammerman (1997) describes as "golden rule Christianity," does not require institutional loyalties of any kind. In fact, just the opposite. "The newer pattern emphasizes looser connections, diversity, and negotiation" by which "people increasingly create a sense of personal identity through an active sequence of searching and selecting" (Wuthnow 1998: 9, 10). And that busy searching and selecting is very much like shopping, the theme of Cimino and Lattin's aptly titled *Shopping for Faith* (1998). For some, the whole world is a spiritual bazaar, their journey through it as exotic as the Indian ashrams and Amazonian shamans they seek. For the rest, spirituality can be as conventional as a sunrise meditation; no longer must anyone convert, commit, or "join up" in any traditional, denominational sense to find inspiration.[8]

A familiar cliché is that Americans are spiritually inclined but, at the same time, not religious. To be "spiritual but not religious" is now rhetorical shorthand for having vague, diffuse feelings that there are important "matters of the spirit," but that churches and synagogues are not the best places for cultivating them. Sociologist Robert Wuthnow (1998) says churches are no longer denominational "homes" as earlier generations understood them but simply way stations along a self-styled, idiosyncratic "journey" (the popular metaphor) toward meeting one's spiritual "needs." Self-enlightenment trumps communal engagement; freedom to choose supersedes ethical commitment; spiritual experimentation claims (falsely, I think) to escape the entanglements of history and context. This "shift from dwelling to seeking" is one of the central attributes of post-1960s religious activism, marked as it is by a sense of the sacred as indeterminate, fluid, and more accessible outside received traditions than within them. Wade Clark Roof (1993) has called the restless souls so engaged "a generation of seekers" for whom inner experience, not creeds or congregations, is what matters, and for whom God or spirit is more likely to be found by looking "within" than "out there" in the human community or aloft in the starry heavens.

Sahlins's understanding of a persistent salvational ethos in Western cultures is consistent with these trends, the hope of deliverance remaining a strong motivator and expectation. His model is useful at a macro level. But we also need a connecting device that links it to the realities of everyday experience. How does such a grand ethos play out in individual lives, and what kinds of evidence tells us that it really is there? Robert Orsi, an ethnographically minded historian, has one answer. *Between Heaven and Earth* (2005) is his account of changes in American Catholicism over the last half century, and he begins the story with a vignette about his mother, who some years ago was terminally ill with inoperable cancer. At the hospital bedside, a frustrated nurse's aide struggled to find a vein in the dying woman's hand. As she fumbled with the needle and tubes, Orsi's father made a comment in Italian, prompting the aide to reply that she was a devotee of the newly canonized Padre Pio and prayed to him daily. That moved the elder Orsi to retell a familiar family story of how in his war days in Italy he had gone to Padre Pio for confession and the priest "miraculously discerned [his] troubles and anxieties without him having to say a word" (2005: 1). As the story was told, the aide kept looking for the diminutive vein and finally had to call in a surgical nurse, who promptly found it and revealed to the onlookers the secret of her technique: "I always say a prayer to Saint Jude before I start looking, and he never fails me."

That scene was a minor medical moment for five people who made three acknowledgements of the supernatural in the space of several minutes, all in a high-tech hospital that was not Catholic. Although Orsi does not invoke Sahlins's theory to frame that event, he witnessed the latter's perduring salvational ethos in action. It is not well-crafted theologies, creedal statements, nor sacred textual sources—the things people commonly say they "believe in"— that define what is "religious" for most people most of the time. "Religion," Orsi says, "is the practice of making the invisible visible, of concretizing the order of the universe, the nature of human life and its destiny, and the various dimensions and possibilities of human interiority itself, as these are understood in various cultures and at different times, in order to render them visible and tangible, present to the senses in the circumstances of everyday life" (2005: 74). Note his choice of words—practice, visible, concretizing, tangible, present to the senses. Religion is specific, in the moment, sensitive to context, and usually performative—an icon acquired at a memorable time and hung on a bedroom wall; the briefest sensation that a deceased friend is quietly present; an unvoiced prayer to the saint of lost causes for help in finding a withered vein. It is about special dress, bodily control, specific gestures, and formulaic utterances, in the presence of a congregation or in the privacy of one's office where no one else would see or care. It is, in an example Orsi uses in his teaching, the Bronx church holy water gurgling from a grotto designed as a miniature Lourdes, and the unlikely place it will be poured. "Bending under the open hoods of cars parked just outside the chain-link fence surrounding the grotto—which gives the site the look of a city playground—men in shorts and T-shirts filled their radiators with Bronx Lourdes water for protection on the road" (1997: 4). Orsi says he would ask his Midwestern university students if using holy water as engine coolant could be a religious act; most said no, and some were appalled at the idea. Religion, they insisted, is not concerned with the materially mundane or with "magical" ministrations; religion engages things "higher" than the traffic on the streets of New York. For them, the boundary between the sacred and profane was clear and certainly watertight.

Orsi thinks otherwise. He asks that we think beyond the customary, culture-bound binaries of Euro-American religious traditions—Protestant/Catholic, believer/atheist, Western/Eastern, and proposes that instead we look at what people actually do rather than what they say they believe. What are the local idioms of expression and practice that their professed tradition makes available to them? How are those usages inflected by class, ethnicity, power, race, and gender? What physical, corporal, and aesthetic tendencies do these little observances reveal? What learning and discipline is involved? What moments of crisis, decision, and action bring them forth? It is not so much sacred texts and holy personages that tell us what a salvational moment might be, but how people deploy what they know in the little chores and tough challenges that get them through a day.

If religious ideation is, as Orsi believes, embedded in the humbleness and immediacy of everyday experience, then Sahlins's salvational ethos ought to be discoverable in many of the routines commonly associated with death—body preparation, memorialization, grief, ceremony, and the like. Of particular interest would be "images of presence," as Orsi calls them, those occasions in ordinary time when the extraordinary seems manifest because relationships with the extramundane are invoked, as in St. Jude helping a nurse find a vein. Such images can manifest themselves in the expected places—in a graveside prayer or the conviviality of a funeral reception. But they can occur elsewhere and frequently do. An exceptionally vivid sunset can be more than a meteorological event, a remembered holiday recipe more than mere food. Even window reflections, shadows on walls, water stains on a freeway overpass, and occasionally the surface of baked goods—all have been viewed by some as more than simply examples of light refracting off mundane surfaces.[9] What is important is not that these incidents play to underlying superstition, magical thinking, or the determined credulity of believers, as the criticisms of the high-minded might go. The issue is that such moments are small, world-building activities invoking a relationship with whatever cosmic realms and agencies we presuppose, authenticating realities that are imaginatively (if not deductively) real. Images of presence are reminders that we can participate in worlds both present and imagined, neither more or less real than the other.

As features of transnatural relationships, images of presence occur in many venues, and the end of life is a particularly fertile one. Instances include family photographs, jewelry and handwritten notes slipped into a casket just before the lid drops; favorite music at a memorial service; strange noises about the house or household objects inexplicably moved in the weeks following a funeral; a dead child's face briefly sighted in a cloud; a framed rubbing from the Vietnam Memorial. These are venues outside formal theological conceptualization and the authorized rituals that reinforce them; they are the kinds of places where the sacred as an image of presence is made real. "The saints, gods, demons, ancestors, and so on are real in experience and practice, in relationships between heaven and earth, in the circumstances of people's lives and histories, and in the stories people tell about them" (Orsi 2005: 18). A well-decorated grave, an urn on a bookshelf, or a ring retrieved from a quieted hand can each become an image of presence, a linking device that through sight, smell, touch, or gesture evokes a web of perceived connections between the everyday and mysterious, far-off realms.[10]

In what follows, I look at a number of contemporary American death practices that, while occurring in a world where traditional religious codes have become optional, are still informed by an ancient, persistent, and religiously inspired redemptive ethos which shapes how we understand the value of life and solemnize its ending. My purpose is not to provide an overview of all end-of-life issues—the field is too large for that—but to give an ethnographic interpretation of some of the things many North Americans do when death is at hand for themselves or for those they care about. However quirky some contemporary practices may seem, they can be understood as modern permutations of an ancient and abiding Western ethos richly endowed with discursive and visual sites for the production of meaning and emotion, something the sociologist of religion Andrew Greeley has called "the imaginative and narrative infrastructure" of a heritage (2000: 16).

2 EXIT STRATEGIES

A COMPASSIONATE PHYSICIAN once remarked that in his neonatal intensive care unit "no one dies in pain and no one dies alone." That was his policy: humane, honest, straightforward. But it is not that simple, as he knew. Like birth and marriage, death is ritually dense in all cultures, creating occasions when belief and ritual are as present and as important as the physician's ministrations. That is because death creates a unique problem: what should one do with a body? In no society do people simply leave the dead as they are and unceremoniously walk away. Central to any death is a living body transformed into a corpse, and for that both medical and ritual technologies of control are brought into play. Despite the routine disclaimers on death certificates, no one dies a "natural death." As culture-bearing primates we do not have that option. In this chapter, I focus on some of the ritual aspects of death that occur alongside modern medical and commercial body management. As the technology of these fields of expertise has changed over the last half century, so have the rituals. We do things to, for, and with dying and dead bodies unimagined just a generation or two ago, and technological innovations inevitably create new moral, and hence ritual, challenges, which are the subject of this chapter. I want to consider first, however, why rituals remain important, even characteristic, of a society where practical-minded utilitarianism is thought to rule.

There are, of course, all kinds of rituals, but those associated with death and crises generally have been labeled "rites of affliction" by theorist Victor Turner (1968). Their purpose is to begin repair to serious disruptions of communal order so that, at least for the moment, further chaos and unpleasantness may be avoided. For example, spontaneous memorials to those who died in the Twin Towers appeared in virtually every American community within a day or two of 9/11, proclaimed as acts of solidarity with the bereaved and attestations of national resolve to face down the perpetrators. Quiet time with a corpse in a mortuary "viewing room" and tossing a handful of earth onto a casket at the bottom of a grave are said to assure the living that the dead really are just that. So too with the photo display at a funeral reception, the choice of an "appropriate" casket, eulogies from family and friends—these and more are reparative acts through which the enduring worth of an ended life is asserted. Ritual in this sense is informative, corrective, and prophylactic; it is one thing survivors can do to recreate order and find whatever meaning they can in something otherwise inexplicable.

All rites, says Catherine Bell, "illustrate complex cultural interpretations of the human condition and its relation to a cosmos of benign and malevolent forces" (1997: 119). As "cultural interpretations," they are meaningful events for several reasons. First, rituals are "overdetermined" in that they pack together in a highly ordered presentation multiple messages linking tradition, current experience, and personal need. They are dense with content and open ended, participants finding in them whatever seems hopeful. Second, as choreography of gesture, sound, and word, they invoke relationships "thought to obtain between human beings in the here-and-now and non-immediate sources of power, authority and value" (1997: xi). Third, rituals assure participants that they are included in those relationships, making everyone a stakeholder in some larger scheme of things. Fourth, rituals sometimes play out in a field of contention where participants assert one interpretation over others. This is especially true in pluralistic societies where older religious ideals compete with alternative systems of meaning. Death in America was once the exclusive domain of religious institutions and individual households, but that has changed. Modern death and the rituals associated with it are now quite likely to occur in medical and commercial venues, on the Internet, and sometimes in passionate public policy debates. My claim is that in these contemporary permutations and expansions which seem to crowd and overtake more traditional beliefs and practices, older salvationist assumptions persist.

I begin with two examples of what reasonably can be considered "traditional" death rituals. They are traditional in the sense that they have historical depth, a shared sense of legitimacy in a community of participants, and they foreground performative elements that are standardized, precisely enacted, and more or less understood by everyone involved. On these three points, they contrast markedly with some newer North American ritual forms that have emerged over the last four to five decades; these valorize diversity and spontaneity of expression, and are not overtly dependent on continuity with the past. They do reference on occasion Bell's "non-immediate sources of power, authority and value" but those "sources" are varied and sometimes optional.

BODIES OF TRADITION

A human corpse inspires curiosity, horror, menace, and sometimes reverence, but outside Hollywood recreations most of us prefer as little contact with them as possible. Cold human flesh is not pleasant to see or handle, even for medical students, whose experiences in the gross human anatomy lab with its rows of bodies and distinctive odor can be a challenge (Hafferty 1991). In preparing for a funeral today, few would volunteer to clean and dress the corpse of someone familiar, even though this was routine a hundred years ago. Sociologist Samuel Heilman, however, did just that. In his forties, it came to him that he and his age mates were quietly nearing the head of the line, that their time was coming. As he puts it, "my anxieties about death were shouting even more loudly than when I had first encountered them in my youth" (2001: 2). To quiet the demons, he volunteered to serve in his local Jewish burial society, a *chevra kaddisha*. Part of what came from that was a brave rarity in modern social science, a religiously inspired ethnography. But *When a Jew Dies: The Ethnography of a Bereaved Son* (2001) is more than the sociology of one corner of Jewish life. It is the reckoning of a baby boomer with the youthful fantasies of his most famous American cohort, one that once believed its own shibboleth that you cannot trust anyone over thirty.[1]

Like many Americans who give serious thought to the end of life, Heilman was dissatisfied with the language of talk-show gurus and self-help grief manuals, riddled as they are with vague therapeutic clichés and distanced from specific traditions, real communities, and a named supernatural. For him, the problem was more than their feel-good mind-set. It was their avoidance of the most important questions that any death inspires: What is the significance of a completed life? To whom or to what does it belong? Do the rituals of the past offer anything of use to modern people? In his volunteer work at the local *chevra kaddisha*, he discovered others with the same concerns. "We seemed," Heilman says, "to use tradition to cleanse death of its malevolence" (2001: 3), exactly what a rite of affliction is supposed to do.

When biological death occurs, an inert body or *niftar* must be purified; it cannot be consigned to the earth in its corrupted condition, for that would give death the victory. Thus the purifying work of the "holy fellowship" of the *chevra kaddisha*. Volunteers recruited from the local Jewish community wash and wrap the corpse, men for men and women for women. "This group serves as the agent for the immediate family, who, according to Jewish law, should not handle these preparations for burial personally but is responsible for seeing it done" (2001: 32).[2] Body purification takes place in a small room used only for that purpose, an unadorned assemblage of sinks, hoses, buckets, washcloths, sponges, and boxes of supplies. Not the decor but the accurate performance of the ritual is what counts. The washing proceeds in a precise order: head first, then face, neck, right hand, arm, chest, stomach, leg, foot, then similarly with the left, ending with the body orifices. Three times the lower gut is washed and drained, then packed with unrefined flax. Why flax? Because "the Chevra was acting precisely in accordance with its venerable rules and procedures, customs that stretched beyond memory and that those who regarded themselves as guardians of that tradition dared not change, especially in the face of death. . . . knowing the reasons was not necessary" (53). With ritual, precedent rules.

Women serve as *chevra* volunteers as well. Andrea Sommerstein posted an online account of the last phase of the washing and dressing sequence for a Jewish woman.

> The final tahara—an immersion in water—was performed quickly. One of the women immediately shook out a fresh sheet and covered Sarah with it. The dressing process was very beautiful. Sarah was shrouded in an immaculate white bonnet, pants, undershirt and overshirt, secured at the knees, waist and collar with three loop bows. The loops represent the tines of the Hebrew letter Shin—the first letter of one Name of G-d. One team member saw to it that the bows lay flat and pretty, while the others offered a poignant supplication in Yiddish that Sarah the daughter of Avraham remember her status as a Yiddishe tochter (Jewish daughter), and that she recall her Hebrew name while on her final course. When Sarah was placed in the casket, she looked clean, warm and cared for.[3]

There is a long tradition behind all this. Burial societies arose at the same time as kabbalistic mysticism, the latter originating in Spain in the fifteenth century and carried to other parts of Europe by expelled Jews. It is associated with the teachings of Rabbi Isaac Ben Solomon Luria, who developed a distinctive cosmology based on Jewish law and on messages he claimed to receive from deceased rabbis and the prophet Elijah. Kabbalists hold that souls preexist the body, that in fact they preexist multiple bodies which they will occupy in sequence. At the death of each one in its turn, purification is required since the resident soul accumulates moral taint (as well as wisdom) which will infect the next inhabited body. Final redemption is not easily attained, but with enough experience through multiple bodies and many lives, and with proper body washing at the termination of each, a soul finally arrives at a state of high moral purity. In the Lurianic formulation, transmigration is the normal course for souls, and while the idea seems to suggest something like reincarnation, it is something different. The translation of the Hebrew word for soul journeying, *gilgul*, is "revolving." How a soul revolves through several bodies has less to do with supernatural judgment of past behavior than with repeated opportunities for restoration. Only when a soul has successfully navigated a stream of multiple body and life experiences, having been duly purified at the end of each one, can it enter eternal life. "In achieving this goal, the individual soul is assisted by all of the soul sparks (that is, wisdom) which have adhered to it in the course of its career" (Gillman 2000: 182), and when all human souls with all their sparks finally arrive at the entrance to eternity, death will be no more and the repair of God's creation will be complete.

Little wonder, then, that a body polluted by the malignancy of its death must be morally refreshed and made suitable for transmitting its inheritance of sparks to a future body. That is what makes the task of the *chevra kaddisha*, in medieval times and now, so weighty. Each volunteer, each Samuel Heilman and Andrea Sommerstein, brings every human being closer to life without death, one soul and one cleansed body at a time.

As with any salvationist ethos, the kabbalistic vision gave expression to historical forces peculiar to its time and place. A doctrine of revolving souls accumulating life sparks over multiple lifespans made sense to persecuted fifteenth-century Jews for it replicated on a cosmic scale the reality of their migrations and exile, exile as historical experience but also as metaphysical destiny. In late modernity, the emphasis is different, less on a soul's travel through a sequence of bodily homes than on the singularity of each soul and body right now. Philosopher and Conservative Rabbi Neil Gillman argues that tahara affirms the sacred worthiness of the physical body itself, not Luria's notion of a bloodless, transmigrating soul. That ideal, he says, runs counter to our experience of ourselves as living beings. "The human body is of ultimate value and significance because it too is a manifestation of God's wondrous power. Would you discover God's presence? Look at the human body!" (2000: 268). In this contemporary view, the work of the *chevra kaddisha* is important beyond making death a holy occasion. It signals a fundamental religious truth: the lived body can be redeemed, even in a culture where death is sequestered, camouflaged, ignored, or denied. Flesh is fully as sacred as the immortal soul residing within it. Bathed in thick ritual, it can be gently reclaimed and made presentable to the deity who granted it life.[4]

BY FIRE AND WATER

There are other ways to purify a corpse. In a setting dramatically different and liturgically distant from that of the *chevra kaddisha*, cleansing of the body is public, and its disposal far more vivid. Governed by as strong a sense of tradition and ritual precision as is the rite of tahara, and very unlike Western rituals, Hindu cremation is intended to efface individuality—no monuments, markers, or burial sites are needed—as the individual's emancipated vital breath merges anonymously with the cosmos. Not water but fire is the purifying agent, and cremation on a riverbank pyre is explicitly sacrificial. The site of this drama is a 200–yard stretch along the Ganges River at the famous stone terraces, or *ghats*, of north India's holy city of Banaras (also called Varanasi and Kashi). To die there, or to have one's ashes taken there and dropped into the Ganges, is the goal of orthodox Hindus. "Death, which elsewhere is polluting, is here holy and auspicious. Death, the most natural, unavoidable, and certain of human realities, is here the sure gate to moksha, the rarest, most precious, most difficult to achieve of spiritual goals" (Eck 1982: 325). As with Orthodox Judaism, preparing the Hindu body for that experience is dense with gestural and ritual significance.

Manikarnika is the most famous of the ghats, the site of a sacred fire which burns constantly and is used to ignite individual pyres. Preparation for cremation begins not with a corpse, however, but with a trip. Dying in Banaras, says Christopher Justice (1997), is a family tradition for those Hindus who can afford it and is the wish of those who cannot. The hostels where the dying and their families stay, *muktibhavan* or "houses of salvation," offer simple, unfurnished rooms, resident priests, rounds of prayer, and private readings from sacred texts. It is assumed that the dying in residence have only days to go, rarely more a week, and their and their family's stay will be short. A sign that death is near, one that *muktibhavan* managers often make a requirement for booking, is cessation of eating. While it is common that those near death have little or no appetite, in the Indian setting, avoidance of food is culturally and spiritually significant. Lack of intake makes death more predictable, and control and predictability are both marks of a Hindu good death. Restlessness and struggle are inauspicious; one should die quietly and peacefully, and a starved body helps make that happen. Photographs in Justice's sensitive ethnography show families gathered around the dead and the near dead at their stark *muktibhavan* quarters. They show gaunt, emaciated, skeletal bodies, an aesthetic of death dramatically different from anything that would be acceptable at an American open-casket funeral. That difference points to a distinctive understanding of what the "natural" is: eating in the Hindu perspective is an inappropriate interference in the normative sequence of dying; the American practice of feeding the dying through tubes is an "unnatural" extension of life beyond its appointed limit. In Hindu expectation, a well-fleshed, well-fed body at the time of dying is a real problem. In a conversation with one of his respondents, Justice says he has "heard that if you have food in your stomach it makes it harder to obtain heaven." "Yes," the man replies, "that is the reason [for self-starvation]. If you have power in the body then the *pran* (vital breath) does not go quickly from the body, you struggle. So it is difficult. And if you are very weak, the *pran* will go very easily" (1997: 230).[5]

Bodies that would be declared newly dead in the Western medical sense are not yet so in Hindu eyes; the pran is still present. So the corpse is carefully washed by close family members, men by men and women by women, and basil leaves are put in the corpse's mouth. Wrapped in a white shroud (some castes use other colors), it is placed on a bier constructed much like a ladder. The gathered family moves slowly in a circle around it, and after a set number of circumambulations, the corpse is carried on its bier, along with rice balls as sacrificial objects, to the ghats.

As with any religious tradition, a complex metaphysics underlies this drama. The ritual reenacts a parallelism between an individual human body and the whole of the cosmos. In the beginning, Vishnu created the world by performing austerities at Manikarnika ghat for fifty thousand years. At the opposite end of time, the world Vishnu made will come to a fiery end at the same spot. Yet nothing will have been lost or gained; all that is and once was is simply transformed. As in physics, the material world never vanishes but simply becomes something else. Sacrifice is the necessary mover of that process. Thus a good death replicates in miniature all cosmic transformations. We have our time, and then, like Vishnu, we sacrifice ourselves at the ghat to become something else. Self-starvation is our last visible austerity, and in our willingness to do that, we too are holy.

Another feature of South Asian sacrificial regeneration is sexuality—not something Westerners usually associate with the end of life. In Hindu terms, life creates the opportunity for death, and death in turn begets regeneration. Jonathan Parry finds the symbolism of embryology in many of these rituals, rituals which he says "might be seen as a branch of obstetrics. Having dispersed

his own body in the sacrifice, the sacrificer reverts to an embryonic state and
is then reborn" (2004: 269). Thus the head leads the body to the pyre just as
it led the way out of the womb; the "vital breath" escapes the skull after having entered it during the early months of gestation; erotic gestures mark the
dance of the mourners on their way to the ghat, their procession described as
a second marriage party. Married couples who die within hours or days of
each other are placed together on the pyre in a sexual position. Esoteric texts
familiar to the Doms, professional liturgists who oversee body disposal at the
ghats, say the smoke of a combusted corpse becomes a cloud, then rain which
enters growing vegetables, and finally semen when eaten by men. The out-
ward journey of the departing soul is a kind of parturition. Hence the rice
balls carried to the ghats. "The word *panda* is used not only for the rice or
flour balls out of which the deceased's body is reconstructed, but also for the
actual embryo" that the released soul will become (2004: 271). Even the
remaining ashes have regenerative power. By way of complex alchemical
explanations, they become the semen of the cosmos. In one text, the god Siva
tells a group of sages, "The supreme purification of the universe is to be accomplished by ashes; I place my seed in ashes and sprinkle creatures with it. . . .
Ashes are known as my seed, and I bear my own seed upon my body. . . . Let a
man smear his body until it is pale with ashes" (David White 2003: 15). Death
is the doorway to new life; ash is critical to crossing its threshold.

Not all deaths, of course, follow prescribed formulas, and ritual adjust-
ments can be made to accommodate individual circumstances. David Knipe
describes a funeral in Andhra Pradesh for a woman who died prior to her husband, not unusual but not what is expected either. A death out of sequence is
not auspicious and requires a reparative ritual. Hers was performed on the
eleventh day following cremation, the eleventh day being auspicious. Men,
including the husband, were not invited but were allowed to watch from the
sidelines. The ceremony began when the dead woman made an appearance in
the form of a crow attracted to rice balls and food spread out on leaves. A married Brahman woman called the *brahma-muttaiduva* acted as her voice and
proxy during the ceremony. At one point, the surrogate was taken to a nearby
pool to be washed and purified, then outfitted as though going to her wed-
ding with flowers in her hair, wrist bangles, a necklace, a marriage cord, and
silver toe rings. When she was ready to receive the *preta*, or spirit, of the
deceased woman, a dab of turmeric paste was applied to the surrogate's forehead. The spirit in the crow then entered the earthly proxy and was ready
to speak. She was interrogated at length by the anxious onlookers: "'Who
are you, Mother'. . . . All ears bend to hear the reply from the mouth of the

brahma-muttaiduva. She should answer 'Gauri' or 'Gauri-devi,' indicating that the ritual has proceeded correctly and the deceased has become a goddess" (2003: 62). The *brahma-muttaiduva* finally voiced the spirit's satisfaction and pronounced a blessing on all the women gathered. Then the *preta* left, known by everyone to have become a goddess dwelling in Gauri-loka, a realm of brilliant yellow light. The unfortunate timing of this death was canceled by a corrective ritual, a potentially bad death made good.[6]

BODYWORK OF A DIFFERENT KIND

In the two rituals described so far, bodies are not presumed to have utilitarian value or to be a resource the living may use for their benefit. Jewish washings and Hindu cremations are about purification and spiritual transformation, enacted through observance of sacred traditions with rites that direct attention to worlds imagined but not seen. What happens, then, when that trust falters, the justifying metaphysics questioned, its loyalists pushed into the role of apologists? Over the last hundred or more years, North Americans have been devising new exit strategies that depart in significant ways from earlier practices inspired by religion. To a significant degree, that has occurred because of sophisticated medical technology, improved public health, increased longevity, and a historic shift in the causes of dying from acute to chronic ailments. The symbolic meanings attributed to death and to the body have correspondingly changed, and ritual innovations have followed. We are now more inclined to "celebrate a life" than "mourn the passing" of the newly dead. Headstone inscriptions are less likely to be limited to a name and a hyphenated time span, spare and hardly informative; now they are more upbeat and include something personal and idiosyncratic, sometimes even a photograph. Religious imagery, if it is there, shares space with information on hobbies and occupations. Nor are the choices of body disposal limited to ground burial or cremation as they once were. Some wonderfully odd opportunities are available to those who want them. To critics, these newer trends are more secular than transcendent, driven by powerful medical and commercial interests. To others, they are newer, better ways of defining the meaning of a body and the human place in the cosmos. I want to begin with one early instance of those changes because, compared to the Jewish and Hindu traditions discussed, and perhaps to religiously derived traditions generally, it is peculiar. Strikingly so. But it anticipates in its garish enthusiasm something that typifies exit strategies that are routine, even exemplary, in our time.

In Paris, in the latter half of the nineteenth century, a group of scientists and intellectuals formed a club. They named it the Société d'Autopsie Mutuelle, and it had one unique purpose. The members pledged to autopsy one another. This they did as a matter of scientific interest and devotion to building the new discipline of anthropology. Their unlikely passion has been examined in detail by Jennifer Michael Hecht (2003) whose impressive social history situates them within the wider context of science, politics, and anthropology in the Paris of their day.[7] The society's members had great respect for science but had other motives as well, including distrust of religion, intense anticlericalism, and utopian devotion to the Third Republic ideals of liberty, equality, and fraternity. The society lasted only a few decades, their overreaching claims quashed by lack of anything of scientific value to show for their experiments. But what they tried to do is worth recalling, not as historical trivia but as an early crystallization of ideological currents shaping end-of-life practices now. The members would recognize, for example, the procedures and equipment common to a modern medical examiner's lab or to the embalming facilities at a school of mortuary science. Certainly, they would appreciate the altruistic donation of body parts, the "gift of life," that enables others to live. Most especially, they would approve of how the language of medical science has crept into the vernacular speech of patients and families, eclipsing the theological in earnest bedside discussions. They saw these things coming and believed that by cutting into each other's bodies and brains they were building toward the future. Their science failed, but their project succeeded.

The Society of Mutual Autopsy was "a club in which one waited for one's friends and fellow members to die and then dissected them—unless they got to you first" (Hecht 2003: 5). A number of prominent writers, intellectuals, and freethinkers were participants, but not to learn dissection techniques. The membership included Émile Zola, Arthur Conan Doyle, Maria Montessori, Hamlin Garland, and Bram Stoker, plus several hundred academics, humanistic scholars, artists, doctors, scientists, socialists, feminists, and ordinary citizens who believed in the cause. Joining was easy. With an application letter and a legal will, the prospective member deeded his or her fresh corpse to the society solely for the pursuit of its scientific aims.

An applicant's letter often detailed motivations, most commonly dislike of religion and a conviction that science is the best way to promote human welfare. One Claudius Chapel, a mathematician who joined in 1878, included in his letter a résumé of professional achievements and publications. He asked the society to do what they wanted with any body parts they chose, distributing what they could not use to his alma mater. Like other academics with a commitment to learning, lifelong and beyond, "he hoped that his skeleton might hang at the Lycée de Nîmes, where he had been a student and later served as a professor. He also mused that the lycée might make use of his heart, liver, and intestines for anatomy demonstrations" (14). Eugène Véron, another applicant, was less grandiose when it came to body parts the society might use: "I attach no type of importance at all to that assemblage of decomposing matter"; and he was adamant that there be no funeral, for a reason typical of society members. He wished not "to contribute, even a little, to the accumulation of the wealth of the clergy, against which I have combated all my life and that never ceases to do to France and to the Republic all the evil in its power." Even more dismissive of his bodily remains and of Catholic clergy, Paul Robin asked in his application "to be put into a hole, naked or in a cloth or in a basket; 'to be buried like a dog' following the charming expression of the priests" (15).

That kind of bombast was legendary among the membership, a group not prone to making deathbed confessions as cautious bets on the possibility of heavenly rewards. And as enthusiastically antichurch and atheistic as they were, they also articulated a hopeful eschatology. In an oration to the society, honoring the steadfastness of longtime (and newly deceased) member Adolphe Bertillon, the speaker quoted from the latter's letter of membership renewal. Bertillon was in great pain and mental torment as death neared, yet he wrote, "To be useful has always seemed to me to be the most beautiful goal in life." In traditional eulogy style, the speaker added that "For him, as for [his friends], the only possible survival was that which resulted from acts and from works. Like us, he knew that the only means of not dying entirely was to dispose to the four winds all that one could of the fire of one's heart and the light of one's mind," an idea reminiscent of Luria's fifteenth-century notion of soul sparks (30). Emphasizing acts and works in contrast to Protestantism's historic doctrine of grace and Catholicism's sacramental salvation, the statement is revealing for its phrases "possible survival" and "not dying entirely." There was some sense, even in a gathering of atheists, that death could be transcended. A homespun poem written by Victor Chevalier in his 1889 letter of application suggested how that might happen. Likely he was inspired by viewing the Society of Mutual Autopsy exhibit at the 1889 Paris World's Fair (18):

> but Anthropology is instructing us, man is marching toward progress its [natural selection's] slow work that is marked off by the centuries the future race will march toward justice and reason under the guidance of science our perfect goal we will address where beings are equal in the universal

formation. . . . my goal is liberty, equality, fraternity in the eternal, just, and reasoned love of nature, the only divinity.

Not only is there respectful dipping into social Darwinism and French republicanism here, but Nature is brought forward as the ultimate source of whatever is sacred. Nature as divinity is the foundational truth to which we can repair as we ready ourselves for the forensic knife.[8]

The society's founder, Paul Broca, was a physician and Protestant by birth, well known to the public and to government leaders for his antireligious, politically leftist views. He was pro-Darwin well before his medical colleagues and at a time when it was professionally risky to say so in public. "I would much rather be a perfected ape than a degraded Adam," he once declared, seeing in the long, slow transformation of our species a progressive, linear improvement. Properly examined, he said, the body will show us how that happened, anatomical form being a better guide to our future prospects than the repressive dogmas of church or state. Broca performed the society's first autopsy and, as a true believer, gave his own body for autopsy as well, specifying that when the time came they should take a very careful look at his brain.

Broca's linkage of body materialism to ideological idealism was explicit. In the late nineteenth century, autopsy was a familiar part of medical training and indigents and criminals filled medicine's need for teaching cadavers. That meant that what was known about human anatomy came largely from individuals, to put it delicately (as the egalitarian-minded members of the society usually did), who were less than stellar contributors to the common good. It seemed to Broca that bodies, and especially the brains of the gifted, people like himself and the members of his club, would reveal new and more interesting possibilities. That being so, brain dissection could be a powerful weapon against both the biological and the social status quo, dramatically proving the worth of the new discipline of anthropology. Hence M. Chapel's inclusion of his academic résumé with his letter requesting autopsy. Correlating specific brain features with evidence of individual productivity would be the first step toward generating a race of bright, socially aware, productive people immune to religious and political blandishments. That all seemed very hopeful, the high priests of anthropology delivering designer brains and engineered bodies so the species could march forward into a wondrous future. Few sensed that a dark eugenics lurked in that vision, its "master race" horrors only a few decades away.

But the characterological evidence alleged to reside in the lumps, nodes, and pleats of the brains of the gifted never materialized. As brain extraction and dissection replaced general autopsy, brain weight became the society's major interest. Weight was thought to correlate with intellectual productivity. It did not take long, however, for that claim to fall apart, especially after the brain of one of the club's star members, the well-known French statesman Léon Gambetta, was measured in 1886. There was a high level of public interest in this, for the society regularly published its findings in a newsletter, members wrote for respected medical and scientific journals, and the popular press was drawn by the high profiles of many who were autopsied. Gambetta was a popular republican critic of the Church ("Clericalism, that's the enemy") and thus his brain was ceremoniously delivered from where he died to the Laboratory of Anthropology by railway and car, apparently held aloft along the way for public view. But unfortunately, it weighed in at a dismal 1,160 grams (most human brains are between 1,300 and 1,400 grams), and remeasure put it at just 1,150. How, then, to square Gambetta's superior intelligence, oratorical talent, legal skill, and well-aimed verbal shots at the establishment with such puny heft? Attention shifted from overall weight to left-brain circumlocutions, still called in medicine Broca's Area (responsible for speech production), and it was alleged that here the Gambetta brain was complex and overly developed. But doubts about direct linkages between brain morphology and personal character, already harbored by some society members, were becoming public, and enthusiasm for the group's anatomical explorations was fading. Perhaps it was out of humiliation, therefore, that Gambetta's heart, not his brain, was sent to Paris's Pantheon of French heroes, where it still rests alongside the more intact remains of Voltaire, Rousseau, and Victor Hugo.

Within a few years, the heyday of celebrity autopsy was over, and the public and scientific community lost interest. By 1930, when the last application for membership arrived, the society itself was moribund, awaiting Jennifer Hecht's scholarly autopsy half a century later. Yet by ennobling its work with a naturalistic (if pseudoscientific) eschatology and the mystique of laboratory-centered rituals, the society's efforts were not without consequence. In fact, they caught exactly the spirit of something just emerging.

The Mutual Autopsy Society is of interest on several counts, and not just because of its eccentricity. First, the members modeled for a wider public the possibility of transforming a pervasive religious ethos into something scientific, secular, and individualistic, creating a recognizable recasting of older salvationist themes. The leaders of the movement functioned as a quasi-scientific priestly class, specifically ministering to those who were ideologically committed—and perhaps needy—in their professed humanism. As high priests, they addressed their flock's ultimate question: what can death mean for an agnostic or an atheist? As with any community of religious seekers, says Hecht, particularly a fledging one, the "role [of the Society's founders] was sacerdotal, regulating the details, issuing text, creating doctrine and liturgy, and, of course preserving relics. [The members'] rewards were sacred if not beatific: when their autopsies and eulogies were published, they each entered into the canonical text of their cult" (2003: 25). It is one thing to be steadfast in one's convictions when the goal is eternal residence in God's paradise, something else when dying means foregoing any hope of personally benefiting from the generous donation of oneself. To maintain hope and trust among free-thinking atheists requires strong leadership and a liturgy that appeals to scientific iconoclasm yet offers some grand sense of purpose, even mystery. To the degree that the society achieved that, it replicated in its own way the classic ars moriendi of centuries past. Humanity at large, not oneself, was the imagined beneficiary, self-sacrifice enabled participation in the vision, and death had a future, not in a celestial heaven with the despised clerics but in the grateful memories of generations to come. The self-autopsy promoters were busy creating rituals of their own—confessionals, canonical texts, justifying doctrines—so that later enthusiasts would know how to carry on the work of the founders. Like their Jewish and Hindu counterparts, they sought ways to neutralize the sting of death through ritual acts that regularized and institutionalized an overarching set of beliefs. That, for believers, apparently, was comfort enough.

More important to us now, the society was something of a sociological canary in the mine, or perhaps more accurately, a canary in the mind. They had the sense, muddled by an implicit eugenics, that death could be imagined scientifically and managed by medically trained scientists. They proposed a new language for talking about death, promoted biomedical techniques for the moral purification of corpses, emphasized individual idiosyncrasies rather than transcendent deities in their memorializing, and held up altruism in death as the best kind of sanctification. The Society of Mutual Autopsy must have seemed to many a quirky aberration. But they were not. In the nineteenth century, modern medicine was coming into its own through standardized educational programs based on physiology, pathology, bacteriology, and organic chemistry. The commanding role of doctors in hospitals was established, their central role in managing dying affirmed. Like the society, hospitals kept accurate patient records and even brought the stereotypical white coat into wider use, adopting it as the medical profession's homage to science. At the time, lab technicians wore white coats, and the wave that carried the Society of Mutual Autopsy transferred control over death from those who

wore priestly robes to those dressed in white ones. We are their ritual reenac-
tors, sans the bogus science. In the remainder of this chapter, I examine some
of the implications of these changes.

A NEW DYING

The members of the Society of Mutual Autopsy were naturalistic reduction-
ists in extremis, reality for them only what can be seen and described. In the
spirit of their reductionism, I begin with a short list of some of the physical
signs typical of human dying. Of course, there are almost as many ways to die
as there are individuals, and Sherwin Nuland's popular *How We Die* (1993) is
a solid presentation of some of them. But bodily changes are only the beginning. Getting dead is more complicated than a stilled heart and a cooling
body.

   We all die a bit every day just to keep ourselves alive, but not all of us
do so at the same rate. Cells die and are replaced on a regular maintenance
schedule, those lining the intestines having the shortest span, just a few days.
Skin cells are constantly shed and replaced as are those of all the bones and
muscles. Heart, brain, and certain eye cells are the most durable, and some are
not replaceable at all. At the cellular level, writes microbiologist Cedric Mims,
"Destruction goes hand in hand with construction, and unwanted cells have
to be killed off and removed. Apoptosis is sometimes called programmed cell
death, and it is the natural process by which the body controls cell numbers
and rids itself of superfluous or redundant cells during development. The cell
also switches on its suicide program when it is infected with certain viruses—
better to die than to support the growth of the virus with the formation of
hundred of extra invaders" (1999: 101). Over time, however, damage control
slows and biological reserves cannot keep up with needed replacement and
repair. Toxins accumulate, organs begin to falter, and the integrity of the
whole is weakened. Malfunction spreads until animate life can no longer be
maintained.

   Mims quips that "everyone dies after their last meal" (1999: 112), but sta-
tistically we are more like to die at night, since that is when metabolic activity is slowest. Apnea, the absence of breathing for a minute or more, is a
common symptom; tissue at the back of the throat collapses, and brain signals to the muscles regulating inhalation do not get through. A "death rattle"
occurs when mucous accumulates and the coughing mechanism does not
clear it. As the brain is slowly starved of oxygen, its cells die off rather quickly.
Eye surfaces then dull, pupils dilate, and the body begins to cool. Blood pools

in the lowest parts, usually the back and buttocks, resulting in skin discoloration. For an hour or two there may be slight movements as tendons relax, suggesting the individual is still alive. Then rigor mortis sets in, starting with the jaw and fingers, as muscle tissue stiffens due to blood coagulation. That condition can last for several days, after which relaxation may reoccur. In an unattended body, one not embalmed or promptly disposed of, the skin dries and shrinks to produce a distinctly skeletal look. Hair and nails seem to grow, but it is skin tightening that makes it appear that way. Microbes in the intestines feed on surrounding proteins and spread into adjacent tissues, producing gas as a byproduct. Like a balloon, the corpse fills and expands, patches of skin slipping off until the surface is breached and internal liquids spill out. Nature's economy returns us to our constituent elements. In food and drink we enjoyed the things of this earth every day we lived. Now the favor is returned.[9]

Every death, of course, is unique in some way, and this list is a simplified compilation, as though death would be obvious in its manifest signs. But death is not always self-evident, a fact that produced a long history of anxieties that anticipated some of the problems we have with death in our own time. In Europe in the 1700s, for example, there was a genuine public fear of premature burial, and it inspired a rich and troubling folklore of hauntings and supernatural revenge. Doctors at that time did not "declare death" for their patients, partly because governments did not collect population statistics and there were no death certificates to sign. The determination of death was left to the family, the undertaker or the village priest. Needless to say, there were occasional errors, "false positives" of the worst sort. To prevent this, homegrown preventives came into use—sticking pins under the nails, scorching the sole of the foot with a candle, and pinching nipples with forceps. One John Snart, author of an 1817 book of medical curiosities, was more systematic than most. He recommended "keeping the corpse warm under close watch for at least a week, with no indecent experiments for twenty-four hours except holding a looking-glass to the mouth or brushing the soles of the feet with strong pickle [acid]; or electricity; or warm baths; or pasting tissue-paper over the mouth and nose; or blowing Scotch snuff up the nose; or pouring volatile tincture of ammonia down the throat with a funnel. If none of these seem conclusive, cut the jugulars, or separate the carotid arteries, divide the medulla, or pierce the heart" (Iserson 2001: 33). Snart would hardly have been faulted by those who, half a century later, posted a warning in an 1884 issue of *The Lancet*, a British medical journal: "It is not so much the undue haste as inexcusable carelessness that must be blamed for the premature burying of persons who are not really dead" (35). Clearly, these things happened, and, sensing an opportunity, entrepreneurial coffin makers applied their ingenuity to the problem, designing models with a periscope-like tube housing a cord attached to an above-ground flag, pointing device, or bell. The bell could be rung from below, inspiring the expressions "saved by the bell" and "a dead ringer." The *Lancet* commentary and these innovative caskets underscored real anxieties that persisted into Victorian times, some of Edgar Allan Poe's short stories offering vivid literary treatments of the theme.[10]

As quaint, perhaps, as these preventive measures seem in retrospect, the medical issues and public anxieties that inspired them have their parallels now. Specifically what, and how much, has to change before "apparent death" —a coma, persistent vegetative state, or even the last days and hours of a slow descent to one's end—becomes genuinely final? Given how most people will die, from accidents, a heart attack, spreading tumors, or in their sleep, recognizing death is not for them an issue. But what of those in a long-term coma or maintained by machinery in an Intensive Care Unit (ICU)? Their dying is forestalled by medical management, sometimes for a long time. Their prospects create new problems and resurrect some old debates about what "life" is and what changes have to occur for it to be clearly, unambiguously no longer there. Margaret Lock calls this the "new dying," death occurring not as it will "naturally" but delayed, managed, and timed (2002). When that happens, death is no longer an obvious biological event. It is a social phenomenon too, culturally shaped by available technology; decisions about its application and withdrawal; and the constraints of medical, legal, and moral standards. There is "debate about what exactly constitutes death, its timing and determination, the technological and ritual orchestration of dying, other parties' competing interests in the body, and the emotional and practical responses of the living to the dying [which] are all moral concerns. Such concerns are the products of specific cultural and historical milieus" (192). What is the background of this "new dying"?

Experiments conducted on animals in the nineteenth century and early in the twentieth, mostly on dogs and nonhuman primates, showed that extracted cells, organs, and even severed heads could be kept alive for a time. Animals put into laboratory-induced hypothermia were successfully resuscitated, suggesting that resuscitation failure could be a reliable indicator that life had ceased. But then a new question arose. If there is a distinctive lifelike period between apparent death and resuscitation, what are its diagnostic features? How could they be measured? What, in a biomedical sense, is "life," and what is that in-between period? Those may be speculative philosophical problems for some, but to clinicians they suggested the possibility of restoration, if it could be known where "life" as an animating force lurked in a seemingly dead body. Somewhere in that hazy borderland, physicians might be able to locate and even extend it. How much resuscitation (or another procedure) would be necessary to do that? What quality of life would that produce? Toward what ends might that be done? Were their ethical, moral, or even religious implications involved? These questions were raised by medical professionals a hundred years ago. And they are still being raised. Every day, anxious families contemplate "pulling the plug" on a life that hovers in a liminal zone between active living and cold death. It is the technology of life support that makes these decisions possible, necessary, and hard. Bodies can be kept alive through heroic measures, but the issue now is more than extending life. It is timing death.

Death as a medically timed phenomenon is fairly new, made possible largely by efficient mechanical ventilators (descendents of the cumbersome "iron lungs" of the 1940s) and ICUs, first established in hospitals in the 1950s. Their successes prompted the ethical, legal, and medical challenges that the early resuscitation experiments foreshadowed: What specifically is diagnostic of life? What parts of the body unambiguously signal its presence or absence? Is a full technological press to maintain life as long as possible always desirable, or ethical? Once started, when should it be stopped? Who is authorized to decide that, and on what evidence? These are practical, medical issues. But in an interesting way, they border on the theological as well. Powner et al. (1996) suggest that historically the medical diagnosis of death has wavered between two perspectives. Those who were "centralists" held that the "soul" or life force was concentrated in a single organ and that when that vital life force was no longer present, the rest of the person died as well. As the common view before 1700, it seemed reasonable, since in fatally traumatized or decapitated bodies the organs die off sequentially rather than all at once. "Because the heart often continued to beat after the lungs and brain had ceased to function, its supremacy was usually reconfirmed in this hierarchy of importance—the 'monarchy of the heart'" (1220). "Decentralists" held that all parts of the body are suffused with a vital essence of life. At death the soul can be restrained from leaving, or induced to return, as their early experiments with resuscitation and electroshock seemed to show. "Because organs wherein sacred vital principles once existed could be lost, but again reclaimed through resuscitation measures, the centralist opinion that a central divine and controlling life force resided in a single organ became less accepted" (1219). By the twentieth century, the centralist position returned: resuscitated lungs and hearts did not necessarily reanimate the brain or its higher cognitive functions. The brain, therefore, and not the heart, must be the residence of the soul, or vital force, or whatever we care to label Life with a capital L. That is the current view (the Mutual Autopsy aficionados would say they knew it all along), but it is not conclusive. Even now, Powner writes, "Physicians currently ponder the same questions and, though they use different diagnostic tools, follow the same process in searching for death, or life, in patients. . . . Does the "vital principle" of life reside in, or is it produced by, a single organ or part of a single organ (centralist theorem) or is the "soul" represented throughout all organs, tissues, or cells (decentralist principle)?" (1219–20). Whatever individual physicians believe, and their beliefs vary, patients and their families have opinions too. And sometimes they clash in spectacular and noisy ways.

THE BODY AS THEATER

Theresa (Terri) Schiavo died in a Florida hospice at age forty-one on March 31, 2005 after fifteen years in a persistent vegetative state. She went peacefully, unaware that hers was the most contentious, publicized death since those of Karen Ann Quinlan in 1985 and Nancy Cruzan in 1990. And like theirs, her death brought to public attention ambiguities in medical interpretation and applicable law that were deeply troublesome to many and seemingly immune to reconciliation. Her case was ensnarled as well in a divisive family feud and hasty, overheated political gamesmanship at state and federal levels. Medically, her death has been declared the most significant case of clinical ethics in recent years, one that dramatizes public fears about the topic, the power of courts to intervene, and the regard and treatment of the disabled (Hook and Mueller 2005). A Florida newspaper editorialized that "she was an international icon, a vessel into which people poured their need for miracles, their convictions about personal liberty, their ideas of democracy and justice and heroes and villains, and their terror of letting go" (quoted in Roscoe et al. 2006). That is a heavy burden for one person and one death.

The byzantine history of this case has its own sizable literature, too large to fully review here.[11] But briefly, Ms. Schiavo had a cardiac arrest at the age of twenty-six; the cause was never determined, but an electrolyte imbalance due to extreme dieting was suspected. She was resuscitated but never regained consciousness. A percutaneous endoscopic gastrostomy (PEG) tube was placed in her stomach to supply water and nutrition because she could not swallow voluntarily. The tube's removal a decade and a half later precipitated her rapid decline into death and was the focus of much of the controversy. The medical examiner's autopsy report stated that Schiavo had suffered extensive, irreparable brain atrophy from which no rehabilitation was possible. Her brain at death weighed 1.35 pounds, less than half that of a functioning woman of her age and size and well below that of Karen Ann Quinlan, who died after ten years in a persistent vegetative state (PVS). Nearly 70 percent of the cortical area was affected, and, lacking functioning neurons, she was probably blind and would have had no cognitive activity or awareness of external stimuli. Only her brain stem continued to operate normally, regulating basic functions such as body temperature and breathing.

Between the heart attack in 1990 and death fifteen years later, Schiavo's personal and family tragedy became a national media event and a cause célèbre for pro-life activists, religious conservatives, and opportunistic politicians. After the heart attack, Schiavo was briefly in the care of her parents, Robert and Mary Schindler, and her husband Michael. But the demands were heavy, and she was moved to a skilled rehabilitation facility for intensive physical, occupational, and speech therapy. Those efforts had no success, however, and she was diagnosed with a persistent vegetative state.[12] During that time, Michael brought and won several malpractice suits alleging a relationship between infertility treatments and her heart attack, most of the award going into a trust fund for her care. Eventually, however, he and the Schindlers had a falling out. He wanted Terri placed on "do not resuscitate" status while they urged she be kept alive at any cost. Saying they wanted her brought home for care and rehabilitation which they would provide themselves, they sued to have Michael removed as her legal guardian. In 1998 Michael petitioned to have the PEG tube removed, claiming Terri would not have wanted to live on in a vegetative state. There was no advanced directive to support his claim, but the courts accepted circumstantial evidence concerning her preference. The Schindlers countered with an unprecedented five-year series of judicial reviews, expert medical reviews, and appeals that eventually went to Florida's legislature, the governor, the U.S. Senate, and the Supreme Court. Even the pope got involved (the Schindlers are Catholic), declaring food and water a basic human right that cannot be denied. During this time of litigation, Terri Schiavo's PEG tube was removed and reinserted twice, in 2001 and in 2003, by court authorization each time. On March 18, 2005, after years of appeals, judicial denials, and amid national media coverage of action in the courtroom and raucous protests in the streets, the PEG tube was removed one more. Terri Schiavo died thirteen days later. Michael arranged for cremation, and her ashes are buried in a Florida cemetery. Of the many commentaries written about this case during and since, perhaps the most fitting is that of Kathy Cerminara, who wrote its legal history: "In the end, there are no winners" (2006: 101).

The Schiavo case is exceptional for the media coverage and political grandstanding it excited. For a time, death planning was a legitimate topic for small talk. What was not exceptional, however, were the difficult end-of-life decisions faced by Michael and the Schindlers, decisions that are discussed, debated, and resolved every day by thousands of families in American hospitals and homes. The language of those conversations is now familiar, more so than it was just a few years ago: patient autonomy, quality of life, prognosis, right to die, palliative care, good death, death with dignity, medical futility, "pulling the plug," physician assisted suicide: the language, as Bill Moyers astutely put it in the title of his 2000 public television series, of modern death *On Our Own Terms*. This is the newer linguistic palette of death management; the language of medicine, ethics, and law bumping (sometimes contentiously) against older rhetorics of religious faith and transcendent realities. It is language that invokes the practical challenges of the end of life: the burdens of family caregiving (Roscoe et al. 2006); surrogate decision making (Ditto 2006); continuing medical treatment when doctors consider it futile (Veatch 2005); the authority of biomedical ethics as a discourse alongside law and religion (Preston and Kelly 2006); the intersections of law and medicine, especially in troublesome cases such as brain injury (Parry et al. 2005); the ethical implications of specific medical procedures such as PEGs (Breier-Mackie 2005); and even debate on whether the dying have disability rights (Johnson 2006). Schiavo's case made these topics acceptable fare for television, tabloid, and radio talk-show scrutiny. But they are only subsets of something else that affects those near death and the rest of us who eventually will be; that is, a general reimagining of the liminal space between life and death, required now that medicine rather than sacred agency regulates the timing. Life and death are not as clearly separated as they once were, and we, not the gods, have arranged that.

Some years ago Barney Glaser and Anselm Strauss described death as "a problem in social definition" (1965). David Sudnow, who, like Glaser and Strauss, researched hospital dying, used the term "social death" to describe the space between responsive aliveness and explicit deadness, "that point at which socially relevant attributes of the patient begin permanently to cease to be operative . . . and when he is, essentially, regarded as already dead" (1967: 74). Sudnow's use of the verb *regard* is essential to the concept. He is describing the period when communication between medical staff or visitors and the patient changes, even evaporates, as when the living speak of and about the dying as though they were not present, as though they were now deaf. It is "the cessation of the individual as an active agent in other people's lives" and is "linked to, but not predicated upon, bodily death" (Froggatt 2001: 320).[13] Terri Schiavo's death dramatized that concept and enlarged it as something more illuminating than simply a withdrawal of communication. Her social death was a huge moral space into which was poured many of the ambiguities inherent in all modern technologies for "managing" the end of life. Hers was akin to the best of television's legal and medical dramas, with the added edge that an unpredictable cast and a host of unruly extras made the outcome uncertain up to the end. Millions in an international audience took in the spectacle and likely pondered their own encounters with dying people, or considered what will happen to them in their turn. The anthropological concept of liminality describes well the fuzzy notion of social death, the stranding of the individual between two states of being, what one was and what one will eventually be. "Liminal entities are neither here nor there; they are betwixt and between the positions assigned and arrayed by law, custom, convention, and ceremonial. As such, their ambiguous and indeterminate attributes are expressed by a rich variety of symbols in the many societies that ritualize social and cultural transitions" (Turner 1969: 95). The problem is that this "new dying" is a recent phenomenon, and "social death" as Americans experience it has yet to be standardized around a "rich variety of symbols" such as those operating at Banaras or in a *chevra kaddisha* washing room. Most spectacularly, the Schiavo controversy was a visualized one, and visualization was central to its symbolic endowment and political enactment. I want to consider that briefly, for the images of Schiavo as a liminal persona are most revealing of the ambiguities of social death at the present time.

SEEING AS BELIEVING

For all that has been said and written, Schiavo's repeated appearances in highly publicized video clips may be what is most memorable about her. In the summer of 2002, four hours of video were made on court order as an aid to determining whether her cognitive functions could be restored. When the video footage and other evidence, including direct medical examination and brain scans, indicated little or no likelihood of recovery, highly selective clips were distributed by the Schindlers to national media outlets, including CNN, Fox, and MSNBC, in the hope that the governor of Florida and state social service officials would be persuaded to stop the court approved removal of Terri Schiavo's PEG tube. Images from those clips also appeared on numerous Web sites, including a newly created www.terrisfight.org (from which they have since been withdrawn). They were seen nationally in newspapers, tabloids, and on protesters' signs waved before news crews and cameras. Over a number of months a huge viewing public repeatedly saw and came to know Terri Schiavo not from four hours of steady viewing but repeated exposure to a handful of clips lasting less than a minute each, many only a few seconds.

They were carefully selected to carry a message to the widest audience possible —the camera does not lie and Terri wants to live.

Several clips were iconic of her predicament. One showed her tracking a floating Mickey Mouse balloon, responding to music and touch, blinking when asked to do so, and opening her eyes wide on command. In another she seemed to acknowledge her mother, who was holding her daughter's head in her hands. Declares one Web site, "You decide. . . . Here are video clips clearly showing that Terri Schiavo is responsive and not in a "permanent vegetative state" as claimed by her husband, Michael and his attorney. . . . Seeing is believing . . . now that you have seen do you believe that this woman deserves to be starved and dehydrated to death?" Says another: "Watch these streaming Real video clips of Terri Schiavo and her parents and ask yourself, 'Was it ok to starve this severely handicapped woman to death by depriving her of food and water? Can you imagine what it would be like to be in Terri Schiavo's position, to be slowly and painfully killed, and not to be able to speak up to prevent it?'"[14]

These images, of course, reveal almost nothing of Terri Schiavo the person or her real medical condition. They were propaganda issued by disheartened parents and politicized supporters who had not got their way in the courts. But that is only backdrop to the issue of interest here. Social death as a liminal space has expanded into something much larger than it was when Glaser, Strauss, and Sudnow were describing it in the 1960s. As a space that is neither vital life nor corpselike death, it is an ambiguous condition created by technology and aggressive medical surveillance, and it invites all kinds of cultural "in-fill," ideologies, narratives, and private interpretations coming from multiple sources, including interest groups with an agenda. With Schiavo, some of that in-fill is recognizable as the stuff of specific religious traditions represented by her parents, conservative politicians, and street protestors, all of whom insisted they were advancing an agenda of the "culture of life." But there is other material there as well, and a careful reading reveals something of the ongoing cultural construction of the new social death.

First, the clips themselves, the "evidence" that Terri Schiavo was very much alive despite fifteen years in a persistent vegetative state. What the public saw was less a species of reality television than what Hendrik Hertzberg, writing in the New Yorker, called "special effects." On the original four hours of video made for court review, Schiavo displays little more than involuntary and random movements. In a clip widely shown, however, she appears to respond to a doctor's request to open her eyes. What was edited out (according to husband Michael's attorney) were eighty to ninety sequentially repeated requests to which she did not respond "appropriately" at all. In the well-known image of Terri Schiavo looking closely at her mother's face, she does so because her head and neck are being held in that position. Where she seems to follow a balloon, it is not clear whether it is an intentional act or an involuntary jerk of her head. "As neurologists who have examined her have explained, the snippets are profoundly misleading. A few seconds of maximum suggestiveness culled from many hours of tape, they are more in the nature of special effects than of documentary record" wrote Hertzberg (*New Yorker*, April 4, 2005). The on-screen/off-screen voices, too, have a manufactured tone, not at all like adult conversation between coequals. She is addressed as though she were a child or a demented elder, repeatedly told how well she is doing, how ably she responds. "How do you feel?" "She doesn't like that, does she?" "You like it?" "Look over here . . . you follow that, don't you?" "Good Job! Good Job! Good job, young lady" (Waldman 2006). She is, in effect, infantilized by her protectors.

Yet for many who saw the clips on Web sites, her living presence was real and convincing. A BlogsforTerri site announced: "Here are video clips showing clearly that JUDICIALLY APPROVED TORTURE victim Terri Schindler Schiavo . . . is NOT in a 'permanent vegetative state' as claimed by Michael and his Death-by-Execution attorney." (Supporters commonly use her combined maiden and married name, presumably out of distaste for Michael.) One blogger responded, "I am glad I saw this, because Terri seems more 'alive' than the media will tell you" while another wrote "If you can't see the live [*sic*] in this woman, something is seriously wrong with you. . . I have seen all the videos." Said another, she "opens her eyes as WIDE AS SHE CAN. Note the WRINKLES ACROSS HER FOREHEAD caused by her also RAISING HER EYEBROWS as high as possible. . . . This action required perception, reasoning and intuition. At the time this video was taken, Terri was keenly aware that Michael and his accomplices were saying that she was practically dead already and *working to achieve that end*." Others were less charitable. "I watched the videos and came to the conclusion that Terri's family were completely selfish in their desires to keep her alive." "You people are crazy. You spend millions to fight to keep a feeding tube in a waste while actual children starve to death in the world." And less kind: "Have you seen her CAT scans, people? SHE HAD NO BRAIN." "It only takes about 10 seconds to see that this is a body with no functioning wetware." Others saw political machinations in the videos. A disability rights activist and feminist spoke for herself and her partner: "If either of us were incapacitated, these right-wingers might argue to keep us alive; but they would oppose our right to stay by each other's bedside."[15] One aspect of the politicization of the Schiavo death, especially during the final weeks of the controversy, was the transformation of the word "vegetative" into something like a racial slur. Politicians and various interest groups were anxious to make the point that no one, and especially not Schiavo, is a vegetable. While that critique worked no detectable change in standard English (although some in the medical community might want to find another word, best Latinized, that will be harder to impugn), it did signal the variety of interpretations that can be brought to the videos and the profound lack of agreement as to what they mean. Seeing, apparently, is believing— believing as beholding.

An interesting interpretation of the nearly visceral power of these images, at least for believers, is suggested by Paolo Apolito (2005) in his study of religious visionary experience on the Internet. His focus is Marian apparitions, their webmaster promoters, and the adoring virtual communities which form around them. The argument is that mediated images of supernatural entities— Mary, Jesus, angels, ghosts, even halos and obscuring oval blobs in photographs of everyday scenes—acquire technosacralization in a number of ways. For example, in times past, Mary (and other supernatural agencies) appeared only to a select few, three child visionaries at Fatima in 1917, Bernadette at Lourdes in 1858, and a single man in Mexico in 1531 when she presented as the Virgin of Guadeloupe. With electronic distribution, however, her pixelated image, her visual presence, is democratized, standardized, and available to anyone everywhere. Appearing now as a cathode ray sweep, her manifestation has no social context, lacks physical placement, is bereft of a shaping social history, and belongs to no particular community, time, or place except the shifting one of the virtual. Her online appearance is not constrained (as were the originals) by historic creeds and legitimating institutional authorities; such forces are not relevant to electronic apparition and adulation. Outside a context, the meaning of the image is entirely dependent on the private, subjective resources of the beholder. Thus the Schiavo blogger declaring that if you are unable to "see the live in this woman, something is seriously wrong with you." In a technosacral presentation, privatized, context-free understanding substitutes for history (the originating four hours of court-ordered video intended only for medical diagnosis) and canonical hierarchies of judgment (the rules of evidence and procedure that constrain doctors, judges, and medical examiners). The private epiphany of the virtual trumps the reality of the painfully lived moment at Terri Schiavo's bedside, much as the online "proof" of the Virgin's vigilance substitutes for the institutional memory of a place-bound event in real human time. [16]

THE DOCTORS RESPOND

A second debate engendered by Schiavo's prolonged social death focused on its precise cause, when she really died, and the role of human action and inaction in her death. One would think her autopsy report, thirty-nine pages of extensively footnoted, highly technical material, would settle those questions. It states, "Ms. Schiavo's brain showed marked global anoxic-ischemic encephalopathy resulting in massive cerebral atrophy. Her brain weight was approximately half the expected weight." Occipital neuronal loss "indicates cortical blindness. Her remaining brain regions also show severe hypoxic injury and neuronal atrophy/loss" (2005: 35). While her brain stem continued to function, maintaining breathing, digestion and sleep patterns, she was blind and lacked the neuronal capability for language, memory, self awareness, knowledge of her current state, and the ability to purposefully interact with her environment. The term "persistent vegetative state" (PVS) was widely used in the public debate, but it is not clear that she died from that so much as *with* that. The medical examiner noted that "Postmortem correlations to PVS with reported pathologic findings have been reported in the literature, but the findings vary with the etiology of the adverse neurological event." So while the *cause* of her death was "complications of anoxic encephalopathy," the *manner* of death was listed as "undetermined." The autopsy did not—and by its nature could not—answer the question central to the public debate, whether a "person" in some sense still inhabited a body lacking the biological machinery for cognition and self-direction.[17]

Nor did the autopsy settle anything as far as the Schindlers were concerned. Following its issuance, they made point by point refutations of the medical findings. They insisted Terri Schiavo was "brain injured," not "brain dead," and still had a strong heart (the latter a finding of the examiner). At terrisfight.org, one of their principle venues, they stated that "Terri's case was NOT an end-of-life case," adding that "The IME's report also confirms that TERRI WAS NOT TERMINAL. . . . THAT TERRI WAS BRUTALLY DEHYDRATED TO DEATH. Second, . . . There is absolutely no evidence that Terri wanted to die of dehydration. . . . Third, the IME said clearly that dehydration, not her brain injury, was the cause of her death. Terri was dehydrated to death before our eyes. The moral shame of what happened is not erased because of Terri's level of disability. . . . As a society, it seems that we have lost our compassion for the disabled."[18] The issues for them were neither PVS nor medical and bioethical judgments about brain death but instead centered on disability and respect for the disabled. In this they had powerful allies in several Senators and Representatives who as physicians made a medical diagnosis supportive of Terri Schiavo's potential for rehabilitation without having examined her directly. (One physician-Representative dissented. And Barney Frank, not medically trained, said of House members eager to take sides, "We're not doctors, we just play them on C-SPAN.") After Terri Schiavo's death, the Schindlers almost disappeared from public view, saying they would establish a foundation to advocate for the rights of those caught in circumstances like hers. During their long struggle with the law, politicians, and media, the Schindlers were befriended by a Franciscan monk, Paul O'Donnell of St. Paul, Minnesota, who told the Associated Press that, "If this is going down, I'm glad I'm here to make the statements and bear witness to what I call the gospel of life," invoking the administration's "culture of life" motif with its pro-life and anti-stem-cell-research overtones. He added that "If people cast us off as fanatics, then they cast us off as fanatics. But that's part of what being a prophetic witness is, to be able to say something is the truth. Whether or not people listen doesn't matter to us."[19] Of course, millions of people did listen, formed opinions, and wondered if the same could happen to them.

Advanced in a language of moral outrage and high theological purpose, social death was reimagined as a disability rights issue. That theme may or may not catch fire, but it certainly eclipsed a quieter discussion that had been proceeding within the medical community on the legal and bioethical ramifications of the Schiavo case. Dr. Timothy Quill, who is well known for research and publications in this area, observed that "The story of Terry Schiavo should be disturbing to us all. How can it be that medicine, ethics, law and family could work so poorly together in meeting the needs of this woman" and he deplored "what can happen when a patient becomes more a precedent-setting symbol than a unique human being" (2005: 1630). He acknowledged that her life could have been prolonged, but believed that the way she died, without food and water, "can be a natural, humane process (humans died in this way for thousands of years before the advent of feeding tubes)," and he concluded, "the central issue is not what family members would want for themselves or what they want for their incapacitated loved one, but rather what the patient would want for himself or herself" (1632–33).

In that last sentence Quill named a key issue, upheld by all the courts involved in the Schiavo case but swamped by political and faith-inspired hyperbole: the priority of the desires of the patient as an autonomous individual. The Supreme Court affirmed in the 1990 Cruzan case that individuals have a "liberty interest" in their own body, an interest that includes the right to refuse medical treatment even when the consequence is death; the Court upheld their "right to die." But clear evidence of the patient's intent is required;

when people are in a persistent vegetative state and cannot speak on their own, other kinds of evidence are admissible, but they must be compelling. Terri Schiavo had no advanced directive, which is not unusual for a younger person, so the Florida court undertook an exhaustive examination and finally ruled that withdrawal of feeding tubes would have been her choice. That effort was legally rigorous and it "produced the highest-quality evidence and provided the most judicial review of any end-of-life guardianship case in U.S history" (Perry et al. 2005: 744). Schiavo had a "right to die," and, given the evidence at hand, to die was her preference. There was no "quality of life" issue to consider, despite the demands of the Schindlers and their supporters. Nor could there be in any legal sense. A study appearing in the *Journal of the American Medical Association* several years earlier found no agreement in the medical literature on what "quality" at the end of life is nor on how it is adequately measured (Gill and Feinstein 1994). The American Geriatrics Society (1997) issued a list of ten quality-of-life concerns such as symptom management, financial burdens and positive communication with family members, but those were useful only as guidelines to professional practice, not as principles of law.[20] At best, what Schiavo, her family, or any of the rest us could realistically hope for is a "least worst" death and good palliative care. But that is not what the Schindlers advocated, nor what the media explained, nor what the courts had to decide. That very large point was missed, despite the fact that discussion of it has been going on inside the medical community for years, traveling under the rubric of bioethics.

Bioethics is a newer specialty within medicine, developed in the 1960s and 1970s and led in part by Albert Jonsen, a former Jesuit who as a professor of bioethics defined and wrote the history of the field (Jonsen 1997, 1998). His religious affiliation is relevant because many of those who established bioethics programs in hospitals and universities were trained in moral philosophy, theology, and occasionally medicine, often in Jesuit institutions. Their value to physicians was in advising on ethically difficult cases, to which they brought a method of formal, dispassionate reasoning and interpretation. The principle of informed consent was one of their early contributions to medical practice. Physicians Tom Preston and Michael Kelly (2006) believe bioethical principles should have been applied in the Schiavo case, and they, like Quill, were "vexed" by the "deep schism over the moral/religious issues inherent in how we die in the modern age of medicine. In our opinion, the political and legal wrangling distracted from the public understanding of the medical and bioethical issues involved in the case" (121). For them, and probably many other physicians, a rational, bioethical critique early on might have spared everyone the media-hyped drama of one helpless woman's dying.

While bioethical reasoning will never hold great fascination for the public at large, it is nevertheless important because it is invoked regularly at the bedside of the dying and in doctor's consultations with their families. Preston and Kelly list four operative principles of bioethics—medical beneficence, patient preference, quality of life, and social context—the first two being salient here. "Using the principle of beneficence, we ask does this treatment maintain life, restore health, and prevent symptoms? . . . Would continued treatment have relieved symptoms of pain and suffering? (122, 123). Since Schiavo's PEG tube for feeding and hydration was the treatment in question, the bioethicist would ask what medical benefits it had for her. The Schindlers claimed (rightly) that the feeding tube was what kept her alive and, further, that withdrawal would amount to torture and murder. Nor did Terri Schiavo ever intend to die from dehydration. For the parents, the tube was an unusual but not exceptional way to receive nutrition, and given their daughter's condition, it was essentially a substitute for a spoon or a straw. That position had the support of the pope, who declared that food is "natural" whether we are sick or not, and providing it is a moral obligation, especially when disability makes normal eating impossible. Specifically, he said,

> I should like particularly to underline how the administration of water and food, even when provided by artificial means, always represents a *natural means* of preserving life, not a *medical act*. Its use, furthermore, should be considered, in principle, *ordinary* and *proportionate*, and as such morally obligatory, insofar as and until it is seen to have attained its proper finality, which in the present case [a person in a PVS] consists in providing nourishment to the patient and alleviation of his suffering. (Pope John Paul II, March 20, 2004)[21]

The bioethicist's response would be that medicine's goal is to maintain life, and as life must necessarily end at some point, doctors must act to prevent an "untimely or inappropriate death" (Preston and Kelly 2006: 123). In Terri Schiavo's case, she had lived fifteen years as a PVS patient, unable to chew or swallow. Most certainly, without the PEG tube she would have died of starvation long ago, just as people in her condition have done for thousands of years. The "naturalness" of food and water is not at issue. The feeding tube is. A tube is not a mere substitute for a spoon. It was there because she was on life support, clearly a medical intervention, and there is nothing "natural" about it. Food, air, and water are natural. But it is unnatural to pierce through the abdomen and place a tube into a patient's stomach, and then pour food through the tube and force it into the stomach with a machine, as it is to use a machine to blow air into a patient's lungs. With artificial breathing, the air at least goes in and out through the natural wind-pipe, while artificial feeding bypasses the natural process of swallowing food through the esophagus to the stomach. The mechanisms of artificial feeding and breathing are different, but one is not more or less natural than the other. (2006: 124)

There was in addition the pope's concern with the "alleviation of suffering." Would Terri Schiavo suffer once her PEG tube was removed—was dehydration a judicially imposed "torture," as some alleged? Beneficence requires that physicians do no malfeasance by imposing treatments that will not lead to better health and that might prolong suffering. Preston and Kelly argue that the medical treatment she received would not restore health, relieve symptoms, or lead to any lasting improvement. It simply maintained a body with a brain so damaged it would never recover. Further medical intervention was, therefore, not indicated. Nor would withholding food and water be a source of discomfort. Terri Schiavo had no capacity to know the experience of pain, as neurologists testified and the autopsy proved. Nor was the option of long-term care in a hospice or at her parent's home a reasonable one. "Although Terri would not have perceived suffering had she remained alive, over the years or decades to come she inevitably would have acquired illnesses associated with aging and being bed-ridden, which would have increased the psychological burden on her family" (2006: 126). Ultimately, of course, and following the principle of patient autonomy, only Terri Schiavo could say whether living that way was what she wanted, or if it would have been a burden to herself or to others. Since she could not imagine that, or speak to it, the "quality of life" argument was moot. At the end of Terri Schiavo's day, all that was really left was the hope that any decision taken had truly been made on her behalf and not that of her husband or parents. Grand pronouncements by politicians and priests notwithstanding, a "one size fits all" formula makes little allowance for individual patient wishes.[22]

Nothing could be more dramatically emblematic of the peculiarity of modern social death as the inscriptions on the Cruzan and Schiavo headstones. Nancy Beth Cruzan's reads, "Departed January 11, 1983, At Peace December 26, 1990." And Terri Schiavo's reads, "Departed This Earth February 25, 1990, At Peace March 31, 2005." Although few of us will die as they did, their experience dramatized how "medical technology could contribute to, could in fact create, bizarre and unnatural forms of human life and could foster new kinds of suffering for the family and medical staff and perhaps for the

machine-dependent person. . . . [that] 'death' could become *a matter of decid-
ing when a person should die and when a person should be considered dead*"
(Kaufman and Morgan 2005: 65, emphasis in original). Sharon Kaufman and
Lynn Morgan estimate that the number of Americans currently existing as did
Terri Schiavo is in the tens of thousands. As the baby boomers age, there will
be many more. Some are kept alive for long periods, many more hover
between life and death in ICUs and hospital wards for only the time it takes
the family to make a decision about them. The complexity of their condition
undermines all easy talk about "death with dignity" and the "sanctity of life."
What kind of dignity? What kind of sanctity? Sad it is, Kaufman and Morgan
say, "that families—who have the least knowledge of disease processes, brain
function, treatment capabilities and the forms of ordinary dying—have the
greatest responsibility 'to decide,' it often seems to them, between life and
death, as though a family member could bring a very sick person back to
health, simply through a decision to stave off death" (2005: 34).

3 THE BODY AS RELIC

AUTOPSIES AND DISSECTION were part of medical training in Bologna as early as 1280. The medieval physicians and their students who studied there were not the only ones with an interest in anatomy, however. Caroline Walker Bynum, who has written extensively on religious beliefs associated with the body in the history of Christianity, notes that "The same period saw increased enthusiasm for boiling and dividing holy bodies in order to produce relics for quick distribution" (1995: 322). Thomas Aquinas's body may have been boiled in 1303, and "An (unboiled) hand given to his sister was, significantly, later found to be 'incorrupt.' Holy bodies were also embalmed because, as witnesses testified at one canonization proceeding, 'God took pleasure in' their bodies and their hearts." Secular bodies were disassembled and distributed as well, "the custom of eviscerating and boiling the corpses of royalty and aristocrats and burying the resulting body parts in various localities" (323) being a common one in parts of Europe. The fragmentation of bodies and display of their parts were thought to be holy acts for lay and clerical figures alike. They still are.

The remains of St. Frances Xavier, Jesuit missionary to India and other parts of eastern Asia, are an example. He died in 1552 and, in recognition of many miracles and healings performed during his life, was named a saint in 1622. Buried in a church in Goa, India, he did not disintegrate; like Aquinas, he was "incorrupt." Perhaps to move the canonization process along, an arm was cut off in 1614 and sent to Rome as evidence. The rest of him was exhibited in January, 1975, brought out of the Basilica of Bom Jesus in Goa for a processional through the streets. A compiler of such appearances says "The right arm, several toes, and other parts of the body are missing, having been removed for relics," and adds that the rest of the saint "is dry and shrunken in size, but there is no corruption and some hairs of the beard are still seen on the dried cheek flesh" (Cruz 1977: 176, 177). His preservation can be attested by the fifty thousand people along the parade route who saw him in his glass coffin. Remains such as his possess power, potentially available to believers for curing disease, increasing crops, and general blessing and merit. They are charismatic, and it does not take much of them to deliver a miracle. A part is as good as the whole, a finger tip the equal of a hand, arm, or complete body. And the many North Americans who know or care nothing of such traditions are not immune to conceiving of the body in roughly the same way. They do so regularly in some of their own body disposal practices.

DEFINING DEATH

To become a relic, a body must first be unambiguously dead. For medievals, boiling assured that. The Schiavo and Cruzan tragedies, however, as well as recent medical history, show how elusive a clear definition of death can be. And not for lack of trying. In the late nineteenth century, it was widely assumed in the medical establishment as well as in popular understanding that the loss of heartbeat and respiration were appropriate and sufficient indicators of the end of life. A physician's pronouncement of death, noting the date, hour, and cause on a certificate, settled it. But the mechanical ventilator, the workhorse of the modern ICU, complicated the natural course of things. Patients not breathing on their own could be kept alive, making respiration and heartbeat no longer useful as diagnostics. So attention shifted to the brain. Might evidence be found there for the presence of life, even in apparently "brain dead" people whose lower brain or brain stem continued to function, maintaining the heart, breathing, and body temperature? Were they dead, partially dead, partially alive? How much brain had to be dead before they could be declared physically, legally, and morally dead? Who should decide that, and on what evidence? In short, what is death and how do we know it when we see it?

Several notable medical commissions attempted to resolve this quandary, dutifully issuing guidelines for physicians and patients alike. Initially, in 1957, Pope Pius XII was approached. When, he was asked, is it acceptable to turn off the machines that keep people alive? His answer was not really helpful. There is no basis in morality for rendering a judgment, he said, and exceptional, heroic measures were not required. He added that "human life continues as long as its vital functions—as distinguished from the simple life of organs—manifests itself" (Jonsen 1998: 237). Did he mean, then, that breathing, digesting, and sleeping as regulated by the brain stem, even in the absence of self-consciousness and any ability to meaningfully interact with the environment, qualified as "life"? That did not move the discussion along, as it gave no guidance concerning when to declare further medical intervention futile. That became an urgent issue when the first successful heart transplant was performed in 1967 and was then replicated hundreds of times in eighteen different countries (Lock 2002: 81). Similar success soon came with other organs as well, including kidneys and eyes. A clinically useful definition of death was critical because the freshest and most survivable organs are those promptly removed from a warm corpse, preferably one with a beating heart. But to justify the rush to gather useful body parts, a donor must be certifiably dead before "harvesting," as it is called, can begin. Thus in 1968 the Ad Hoc Committee of the Harvard Medical School to Examine the Definition of Brain Death was formed to settle what death as a singular phenomenon is. But they sidestepped that goal in order to accomplish something else. Their opinion appeared in the *Journal of the American Medical Association* (*JAMA*) on August 5, 1968, and began, "Our primary purpose is to define irreversible coma as a new criterion of death" (1968: 85). Narrowly defining coma as a "new" criterion avoided the larger question—What is death?—and solved instead a clinical transplant issue by defining the permissible circumstances for organ harvesting. The state of the brain, not the heart, was the center of their attention, and that triggered another debate. How much brain has to be dead before its owner is really, truly, absolutely dead—all of it, some of it, or just the "higher" centers of consciousness? Even the editors of *JAMA* were stymied, writing later that year that "It seems ironic that the end of existence, which ought to be clear and sharp as in a chemical titration, should so defy the power of words to describe it and the power of men to say with certainty, 'it is here'" (1968: 539–40). Despite these doubts, brain death, however construed, quickly became the criterion adopted in many state legislatures, sometimes supplemented with heart and respiratory failure as additional criteria. Thus "It [became] possible to be dead one way in one state and dead in another way in the neighboring state. The confusion that the Harvard ad hoc committee had hoped to dispel returned" (Jonsen 1998: 240).[1]

One thing that is clear about these medically oriented attempts at definition is their devotedly materialist focus. Death is about cells, organs, body systems, and functional integrity, the end of life being the province of scientific medicine. That is not wrong, given that the aim of medicine is to preserve health. Yet not all body parts are created equal, and just as the members of self-autopsy community valorized the brain, more recent investigative commissions have arrived at about the same place, and for comparable reasons. The brain is the physical site for what we essentially are, the "self" mysteriously embedded in the stuff between our ears, or at least selected parts of it, and when that fails, that is death. While useful for laboratory purposes, perhaps, this is nevertheless not the only way of defining death.

For many clinicians, writes Margaret Lock, "death is not a self-evident phenomenon. The margins between life and death are socially and culturally constructed, mobile, multiple, and open to dispute and reformulation" (2002: 11). What kind of "reformulation" might that be? In the 1980s, sociologist Lindsay Prior was interested in that question and began looking at how death was understood in practice in Belfast, Ireland. He examined medical literature and public records, the vocabulary of causation, the named types of dying, descriptive accounts of pathology, and the medical and bureaucratic uses of that information, calling these varied formulations "schemes of knowledge." He also considered what doctors, hospitals, patients, and families did with regard to body disposal and cemetery usage; and their feelings about their choices. Taking into account things beyond the body's "imprison[ment] within physicalist assumptions," Prior concluded that

> death is primarily defined by the social practices which encompass it more than by the presence or absence of any given set of physiological processes. In that sense, death is not, and never can be, characterised simply according to biological "facts." . . . Indeed, death is always, in part at least, defined by a whole array of legal, social, religious and political practices not withstanding the fact that such practices may be historically and culturally variable. (1989:12–13)

To understand what death is, to imagine any definition of it, requires looking at the body as a physical construction but also at those practices and "schemes of knowledge" that, like medieval boiling, construct the context for being dead in some way. In the remainder of this chapter, I look at several schemes—the body at the end of its road, as a useful relic, as an aesthetic one, and as an object for ritual experimentation. Each of these schemes of knowledge defines in somewhat different ways what death is for many contemporary Americans. It is not just cell failure, nor is boiling in oil required.

AT JOURNEY'S END

Hospitals are where most people die, and while some will have the peaceable, uncomplicated departure they expect, many will not. In her ethnography of modern hospital dying, *And a Time to Die* (2005), Sharon Kaufman describes why that is so. Hospitals are complex bureaucratic cultures, where patients and families arrive as strangers and usually leave the same way. As somewhat bewildered "house guests," they are under pressure to make life and death decisions even when they do not clearly understand the consequences of their choices. They know little of what "life support" means in a practical sense; that cardiovascular resuscitation is rarely successful; that prognostication is always iffy; that a mechanical ventilator once applied is difficult to unhook, at least in a moral sense; and that the dignified, self-affirming "control" implied by advanced directives and guidelines on patient autonomy are rarely present at the bedside. Even the well educated have little knowledge of human anatomy or how specific diseases progress toward biological death. Consequently, they often resist the prompt, critical decision making that professional staff would prefer, in part because they do not understand "the way hospital treatment and hospital logic work to prolong life, stave off dying, and then make death happen" (2005: 59). They most certainly are unaware of the implicit institutional expectations and internal professional dynamics that are in play on and off the wards. Kaufman provides a roadmap through this complicated cultural terrain, only some of it obvious to the dying and those who accompany them on the way.

Physicians, of course, control the critical intersections in this landscape; they direct the traffic. They are trained to prolong life, not to act as though death is inevitable, and so they ask for tests, get advice from other specialists, and prescribe treatments that may be helpful. There is great pressure from families and from peers to do just that. Patient care is as much a matter of negotiation as of medical necessity, and that becomes more evident as patients deteriorate and move more quickly toward their death. "In many instances the line between some ideal notion of 'humane' end-of-life care and aggressive medical intervention that delays death is not clear to physicians *in practice*"; and thus, one physician told Kaufman, instead of simply withdrawing treatment and waiting for death, "the quickest way out of this is to get (the patient) over these little humps so then I can get him out of here" (39). The intent of treatment is to stabilize the patient, while death is rarely discussed until it is imminent and obvious to all. Surprisingly, says Kaufman, "I rarely saw dying declared by anyone—doctor, patient, or family member—more than seventy-two hours before it happened. More often dying was named much closer to death's actual arrival. Dying did not become institutionally recognized or named, and thus is not really happening, until medical staff interpret discrete measurements as irreversible and fatal. . . . Death is mostly *decided*, not waited for" (92–93).

As one subculture within the hospital system, nurses have their own understanding of what patients are experiencing as they move toward finality. Kaufman notes that they use the words "comfort" and "suffering" more often than doctors. Doctors are diagnostic and treatment oriented, focused on organ and system failure. Nurses attend to pain. They have technical skills for doing that, particularly on display in the ICU, and many nurses told Kaufman they saw their work as providing relief, not cure, and not prolonging life simply to avoid death. One described ICU patients as "trapped in a disease, in their bodies," adding that it was not up to her to change that: "I would say, what are the chances of this person living? At what point are we being futile? How many days are we going to pursue this treatment? And if we really did something less elaborate, maybe one out of a hundred would live, but the other ninety-nine would not be tortured" (42).

These ambiguities, which became more evident as death approached, created what Kaufman calls a "zone of indistinction" that is filled with contradictions. For example, the "good death/bad death" imagery that dominates public discourse is almost irrelevant at the bedside and in the ICU where other realities dominate. Patient autonomy and informed consent, as legal and moral ideals, may or may not have relevance for patients in critical care, since the exigencies of dying can change daily. Patients cannot always speak for themselves, and even when they do, or when an advanced directive does it for them, they can change their minds with their mood and options. Their preferences, written or oral, can be contested by family members, and they sometimes are. When old family grievances stir, the medical staff wait, taking necessary (as they see it) measures to prolong a failing life and hoping that a consensus will emerge. They do this because the medical imperative, professionally and technologically, is to extend life if possible. For some patients, that will mean an open-ended, perhaps lengthy attachment to a mechanical ventilator, morphine drip, and feeding tube. "The organization of the institution," Kaufman observes, "pushes everyone toward lifesaving treatment, even when hospital staff, patients, or their families do not want to prolong dying." And a bed occupied is, of course, one that could be used by someone else. She adds, ironically, "dying people are not wanted in medical institutions, and it shows" (29).

The freeway of Kaufman's ethnographic roadmap is what the professional literature calls "the dying trajectory." It is the road through her zone of indistinction, and it has two, somewhat separate lanes. The first, that of "heroic intervention," usually begun in the ER, is the route of those who will leave the building wrapped in a shroud. In the ER, they are intubated and moved to the ICU. Diagnostic tests begin, and a treatment program is established and monitored. If they improve, they are discharged (put on lane two), but for those who are terminal and maintained on machines, there is a period of waiting to see what comes next. Waiting, however, is not simply "down time," although families and visiting friends often perceive it that way. Kaufman masterfully depicts how "down time" is structured in hospital culture, how particular events are spaced along the "heroic intervention" lane. For example, doctors normally tell "the truth" to patients about their condition, but they do so in terms of the treatments they want to use, not in terms of the nearness of death. What families usually hear them saying is that there is more time than there really is. If one treatment fails, the physician then proposes "trying something else"; thus patient hopes are maintained, the dying trajectory lengthened, the waiting extended. When families or patients are confrontational or stalled by indecision, staff members usually let them have their way, at least for a time, further extending the wait. Those who do not expeditiously "move along" their lane, who "linger" or avoid hard decisions, are said to be "in denial." Where doctors and nurses see life ebbing, anxious families search for tiny glints of hope—the shift of an eye, the smile that may be only an involuntary response—and these delays are tolerated because of liability issues. But they pile more time onto the wait. Eventually, without signs of improvement, staff and family turn to negotiating agreements about "what X would want" or asking whether "the person we knew is still there." Medical personnel may gently channel this conversation by suggesting that "prolonged suffering" is now the issue, not stabilizing what is left of life, as the medical problem is transformed into "facilitating" a comfortable death. That will mean resolving uneasy distinctions between killing and deliberatively ending treatment. Movement along the heroic lane often stalls at this point until someone decides it is time to "pull the plug," stop the ventilator, move the patient to palliative care, or up the dosage to numb pain, knowing that these moves silently edge a comatose spouse or parent toward eternity. In the jargon of medical ethics, that is the so-called secondary effect: death per se is not intended, but it is the outcome anyway. The end of the trajectory arrives, not from waiting out God's will as in former times but as it has been "managed" within the culture of the hospital system.

Lane two on Kaufman's map zigzags back and forth through a revolving door. Again, a patient is admitted and examined by specialists, tests are run, and symptom relief is prescribed. It is possible that the patient will enter the land of heroic intervention, but usually these revolving door travelers instead make many short visits to hospitals and clinics in the final year of life. They are usually under the care of a family physician who coordinates with various specialists he or she uses at local clinics and who as a team intermittently encounter the patient during a long period of slow decline. Tests are run on each pass, and pharmacy bills quickly move toward the stratosphere. The number of specialists may change and even grow as conditions worsen, but there will not be enough wrong with the patient to justify permanent occupation of a hospital bed. In-home nursing care and adult family homes are alternatives, and this lane requires some degree of financial wherewithal on the part of the patient. Death may end in the hospital during one of the patient's short visits, but there is less intensive involvement by medical staff than is typical of heroic-care cases.

Kaufman's point is that each lane of the dying trajectory is a piece of the culture of the hospital and has a logic and a dynamism that neither patients, families, nor medical professionals can easily escape. She likens it to the moving walkway of an airport, one with high walls, and even those patients who want off and want to die are surrounded by families and doctors reluctant to end medical support. Expensive technology and aggressive intervention signal hope, and no one wants to feel they were the proximal cause of hopelessness and premature death. Critics may rail against high-tech dying and its alleged artificiality, but when their wife, their parent, their favorite uncle is at risk, they want something done.

Both heroic intervention and repeated visits through the revolving door imply that help is on the way, that hope can be sustained. They distance the notion of death so no one has to think about it until it is almost in the room. Few are able to lift themselves off of either track. But Kaufman cites one instance where that happened, and it is touching to read. She quotes novelist Philip Roth, who in his memoir *Patrimony* describes how he met early one morning with the doctor treating his father. Heroic measures were proposed, including putting the elder Roth on a ventilator. That would not have solved the problem of the tumor interfering with his respiration, but it was the only thing to do at that point. The doctor added that, once connected, the ventilator could not lawfully be disconnected until the patient could breathe again on his own. Visualizing that, writes Roth, "I thought about the misery that was sure to come, provided he could even be kept alive on a respirator. I saw it all, all, and yet I had to sit there for a very long time before I leaned as close to him as I could and, with my lips to his sunken, ruined face, found it in me finally to whisper, 'Dad, I'm going to have to let you go.' He'd been unconscious for several hours and couldn't hear me, but, shocked, amazed, and weeping, I repeated it to myself again and then again, until I believed it myself" (101).

THE USEFUL BODY

Grim as hospital endings can be, they need not be the end of "living" in some sense. Like the members of the Mutual Autopsy Society, Americans respect the useful and the practical, and that does not subtract from the moral sentiments they associate with death. In fact, it can add to them.[2] The National Donor Memorial home page explicitly declares what is at stake. "Organ and tissue donors leave a miraculous legacy. They are living proof that death can bring life, that sorrow can turn to hope, and that a terrible loss can become the greatest gift of all. Every day they lead us on a journey of hope, renewal, and transformation."[3] The U.S. Department of Health and Human Services estimates that 89,000 Americans "are waiting for the gift of life" and that every day 74 of them receive a transplant while 17 die because of organ shortages. In the first eight months of 2005, 11,523 patients received organs from almost 6,000 donors, according to the United Network for Organ Sharing. Donation is a big and growing business, and its appeal to the bereaved, offering the transformation of "a terrible loss" into "the greatest gift of all," is a powerful message. As a newer scheme of knowledge within prevailing death practices, its language of "gift," "miraculous," and "legacy" is not as transparent as it seems, however.

What is a gift? The classic anthropological source on that is Marcel Mauss's *The Gift* (1967), first published in 1925. Mauss argued that gifts are units in economies of exchange that are different from the market-based "cash nexus" of everyday commerce. In offering a gift, one offers part of oneself, perhaps out of altruism but also with the expectation that it adds to an enduring relationship with future reciprocities. Gift goods are anthropomorphized and fetishized, believed to carry some modicum of the essence of the giver. There is, consequently, a moral burden on receivers to respond in some appropriate way. Gift giving, in Mauss's view, is never purely altruistic, for it always harbors an element of self-interest, the anticipated return. That works well with holiday gift giving, but when the offering is the "gift of life," how does one give something back, either to the dead or to the bereaved who consented to a donation? Early on, this was a serious issue in organ transplant work, when physicians noticed their patients' anxieties about returning something, anything, for what they had received. Yet when donor families and recipients were able to meet, participants were not always comfortable with it, each side feeling locked into what Renée Fox and Judith Swazey call "the tyranny of the gift." The need "to express gratitude to the deceased donor's relatives, along with their desire to know more about the person from whom the organ has come, may impel [recipients] to make personal contact with the donor family and to become involved in their life" (1992: 41). Similarly, donor families seeking "closure" may seek out recipients, "especially with heart transplants, to relate to the person as if he or she embodied the living spirit of the donor. However painful it may be for recipients and their families to be united with their organ donor's kin, they are likely to feel obligated to yield to them because of their ineffable sense of indebtedness for the gift they have received through death" (41–42). A "creditor-debtor vise," as they put it, binds the parties in ways neither side to the exchange may want.

The "miraculous legacy" that each donation is can be problematic in itself. Lock (1996) interviewed a number of transplant patients, about half of whom quickly adjusted to the fact that they had a new organ and felt it comfortably belonged to them. "However, the other recipients produced emotionally charged accounts of their donors (about whom they actually knew very little), the particular organ they had received, and often about their own transformed identities" (320). An Anglo-Protestant who received a kidney from an Italian discovered a newfound taste for garlic, or so he alleged. Some men who received kidneys from women feared they might become feminized. A woman who received two kidneys said, "You know, I never liked cheese and stuff like that, and some people think I am joking, but all of a sudden I couldn't stop eating Kraft slices—that was after the first kidney. This time around, the first thing I did was to eat chocolate, and now I eat some every day. It's driving me crazy because I'm not a chocolate fanatic" (323). Perhaps such imagery is simply a variant on the belief that "you are what you eat," but it goes beyond food. "Recipients of cadaver organs, like those with organs from living relatives, often express the sentiment that one can acquire the donor's emotional, moral and physical characteristics. Such qualities can be elaborate and imaginative, especially when the donor was an anonymous stranger. Some patients live in fear of the independent or animate qualities of their new organs" (Sharp 1995: 372). Musical, artistic, and even criminal imagery occupies the thoughts of some. Did they receive the heart of a good (if unintentional) Samaritan, or that of a neighborhood bully? To escape that dilemma, one can, as many patients do, objectify the new organ as an off-the-shelf substitution. The view, common enough, that the body is a kind of machine, accommodates that kind of thinking as well as preserving the traditional Western body/soul, physical/spiritual dualism. But it does not always eliminate a countervailing notion. Eyes and hearts are emblematic of the individual who was their source, far more symbolically loaded than kidneys. When a body part is replaceable machinery, the donor is objectified, and that is not quite the "gifting" imagery the language of organ procurement campaigns promise. As Mauss foresaw, all gifts come with entanglements, creating recip-rocal obligations that are not necessarily met or even welcomed.

The innocent language of altruism and gifting, used in heavy doses to attract donors, exists to solve a chronic supply and demand problem. Over time, the categories of persons deemed eligible to donate has grown, simply to create a larger donation pool. Medical staff in many hospitals are expected to raise the subject of donation with the families of those who have just died. Yet the "dead donor" rule, that a donor must be clearly and explicitly dead, sometimes founders on precisely the ambiguities in defining death already discussed. When is a patient "dead," or "dead enough," to justify harvesting? To speed procurement, should some patients be quietly "allowed to die" on the utilitarian notion of the greater good, while others receive heroic interven-tion to the finish? Who decides that, and for which patients? These are points of contentious discussion in the medical literature. Families have their prob-lems, too, and for them the suggestion that a gifted legacy will miraculously live on in the body of an anonymous other may seem the best solution to a sad situation. Their need is to salvage something that "creates meaning," espe-cially when death is due to an accident. If spare parts and memories are all there is to work with, that is the limit of their choices and that is what their discussion of the meaning of a death will be about. A part as relic can live on, emblematic of the whole.

THE AESTHETIC BODY

Dying is hard work, and messy. But no one has to leave this world looking bad. Funeral directors are paid to make bodies presentable, and embalming, their most important service, is basic to the funeral industry as it has been since the Civil War. Modern preservation techniques originated with battle-field casualties and the assassination of a president. Lincoln's funeral, writes historian Gary Laderman (1996, 2003), was the first recognizably modern one, the president's body chemically treated much as were the corpses of Northern soldiers dying on Southern soil. At the beginning of the war, and following a military engagement, bodies were quickly buried where they fell. Respect for the dead did not allow abandonment, and the sights and smells of a battlefield days later were powerful incentives to get remains underground. Special units were assigned this unpleasant duty, and wary soldiers sometimes pinned their names to their clothing (the precursors of military dog tags) so relatives could be informed if they fell. Most of the war's battles were fought in the South and Northern troops were buried there, in enemy soil, rather than back in Vermont or Illinois where their families wanted them. Human remains were sent home only when convenient, and relatives sometimes traveled to retrieve a body themselves. But that was difficult, expensive, and hardly sanitary, especially in summer heat and humidity. One solution was to pack a body in a cask of whiskey, always available; another, to stuff a corpse with sawdust or charcoal. The new science of embalming promised an improvement. Arsenic-laced embalming fluids had been used in medical schools for several decades, and their use in wartime quickly became popular. Laderman notes that "Washington became the nation's embalming capital" because of the army hospitals located there. For casualties further afield, and in the spirit of American enterprise, freelance embalmers followed the troops, even posting their advertisements on trees along the line of march (1996: 114).

The assassination of President Lincoln, however, was the signal event in demonstrating the embalmer's new cosmetic skills. After an autopsy by army doctors, Lincoln was embalmed by a private Washington, D.C., firm, and Laderman quotes a New York newspaper's description of their success: "The long and bony body is now hard and stiff. . . . The scalp has been removed, the brain scooped out, the chest opened and the blood emptied. All this we see of Abraham Lincoln, so cunningly contemplated in this splendid coffin, is a mere shell, an effigy, a sculpture. He lies in sleep, but it is the sleep of marble" (1996: 159). Marble-like or not, he did not hold up well. Lincoln took a final train ride, leaving Washington on April 21 and arriving in Springfield two weeks later on May 4, 1865. His body was on display, and thousands viewed him in several northern cities along the route. His closest companions were his wife, some government dignitaries, and an embalmer who consulted with funeral companies at each stop. Some described the naturalness of his appearance, but as the trip progressed others commented on discoloration and the increasingly gaunt and skeletal look of his face. Disintegration was soon evident and in the last viewing, at the Illinois statehouse, only a thick application of powder hid the inevitable. Yet the public seemed satisfied, embalming having created for them what Laderman calls Lincoln's "hallowed" body, a visual device linking personal tragedy to national purpose, to history, and to the Christian epic. An innovation critical to future American funerary practice, the "memory picture," was born. And so was something else—the control of death and body removal, traditionally the responsibility of families and usually of the women in them, was handed off to men trained in the embalming art. Working out of commercial establishments, they were pioneers in the nascent funeral industry.

Embalming is largely an American phenomenon, practiced to a lesser degree in Europe. It is not legally required except in a few states where interstate shipment of a body or use of a common carrier is involved. Nor does embalming provide any public health benefit, although industry promoters often claim it does.[4] They argue embalming is necessary for the safety of those who handle bodies and, by extension, is a good public health measure. There are other justifications offered as well but they are selling points, not health issues. One is historical precedent. Egyptian mummification is a favorite, probably for its "classical" associations, although the technology of the ancients was different, and their purpose was hardly sanitation. Nor is the long-term preservation they achieved even remotely possible with modern techniques. Contemporary embalming maintains the appearance of a body for a week or two at best. Another benefit claimed is the extra time embalming gives families to gather, view the body, and share their love of the deceased. In effect, embalming promotes healthy grieving so the bereaved can see that the dead are just that. Many deaths, however, especially among the elderly and those who have suffered chronic terminal illnesses, are expected, grief usually having begun well before the individual expires. An additional rationale, if one follows the critical line of Jessica Mitford (1963, 1998), is that embalming is what the industry has to sell, since other services are available elsewhere in a competitive market. That might be more true now than when she first wrote. Caskets can be purchased online; cremation is the growing preference of North Americans; burial societies offer low-cost, no frills services; and private, do-it-yourself home funerals are a growing trend. The industry is under pressure to emphasize the value of its products and expand the range of what it offers. Forward looking funeral companies now do just that.

Embalming is science and cosmetic art, and it does require skill and training. It begins when a corpse arrives at a funeral company's embalming room, a laboratory-like place familiar to all fans of the television series *Six Feet Under*. The corpse is undressed, jewelry removed and inventoried, and the body laid out for washing on a stainless steel or porcelain table, the head slightly elevated and hands and arms resting at the sides. Messaging and flexing remove rigor mortis, giving the corpse a more relaxed look. Two procedures are involved, beginning with arterial embalming. A cut is made on the lower neck to access the carotid artery and jugular vein, and a tube is inserted into each. The one in the artery is attached to a pump and tank of embalming fluid, the other drains blood as it is forced out. Pump pressure is kept low, steady and is closely monitored since blood clots can form blockages, back up fluid, deprive some areas of preservative, and (even worse) puff up the face so it requires remedial work later. Dyes are added to the preservative to adjust skin color but that is tricky since they can interact unexpectedly with medicines still in the body, creating unwanted coloration effects. Creams and powders can hide these if necessary.

After draining, cavity embalming begins. A cut is made just above the navel and a trocar inserted. A trocar is a sharp, pyramidal-shaped blade at the end of a metal suction tube about eighteen inches long that is used to "aspirate" (the technical term) the organs of the gut and chest. That means vigorous puncturing and slicing so that fluids and gas trapped in intestines, the stomach, bladder, lungs, and adjacent organs can be suctioned out. Then full-strength embalming fluid is pumped in. If during this procedure the chest collapses, it is stuffed with packing material until it returns to its original appearance. The anus and vagina are packed as well so that fluids will not leak out.

With the body clean and filled with formaldehyde preservative, cosmetic work begins. This is the art in the job, requiring skill and a steady hand. Eyes are closed by pulling the lids over thin plastic "eye caps" placed on the eye that have a rough convex surface to help hold the lid in place from the inside. One mortician explained to me the difference between the work of a neophyte and a pro. The pro brings the top and bottom lids neatly together, just touching and no more. The less assured practitioner slightly overlaps them, bringing the upper lid a bit over the lower. In either case, both glue and eye caps hold the lids in place. The mouth, however, is the real focal point and, along with the nose, influences how viewers judge the accuracy of the embalmer's recreation. (Embalmers commonly ask for a photograph to guide their reconstruction, especially important if there has been trauma to the head or face.) Dentures are reinserted and additional packing material is used to keep the mouth and nose from sinking. The mouth must be closed and kept that way, and there are several closure techniques. One is to run a long, curved needle with heavy thread through the gums of the lower jaw just under the front teeth, up through the roof of the mouth on one side, then back down through the other. The thread ends are pulled firmly to close the mouth. The thread ends are then tied in a knot, trimmed, and hidden under a lip. A spot or two of glue keeps them there. According to the Web site of one company, "The prime consideration is to have the lips meet naturally. If the mouth is closed too loosely, the funeral director cannot produce a pleasant look, and if the mouth is closed too tightly, the area under the nose puckers, giving the upper lip a distinctly unnatural expression, sometimes appearing to scowl at the mourners. The funeral director will occasionally widen the lower lip to improve a face's appearance."[5]

Embalmers are challenged by bodies emaciated after a long illness or facially damaged by trauma, as from gunshots or drowning. They want to create a positive "memory picture" and are sensitive to the expectations of families. A photograph is helpful as a guide. They can repair sunken eyes, cheeks, a mandible, a misshaped nose or bony protrusions. Feature-building pastes and liquids are inserted with a needle to plump up sunken areas. Creams and waxes hide pallor and prevent further dehydration. Where skin is missing, even from large patches, surgical gauze is laid over anchoring tissue, or bone and paste is applied to build up the surface. The surface is smoothed, and when it is dry, cosmetic creams are applied that match surrounding color and appearance. One critical area for accurate restoration, immediately noticed by survivors if they think the look of the deceased is "off," is the nasolabial fold. That is the crease running from the side of the nose to the corner of the mouth, separating mouth area from cheek. A lifetime of talking, smiling, laughing, and chewing gives it depth and shape. A good embalmer will inject feature-building material into the cheek by going in through the nasal passage on the opposite side, filling it out and messaging it to get a crease matching that seen in life. If the crease is obliterated, viewers will perceive the deceased as unnaturally fat in the face, and if too deep, as painfully shrunken and not comfortably "at rest." Fingers, too, get some help, since like the face, they are visible at the final viewing. Filler material is injected into the middle joint of each finger from the palm side, the finger then massaged to move it toward the sides, creating a less bony appearance. Finally, before the body is dressed and moved to a casket, the hair is washed and styled, the hands and nails cleaned. An embalming job well done creates "respectful viewing," according to one industry supply-house instructor. "We need to make all our viewing easy to look at. If the signs of sickness and disease still exist, viewing is hardly easy. Families should be proud to greet friends at the casket, and they should be comfortable while hearing stories about the deceased to be able to glance respectfully at their loved one. If their deceased mother looks beautiful, it's easy for them to feel great about this open casket experience."[6]

A body well presented for "respectful viewing" is also a body worthy of a "memory picture." The idea of photographing the dead may seem ghoulish, but it is built on precedent. Posthumous paintings of the dead have long been popular with wealthy and middle-class Europeans and North Americans. The invention of photography in 1839 made that privilege available to everyone. The definitive work on death photography is Jay Ruby's *Secure the Shadow* (1995). As a visual anthropologist, his interest is in the social uses of photographs as well as their aesthetic features. Photographs of the dead were sometimes made to guide a commissioned painter but more often they were solely for family display as valued keepsakes. Ruby quotes from an advertisement in an 1846 Boston business directory: "Our arrangements are such that we take miniatures of children and adults instantly, and of DECEASED persons either in our rooms or at private residences. We take great pains to have Miniatures of Deceased Persons agreeable and satisfactory, and they are often so natural as to seem, even to Artists, in a deep sleep" 1995: 53). Two things are notable about this ad. First, photographs of the dead are taken quickly, there being no refrigeration or embalming (although ice might be available), the death, funeral, and burial happening within a day or two. Second, the aesthetic goal of the photograph is less to show the person as a distinct individual than to show someone sleeping. Death to the Victorians was "sleep" and that is how they wanted the pictured dead to look, in restful repose. The unpretentious, almost utilitarian feel of many of those photographs is striking. Old people are shown at home in their deathbeds; children (of which there are many), in their mother's arms, propped up in chairs, or laid out on family couches.

Commercial photographers were usually mobile, traveling from small town to small town to photograph weddings, elderly couples, large multigenerational families, and the newly deceased. Michael Lesy's *Wisconsin Death Trip* (1973), something of a cult classic, is a collection of these old prints, all of them showing the modest, homey settings of their subjects. Photographs of the dead were sometimes expensively framed but more often they were slipped into a cheap cardboard holder with black edges, the photographer's name and place of business printed across the bottom. Stereographic images were popular as well. Increasingly, however, photographers began working closely with funeral directors, and the look of the images changed into something more formal than an unadorned family parlor setting. Floral displays and background curtains were added to the scene, revealing the locale of the shot as the funeral company's viewing room. In these photos, family members posed at the casket, sharing visual space with flowers, drapes, and the dearly departed. The image portrayed an event, less the singularity of the deceased, and even the casket, no longer a "coffin," was a feature of interest in its design and suggestion of expense.

One of the most innovative photographers of this genre was James Van Der Zee, an African American who opened his studio in Harlem in 1916 but received little recognition outside the black community until late in life. His strong compositional sense was matched by darkroom skill and, well before the age of computer-manipulated imagery, he was using sophisticated techniques to create an ethereal mood in his memorial photographs. He superimposed above and around the deceased familiar images of angels, Jesus, bits of text, and views of the subject when alive. A peaceful sleep with dreamlike suggestions of heaven were his visual metaphors. They softened and concealed the facts of an individual death, portraying their subject in transcendent glory as counterpoint to the gruesome reality of black deaths in Jim Crow America.

Writing of that aesthetic, Karla F. C. Holloway, a historian of African American mourning, says that "Perhaps as a testament to the familiarity of the experience, African Americans upheld the tradition of formal portraiture of the dead in final sleep, a tradition Euro-Americans did not continue" (2002: 27). Other African American memorial photographs have had a different impact. A photograph of the murdered and beaten Emmett Till became iconic of the civil rights movement when it was published in *Jet* magazine and by *The Chicago Defender* (but not the national press) in September, 1955. Fifty years later, the maker of a new documentary film on the killing (*The Untold Story of Emmett Louis Till*) said of that photograph, "It was an educational tool that was told to many African-American men, to teach them about the racism that exists in society today. This has been a major part of our makeup growing up in this country" (*New York Times*, August 28, 2005). Holloway, too, discusses the educational power of images of early death; a particularly affecting one shows four very young children peering into the open casket of an eleven-year-old.[7]

Pictorial memorialization is hardly limited to cadavers, however. Laser etching is now common on headstones, as are photographs embedded in plastic. Unlike headstones of the 1950s and 1960s, featuring little more than a name and the dates of birth and death, newer styles revel in the idiosyncratic and individualistic, often on both sides of the marker. My own modest collection of headstone images includes a hunter in fatigues with his deer rifle; a complete will etched across the back of a large marker ("I give my fishing things to my mom," and so on); a serious Bruce Lee looking out from exquisite pink granite; and the image, designed by a hiking companion who was also an art student, of a young man who loved camping, shown in silhouette as though he were a mountain cliff above a lake. Occupations (machinery in a wheat field; a logger's boots and axe) and hobbies (musical instruments, boating) are now almost routine. As miniatures, they freeze-frame another time and place, re-embodying the dead not as dead but still alive, at least to memory, doing what they loved most. In their emphasis on the personal, they suggest the devotional just as did the body parts of saints in medieval times. Photographs and imagery on headstones make them something more than markers; they are little shrines inviting the family faithful to visit, leave small offerings, and share social as well as eternal time with the dead. Like holy relics, they make the dead physically and intimately available beyond what a mere name inscribed on stone can do. "The current use of photographs at the site of graves embeds them within an unfolding set of material relations and exchanges which sustain the dead as socially living persons" (Hallam and Hockey 2001:152). In that sense they have salvational pretensions and effects, Orsi's sense of presence, little assurances that the dead are far but near, away but aware. That has been confirmed by an insightful study of visitors to London cemeteries. Anthropologist Doris Francis and her colleagues found that mourners often held that souls resided in an eternal place but existed in "linear time" in association with their grave site as well. Once the gravestone is installed, "it may take on the persona, the 'presence,' of the departed. Grief may be transferred to the monument, at which mourners talk openly. . . . For many the memorial *is* the departed, but the marker gains this attribution only through its proximity to the bodily remains." They quote one visitor, "When I talk with him I tell him things that happen (I think they already know) about So-and-so is on holiday, people who got married" (2005: 123–24).[8]

One form of posthumous portraiture commonplace in the nineteenth century but out of fashion for a hundred years, that of deceased children, has been rediscovered and revived. Ruby describes how photographs of the dead as dead were once routinely displayed in the parlor alongside the family Bible. They were topics of conversation with guests and no one thought that unseemly. But as that kind of parlor conversation became "inappropriate" for polite company, pictures of the family dead were secreted inside bibles, storage boxes, and file folders. Ruby found in interviews with contemporary families great uneasiness about acknowledging or revealing their mortuary photos. Yet in the 1980s, neonatal clinics were beginning to use photos of stillborn infants and those who died within days of birth not only for archival purposes but as therapeutic tools with grieving parents. Not only were parents glad to have them, but as snapshots they were easy to share with other family members. Bereavement counselors began recommending neonatal hospice photography to their clients. Infants were photographed with blankets and toys because, as with photos of the elderly on headstones, a body is necessary for memory. Awareness of a body establishes identification, treating the child as person rather than tragic mishap, and Ruby quotes a psychiatrist who advises, "Mourning a stillbirth is an even more complicated and difficult task. To facilitate mourning, I recommend that a stillbirth be managed by making the most of what is available and can be remembered. The aim is to make history, to make memories that can be thought about and talked about, which will then fill the emptiness that impedes the mourning of a stillborn" (1995: 181). Nothing makes history so real as a photograph.[9]

AND NOW FOR SOMETHING COMPLETELY DIFFERENT

The deceased embalmed and "at rest" in a tastefully chosen casket, a formal service that "celebrates a life," and a reception where personal artifacts are on display is, for most Americans, the formula for a proper send-off. And not too many years ago the formalities concluded with a motorized procession to a cemetery (car headlights on, motorcycle police escorts) for committal at the graveside.[10] Central to all of that, as promoted by the funeral industry from the time of its beginnings in the late 1800s, was the prepared corpse. "The true anchor of the American way of death [is] the visible, embalmed body, put on display either before or during the religious service" (Laderman 2003: 78). Anything less would not be proper, respectful, or patriotic. There are now, however, many more choices, and some, frankly, that are a lot more interesting. Breaks with death traditions are often controversial, and that was true of the first North American cremation. It occurred on December 6, 1876, in the village of Washington, Pennsylvania. The hero of the hour was one Baron Joseph Henry Louis Charles De Palm, a theosophist and Austrian immigrant who claimed aristocratic status. He had asked his well-placed friends to arrange a cremation, but when that came to public attention all right-thinking citizens were scandalized. Newspapers around the country were hostile, the *New York Times* predicting that when the novelty of cremation wore off it would disappear. The locals certainly hoped so. They feared the fallout of smoke and ash would damage their fields but, more fundamentally, that incineration of human remains was a blasphemous reversion to heathenism. Equally troublesome was the effect of fire on an immortal soul—would it too become ash? The morning of the cremation, a gathered crowd of protesters "lent to the occasion the raucous air of a prizefight or an execution" (Prothero 2001: 32). Cremation proponents countered that what they were doing was hygienic, that they were merely concerned with public health, and disposal by fire would make unnecessary the dank cemeteries with their "miasmas" (toxic fumes) and fouled runoff, sources of disease. But at the heart of all this were issues of privilege and social class. "Cremationists were, by and large, genteel elites, and their cause was a genteel endeavor" appealing to philanthropists, lawyers, professors, temperance crusaders, women's rights advocates, Unitarians, Transcendentalists, liberal ministers, freethinkers, and devotees of Eastern religions and the Ethical Culture movement (20). They knew better than ordinary folk. The cremation that day went ahead, yet in some parts of the country, notably New England and the South, ground burial is still the preference of most Americans.

Almost a century later, another challenge to funeral and body disposal orthodoxy was made, but this time on behalf of the ancestors of those ordinary folk who protested cremation in the late 1800s. Jessica Mitford's broadbrushed attack on the funeral industry, *The American Way of Death*, appeared in 1963. It too created smoke and fire, and it inspired defensive protests from the industry—that she exaggerated how the funeral industry priced its prod-ucts; played loose with stereotypes of unctuous "undertakers" manipulating grief-addled widows; and worse – she was a foreigner and a Communist. (She was. And also a radical English aristocrat who left the party in 1958 but remained a muckraking crusader.) The consequences of Mitford's attack, like those of the early cremationists, were enduring. By the 1970s, amid much unwelcome publicity and investigations by the Federal Trade Commission, the industry was required to change some of its practices. Fees could not be hid-den in the price of the casket; consumers could choose from a menu of choices what they wanted, and could reject "package deals"; local legal requirements (embalming is not generally one of them) had to be disclosed; and the wishes of those who wanted minimalist services (body pickup and cremation only) had to be respected. Progressive funeral directors began to refashion them-selves as grief specialists, something more than the stereotypical body handler and casket salesman.[11] Even a member of the fraternity, Michigan funeral direc-tor Thomas Lynch, an established essayist and poet (1997, 2000), continues the tradition of funeral industry critique and reform, although in a more sober and kindly way than Mitford would have cared for.

Predictably, unhappiness with commercialized handling of the dead has led to countermovements outside the industry, and they are beginning to appeal to North Americans. Best known, perhaps, are funeral service cooper-atives whose members prepay for body transportation, refrigeration, and cre-mation. No casket need be purchased and cemetery burial in a plastic urn is at the survivor's discretion. Typically, the cost is under $1,000. Consumer advocacy organizations also exist. The Federation of Funeral Consumer Infor-mation Societies lobbies legislatures and maintains state-by-state updates on applicable laws, provides ombudsman services for members, advises on costs, publishes preplanning information, and promotes itself through a newsletter, the *Funeral Consumers Alliance*, and a Web site that includes (mildly) humor-ous death jokes and, of course, T-shirts and latte mugs.[12] And there are emerg-ing options more interesting than that.

One is the modern ecoburial movement, variously promoted through woodland cemeteries, ecocemeteries, memorial nature preserves, and green burials. These services are less expensive than conventional funerals and aim to be environmentally responsible. They are an English invention, the earli-est being the Carlisle Cemetery, developed by Ken West in the 1980s and win-ner of a number of awards. In an older, city-owned cemetery begun in 1855 and immaculately maintained, West added a special section for people who preferred something "natural" and less costly. A number of his innovations have become standard in the movement. Embalming, of course, is out. Some very strict green burial grounds also prohibit nonbiodegradable items such as metal jewelry and synthetic clothing. Bodies must be wrapped in a cotton shroud or placed in a biodegradable coffin. Cardboard, bamboo, some kinds of chipboard, and unfinished wood (preferably from managed forests) are acceptable. Carlisle's "woodland burial" is on the perimeter of the cemetery proper, outside a wall and presenting an impressive visual expanse of open fields, clouds, and quietly grazing sheep at a distance. After burial, of a body or of ashes, the soil is allowed to settle before wildflowers and a native oak sapling are planted. The area is intended to return to woodland and fertilizers and chemical weed control are not used. The cemetery brochure states that "It must be appreciated that the traditional 'neat and tidy' appearance of our cemeteries will not apply to this burial area." A "strewing area" in the open fields is available to those who want to scatter ashes. There are no grave markers in the woodlot, walking in it is discouraged (since the location of each grave is not evident), and leaving flowers or items of remembrance is not allowed. Nearby is a low brick structure in the shape of a "C" modeled after a traditional sheep holding pen. On its wall are nameplates for those buried in the woodlot and benches for quiet contemplation among the bluebells, young trees, and lowing sounds of sheep a quarter mile away. The cemetery brochure advises that the space "will be chosen by those who love birds and wildlife and who wish to create a woodland and provide environmental benefits for future generations." [13]

An important advocate of green burials is the Natural Death Centre in London. An all-purpose, end-of-life advocacy organization founded in 1991, the Centre has been successful in arranging the use of farm woodlots as permanent cemeteries. Individual farmers agree to preserve their forested land in perpetuity in exchange for burials for which they take a modest fee. Since decomposition is achieved in a few years, the plots can be resold and reused on a regular basis. The strictest biofriendly practices are enforced, with graves often marked with little more than a ribbon on a nearby tree. An unexpected side effect has been the relationships that develop between some farm families and those who use their land. The Centre reports seasonal gatherings hosted by the farmers; those who have buried loved ones gather at the woodlot for a day of food, music, and getting-to-know-you conversations. In addition, some modern Druids have a liking for the woodlots where funerals and burials are "natural" rather than commercial. There are currently about 150 green burial sites in the UK.

In this country, two American companies have their own "unique business model," as they call it, for conserving land through green burial. Memorial

Ecosystems Inc., founded in South Carolina in 1996, and Forever Enterprises, based in California since 1998, offer what they call "interment rights." "The concept is to sell interment rights on 5 percent of the land and use the endowment from that 5 percent to preserve the rest as open space. In essence, we will use existing cemetery law to conserve land and protect it in perpetuity with a conservation easement." [14] Apparently the idea has appeal, for they now have a number of sites and in California a waiting list of over 500. They also consult with existing cemeteries wanting to establish green burials on their own land; recommendations include replanting with native species and appointment of an on-staff "steward" to supervise green development. The California operation proposes something additional. Visitors wandering in deep coastal woods lacking markers of any kind will find their loved one's burial with a hand-held GPS device. A service in Montana, Ladies in White, adds to this environmental emphasis a feminist one. Their web site declares: "Ladies in White reasserts women's role in death care" (ladiesinwhite.com). Three women dressed in white hike into remote country to scatter ashes at the type of location a family prefers. Examples shown on their web page include forests, ridgelines, lakes, waterfalls, meadows and rock outcroppings. The service is for those who not only want something green but seek the anonymity of wilderness. Finally, green burials are meant to be competitively priced. At the Ramsey Creek Preserve in South Carolina, a full body burial is $1,995; ashes go under for $500; a large dog requires a mere $75; and a cocker spaniel or a cat, only $50. What do these places look like? Go to the Glendale Nature Preserve at http://www.glendalenaturepreserve.org and click on their photo gallery. Clearly, nature is the theme.[15]

Do-it-yourself funerals are a related development, an ecoburial spin-off. DIY funerals are cost effective, often less than $1,000, the largest expense being the cremation. But the real attraction is the focus on domesticity and family care without the intrusion of commercial body handlers. A body can be kept at home for several days without difficulty. Typically, it is washed, dressed, and placed in a personalized, homemade casket, as inexpensive or as elaborate as desired. Caskets are usually simple constructions of cardboard or plywood, and painting and decorating by hand are part of the ceremonies. After visitations and an informal ritual, the body is taken to be cremated or buried. A family member with durable power of attorney for health care can substitute for a funeral director and no embalming is required. It takes planning, more than most people want to do, but is a legal option in most states.

There are several sources for those wanting advice on DIY departures, including Final Passages of Sebastopol, California, and the Funeral and Memorial Society of America (FAMSA), the latter claiming to have 140 affiliated chapters. Their most effective promotional tool to date may be a well-received documentary shown in the PBS series *Point of View* in 2004. "A Family Undertaking" depicts in a sensitive way several home funerals, including that of Bernard Carr, a tough, poetic rancher in South Dakota. In one scene, his sons take him out to the barn in his wheelchair, and with a heated iron he applies his cattle brand to the sides of the elegant casket they have made for him. The film is a collaboration between Lisa Carlson, self-described "full-time consumer activist and some-time hell raiser," who is the president of FAMSA, and Jerri Lyons, who founded Finals Passages in 1995. Both women describe themselves as "midwives of death" who promote literacy on consumer rights and run workshops on planning DIY funerals. Only a tiny percentage of all funerals are DIYs, but the movement may become as important to the boomer generation as Jessica Mitford was to her sympathizers in the early 1960s. They carry on the Mitford heritage by emphasizing choice, family, and individuality, values just as American as those held by the hometown entrepreneurs who launched the commercial funeral industry over a century ago. Even funeral director Thomas Lynch has one foot in their camp. "I embalmed my own father. And it was something that I could do for him. Other people make casseroles."[16]

REIMAGINING THE SALVATIONAL

How far are we from that time and place where, Philip Ariès believed, death was "tamed" by the cautionaries of religion? The body handling of Heilman's chevra kaddisha and the rituals at the burning ghats explicitly reference the transcendental. That is expected in communities where there is a common metanarrative of death and the larger realities it names. But America is pluralistic, containing many visions of what happens to us as we die and of where we go, if anywhere, after that. The historical imagery of Christian eschatology now competes with revived Native American traditions; vigorous imports from Hinduism, Buddhism, and Islam; and the late twentieth-century shift from formal, denominational "religiosity" to all-purpose "spirituality."

A variety of factors enumerated so far—medical, legal, demographic, technological, political—have converged to redefine the sacred and relocate salvational possibilities in a wider range of narratives, something the members of the Mutual Autopsy Society well knew and appreciated. Now, however, heartfelt discussion of advanced directives, medical choices, insurance coverage, hospice care, and funeral company arrangements are the modern ars moriendi. Medical intensivists, ICU teams, and palliative care physicians and nurses are the liturgists. The language of bioethics is the emerging scripture of modern dying, the treacly meanderings of pop-psychology grief guide a contemporary midrash. Even the body as dead and unlovely has its partisans, as the book sales of Mary Roach and Sherwin Nuland show. The failing, autopsied, and decorated body still has its mysterious wonders.

Orsi's notion that beholding the material is a way of "concretizing the order of the universe" seems especially applicable to a corpse. "Once made material, the invisible can be negotiated and bargained with" (2005: 74), and that seems an apt description of the work of a relic. A cold body is a space for affixing "imaginary futures," Orsi's variant on Anderson's well-known "imagined communities." Every culture has its favored locale for the dead, its stock answer to the question, Where is she now? The dead are ancestors, ghosts, on a celestial journey, permanently residing in a utopian or a dystopian place, reborn as someone or something else, anonymously absorbed into the All, a memory trace in the mind of God, nowhere because there is no afterwhere; or as some believe, the dead are simply a residue of memory. All such schemes, of course, are conventional imagery, culturally and historically shaped, no one of them more or less right than any other. The power of the relic, its charisma, is to vouch for the truth of whatever is claimed.

A body, then, is mysterious because it is a site for the play of imagination, most especially in its stunning silence as a corpse. Feminist theologian Paula Cooey (1994) has proposed an interesting way of thinking about that. A sense of the mysterious is important not because it suggests the truth of extranatural realities but because it engages more tangible moral concerns. "Namely, to what extent do such experiences sustain, advance, enhance, or extend a socionatural environment conducive to perpetuating further human creativity itself?" (116). The mysteriousness of the body as relic has to do with how a specific life was enabled or stunted, how it was known and experienced by others, how the wake it leaves will be observed, how we will be regarded in our turn.

The anthropological lesson seems obvious enough. Death is a process, not an event, as much sociological as biological, and there is very little that is natural about it. Some years ago, Nancy Scheper-Hughes and Margaret Lock (1987) argued that we each have three bodies. There is a phenomenological, individual body-self, the one that craves, itches, and demands to be fed. The second is the social body, and it takes on the stuff of culture, becoming a constructed artifact with age-, role-, and gender-appropriate plumage. The politicized body is a site for regulation, surveillance, and control. A dying body is all these, transformed in its final days and hours from an animated being into a relic.

4 SOULSCAPES

THE ENGLISH DISSENTERS who beached at Cape Cod in 1620 arrived well prepared. Packed into a ship previously used in the wine trade were their clothes, tools, pots, seeds, and a store of "victuals" sufficient for a return. On board, too, was a distinctive vision of divinity and an explicit notion of humankind's place in this life and that to come. Since then, Americans have carried on a conversation framed by these seafaring Separatists about the nature of the afterlife and, maybe more important, who will be rewarded there and who will not. Two views about the afterlife have been in competition for much of the time since. Is our destiny a celestial gated community with strict entry requirements and an omnipotent Ruler showered with adoration by the assembled chosen? That is the traditional understanding. Or is it grand in a more democratic, contemporary way, a restful, almost domestic place where the inhabitants abide with family, friends, even former pets, the whole surrounded by a perpetual glow of Great Love welcoming all to their final "home"? These two models hardly exhaust the possibilities, but they are recognizable and commonly held variants among the postmortem worlds many Americans imagine. More than that, they exemplify an enduring conviction that something "up there" awaits, however unclear our perception of its spiritual landscape. Given the utilitarian, commonsense style most North Americans endorse, it is remarkable that they would invest their cosmic hopes in vague, ethereal realms beyond the present and over the rainbow.[1]

Beliefs about such realities are widespread in human cultures, and as long ago as 1907 the French anthropologist Robert Hertz proposed a model for analyzing them systematically and sociologically (1960). He argued that any set of death practices involves three essential components: the survivors, a corpse, and a realm of postmortem experience. These can be imagined as the three points of a triangle, but what was crucial for Hertz was not the named points but their connections, the relationship of each to the other two (Metcalf and Huntington 1991: 79–85). For example, if survivor-to-corpse is the base leg of the system, display and body disposal arrangements are central as the ritual enactments of that relationship. The resources and social standing of the participants are on public view, as are their aesthetic choices as to what is "appropriate" to the occasion. Most North American funerals, for example, follow a recognizable script and reception-line conversations often involve judgments on how it was ornamented: open casket or not; things said and unsaid in the eulogy; choice of music; how other mourners comported themselves; what the deceased would have thought of it all. Aesthetics and display are important, both as markers of the status of the living and as measures of esteem for the newly deceased. The difference in scale between a pauper's funeral and that of a president exemplifies the extremes of what we all do when we make "appropriate" and "proper" arrangements for dispatch of the one we love. Nor is that labor "just ritual" as the utilitarian-minded allege. Reynolds and Waugh suggest that "Death rites not only transform the dead to their proper levels in the world beyond but transform the living into creators of the order in which everyone may find a place. The ritual participants operate at a level of cosmic significance far beyond their role in the ordinary scheme of things" (1977: 9). The performance of ritual is critical, not just for expressing our sense of loss but in the workings of the two other components of Hertz's understanding of death as a kind of system.

The second element of the model, linking the corpse to postmortem experience, invokes concepts of the self, and beliefs concerning its survival and transmutation into something else—an ancestor, a spirit being, an animal, or even, as we will see, something of a god. Two things are important here. First, and again referencing the body, there is the manner in which people think of themselves as animate beings. Do they imagine their corporeal selves having an essence, a nonmaterial force such as a spirit or soul, multiple souls, an embedded personality, a surviving memory which relocates somewhere outside a failed body? If so, where within us does such agency reside, when in the dying trajectory does it separate from flesh, from what point does it exit the body, and how do we know it has left? Is there a sound? A little pop? A last sigh? Something visual? Uncanny sensations felt by those gathered at the deathbed? Do newly released souls hover nearby? Can they read our thoughts? Do they wait to view their funeral before finally leaving or do they come back to frighten or warn us, like poor old Jacob Marley? These and countless other possibilities have been devised by our species, probably for as long as we have been Homo sapiens, maybe longer. It is even possible that evolution has hard-wired us to speculate this way, that capability an epiphenomenon of higher-order cognitive functioning. It is also possible that extraordinary postmortem realities really do await and that the spiritually astute have foreseen them and given us fair warning. Lacking verifiable evidence either way, at least of a kind that would pass as scientific, we may be comforted in knowing that post-death journeying is a common feature of death systems in many cultures. The dead are presumed to go somewhere rather than nowhere. The ultimate goal of their postcorporeal travel may be vague, as it is for the many Americans who say simply that they hope (the operative word) to arrive somewhere pleasant. Or eternity may be exquisitely mapped, as was done in medieval Catholicism, dramatically so in Dante's fourteenth-century poem *Divina Commedia*, with its graphic eschatological tour of hell, purgatory, and heaven. Among some Melanesians the dead become ancestors who can harm or protect and are all about as unseen beings inhabiting dark groves in the forest and appearing to the living in dreams (Keesing 1982). By contrast, Theravada Buddhists in northern Thailand reject ancestral spirits altogether, since for them the journey of the deceased is toward a karma-driven rebirth, not a reappearance. The journey begins not at the moment of death but in the present life, with the assiduous accumulation of merit, assuring a rebirth that is favorable (Keyes 1987). In these and other instances, whatever a culture's configuration of the afterlife, a proper ritual dispatch at the first leg of Hertz's model is the necessary prelude to success at the second, in which the dead are sent on their way.

Finally, the third element of Hertz's model concerns the continuing relationship of the dead with those left behind. In some instances, Chinese reciprocities with ancestors, for example, and spiritual visitations during the Mexican Dia de los Muertos, the deceased have a continuing, active interest in the living. In other locations, including much of North America and Western Europe, the dead are largely confined to memory, although the mechanisms for remembering are complex and varied. In parts of eastern Indonesia, specific features of the dead are "recycled," their names and personal qualities returned to life in the newly born. Something similar happens in North America, at least if we take seriously the claims of some organ recipients that they have inherited attributes of the person whose donated organ they received. The dead may continue as unwanted presences; an intrusive "haunting," for example, reported for modern England (Bennett 1999). Or the dead may be linked with mass terrors such as slavery in the United States or the plight of those who became *desaparecido* (disappeared) in Argentina in the 1970s (A. Gordon 1997). For most Americans, however, postmortem presences are brief and hardly supernatural: a favorite picture of the deceased on the bedside table, a yearly visit (if convenient) to a grave on Memorial Day, a favorite holiday dish once associated with the deceased.

Taken as a whole, the three elements of Hertz's model define a coherent death system and suggest an organized way of approaching the diversity of beliefs, rituals, and body-disposal practices that occur in human societies (Metcalf and Huntington 1991). Approached comparatively, the worldwide variety of death customs and beliefs takes on an orderliness not immediately apparent. It could be useful to know about that, if only to make heaven easier to recognize for those planning to travel there.

HARANGUING THE DEAD

If the polls are right, heaven is real enough but there is confusion about the admission requirements. As noted in Chapter 1, most Americans believe in an afterlife, including the possibility of hell. They foresee being judged at entry in accordance with a mix of criteria: everything done over a life span (84 percent), their spiritual condition at the time of death (78 percent), a critical "spiritual awakening or decision" (69 percent), and rituals performed at the time of death (43 percent) (Gallup and Lindsay 1999: 31). Many apparently feel that being "a good person" will do. Things are hardly different in the UK, where in 1996 the Church of England declared its doubts about the reality of hell. In response, the Catholic Church as well as theological traditionalists under the banner of the Evangelical Alliance replied that hell is indeed real but what happens there is unclear. They acknowledged debate within their ranks, disagreements as to whether punishment is eternal or proportionally adjusted to the misdeeds of the sinner, but agreed that older notions of fire and brimstone are no longer helpful.

There are societies, however, where much more precision than that is expected. One is the Sora, a "scheduled tribe" or ethnic group of over 400,000 living in rural enclaves in eastern India. Their presence in South Asia long precedes that of the Hindu majority with whom they have cautious and sometimes hostile relations, and their language suggests affinities with tribal and hill peoples as far away as Southeast Asia. The Sora are interesting because for them access to an afterlife is not a matter of voluntary belief or vague hope. In fact, what the dead spend their time doing, where they do it, and what they think of the living is self-evident, almost every day, and is not always pleasant. Postmortem conversations with deceased individuals happen regularly, daily, even hourly, at springs, in paths, groves, and the dark corners of houses. Several categories of shaman facilitate this ghostly discourse, mainly powerful funeral shamans (always women) who travel in trance states to the Underworld where the dead abide, and shaman helpers (both men and women), whose ritual duties include washing corpses, doing cremations, and helping the living and dead to speak with one another. These practitioners learn their skills as apprentices, and one, Cambridge anthropologist Piers Vitebsky, was so trained during his fieldwork. Having talked with a good number of dead Sora and conveyed their thoughts to the living, he knows some of what they know, what grudges they keep, and what is likely to come up in their next conversation with survivors (Vitebsky 1993: 23).[2]

While the geography of the Sora afterlife is not complicated, relations with it are. Sora think of the deceased as having two aspects, an "Ancestor-sonum" through which features of individual identity are recirculated through births in the patrilineal line, and an "Experience-sonum" which threatens survivors with disease and death after the manner that was experienced by the newly deceased. There is nothing comparable to "sonum" in English, and terms like "spirit" and "soul" are poor substitutes because they suggest a distinctive entity originating in and modeled vaguely on the human body. For the Sora, the dead are thought to be a state of continuing consciousness. Death ends one's material manifestation but does not annihilate personhood; it is simply one event in the total experience of consciousness typical of all humans. Ancestral and Experiential states are two of several modes of postmortem consciousness. Over time and with effort the newly dead, who manifest themselves first in their dangerous Experience-sonum consciousness, evolve into their more nurturing Ancestor-sonum form, and after passing distinctive features of themselves into newly born descendents, they turn into a small creature that is common in the local landscape. At that point, their consciousness persists but is beyond human contact and they are forgotten. An example will make this clearer.

Vitebsky describes a conversation between a distressed young mother and her dead daughter. The daughter, who apparently was disfigured during her short life, is abrupt and accusatory in her Experience-sonum mode, demanding to know the whereabouts of her nose rings, items of jewelry that are important symbols of Sora identity. Through the aunt, her mother responds: "They must have burned in the pyre, darling, we looked but couldn't find them. . . . They were so tiny." The daughter is not satisfied and, through the shaman, taunts her mother. "Mother, you were horrid to me, you scolded me, called me Scar-Girl, you called me Leper-Girl, you said 'You're a big girl now, why should I feed you when you sit around doing nothing? . . . Why can't I have my nose rings?" The aunt pleads for the girl's grieving mother: "She didn't mean it, she couldn't help saying it: after all, you were growing up and there were such a lot of chores to do. . . . So don't you pass it on, don't you give it to your mother and little sisters! . . . Your cough your choking, your scars your wounds, don't pass them on." Still the daughter is not satisfied. "My mummy doesn't care enough about me." She abruptly ends the conversation and goes back to the Underworld (3–4).

There will be more meetings like this, many in fact, through the shaman and with multiple audiences. As a continuing consciousness, the daughter has grievances to settle, and negotiating them will take time and numerous, contentious discussions. At these events, open to everyone, a variety of remembered family issues and grievances are revisited (which in small-scale communities like the Sora are also communal issues), explored in lengthy and sometimes dramatic dialogues between the dead and the living. These are tense occasions, as the recently dead are in their threatening Experience-sonum phase. They are mindful of how they died, sensitive to how they were treated while still alive, and dangerous because they can cause others to die in the same manner. Since the dead are ubiquitous, inhabiting all manner of things and places—including trees, animals, stars, wall paintings, and even pottery—they cannot be ignored. Observant of what the living are doing and inclined to be vengeful, they regularly comment on current family and village affairs. These spiritual border crossings are never easy and frequently unnerving. Vitebsky says that as a trained shaman and participant-observer, he never put himself outside these dramas: "Indeed, I still find it difficult, several years later, to listen to their tapes with a dry eye. All [were] unsettled not only cosmologically but emotionally" (179).

The goal of these disputations between the living, who are here, and the living, who are dead and there, is transformation of the threatening Experience-sonum into its more friendly aspect as an Ancestor-sonum. Vitebsky emphasizes that the movement from Experience-sonum to Ancestor-sonum is a gradual one. The habitus of the postmortem Experience-sonum is real relationships, felt wrongs, and occasional satisfactions. That of an Ancestor-sonum is social continuity, restoration of relationships (Vitebsky sometimes uses the term "redemption"), and orderly generational succession assuring the perpetuity and prosperity of kin groups. Vitebsky prefers to use the term Memory with a capitalized M rather than our conventional "soul" or "ghost" to describe what the sonum are. As Memory, they are less stored information, the usual American sense of the word, than competing perspectives on what once "really happened," voiced through shamans. Eventually, however, each sonum must fade, as living rememberers themselves die away and there are fewer opportunities for dialogues that anyone would find meaningful. At that point, a sonum as Memory returns to its hazy Underworld for the last time. There it is transformed into something else, something final.

> At times, the shady lower branches overhanging a stream are settled with swarms of butterflies. Sora people say that butterflies are indestructible, since when they flock to a pot of sweet wine they apparently drown but when pulled out they come to life again and fly away. But they are also inarticulate and characterless. Butterflies are beyond the reach of dialogue and they receive no cult. . . . A butterfly is a consciousness which cannot cease to exist, but which has no attributes because nothing can be known about it. Incapable of activity and action, liberated from passivity and passion but also deprived for ever of company, butterflies are Memories without rememberers. This, at last, is the final death of the person. (235)

Hertz probably never knew of the Sora, but he would have been impressed by the logic and highly social nature of their cosmology. Its assumptions easily map a death system much like the one he proposed. Life and death are a career, the influence of one extending into the other, with consequences for individuals on each side of its dark divide. To which a Sora might reply, "How could it be otherwise?" The hostility of the newly dead in their Experience-sonum consciousness, angry at their own death and wishing to inflict the same on others, recalls Hertz's attention to the centrality of the body and its relationship with survivors, the foundational leg of his triangular scheme. Sora death does not destroy consciousness but relocates it, leaving the dead free to move to and from their Underworld, observe the living, and make their views known through expert shamans. In that respect, Sora dialogues with the dead may be one of the most intense forms of dead-to-living and living-to-dead communication in the ethnographic literature, grandly fulfilling Hertz's proposition that some kind of communication across the greatest of all divides is a feature of death systems generally. So very different from the death practices of urbanized Western democracies, the beliefs of the Sora are not irrational, and theirs is a cultural logic as convincing as any other. It is not an easy logic, sometimes even a threatening one, but survivors live with it, knowing with certainty that something rather than nothing awaits them.

BELIEF AS CULTURAL KNOWLEDGE

It is evident that the Sora really do talk with the dead, or at least believe they do.[3] Vitebsky, too, says the speaking dead are real because he has heard them, made audio recordings of their messages transmitted through shamans, and talked with them himself. But in saying that, has he, a European, come to believe in the reality of sonum as the Sora do, or is he addressing us in his anthropological, participant-observer voice, one foot in and one foot outside the circle of true believers? When ethnographic researchers, tourists, and casual readers of travel magazines come across something called a "belief system," there is always an implicit question: but is it true? Is it possible that of all the human conjectures about an afterlife, imagined by people in all cultures everywhere and at all times, the Sora alone got it right? Or should we qualify that with a liberal, generous, maybe patronizing, "Well, right for them"? What is meant by "belief" when bereaved Sora insist on the edgy truth of Experience-sonum, or when English speakers say they expect a reunion with loved ones after they die? Before moving to ethnographic cases closer to home, where different beliefs in immortal souls and their place of final residence are at issue, we need to ask if Sora practices hint at something about belief generically, something applicable to how we "believe" as well. I think they do, but we will not see it if we rely on conventional definitions of what, in Euro-American practice, qualifies as belief, including belief in an afterlife.

Traditionally, one of the most widely used religious formulas for expressing belief among Christians begins, "I believe in one God, the Father Almighty, Maker of heaven and earth, of all things visible and invisible." The Nicene Creed, recited in the liturgical churches of the West since A.D. 325, contains a large cultural assumption, namely, that belief is the individual's voluntary assent to a set of propositions and, by extension, the authorized teachings which support them. Belief and assent are inner states, often called "faith," publicly affirmed in endorsements of sacred texts by individuals and congregations. Belief is, initially, an inner condition. For example, *Webster's New World Dictionary* defines belief cognitively, as "acceptance that certain things are true or real" even where "absolute certainty may be absent." Similarly, the *New Catholic Encyclopedia* says "faith means belief in God and acceptance of His revelations as true." The *New Dictionary of Catholic Spirituality* combines commitment with the cognitive, "faith as both trusting surrender and a loving assent to God" and a "clinging of the whole person" to Deity as well as to "true intellectual content by which we intimately know and confess" the historic creeds. The *Anchor Bible Dictionary* adds a social dimension, belief "characterized by a lifestyle consistent with apostolic teaching." In theologically traditional circles, the biblical story of Thomas, the infamous doubter, is often used to admonish the faithful on these points. If, unlike him, they can believe without seeing, they are doubly blessed. The subtext there is hardly obscure: material seeing and "spiritual" or inner believing are two ways of knowing, and the latter is more commendable.[4] Belief and faith are a complex, heady mix that has generated a theological paper trail two millennia deep. Conventionally, they are associated with revelation, inner transformation, devotion and obedience, trust, and intimate knowledge of the godhead, all matters of private conscience. They have, of course, their public expression in quests, pilgrimages, social activism, and various kinds of "witnessing" and proclamations of "good news." But in the grand mix we like to think of as American religious pluralism, belief is generally something personal, occasionally idiosyncratic, and thought to be a necessary precondition to true knowledge and right conduct.[5]

Considered historically, belief and faith so understood are conceptual set pieces, critical notions in the competing, contending discourses that have riled European civilization for centuries as well as many of their offshoots in North America. They spring from and belong to a specific historical tradition, something that raises key anthropological questions: Is belief as Euro-Americans understand it a universal experience, a useful cross-cultural category for describing religious sensibility and practice in other cultures? Or is it culture-bound, appropriate to its historical context but misleading when used in inquiries into the beliefs of people in non-Western traditions?[6]

At some point, that may have crossed the minds of the Baptist missionaries who once sought to convert the Sora, a people who must have seemed to them spiritually obtuse. Belief in the reality of the sonum does not require affirmations of things unseen since it is so obvious to the Sora that the dead appear regularly and on a schedule. That the dead speak as well must be far more convincing to Sora than the claims made in two-thousand-year-old texts, however venerated by cultural outsiders. Ghostly conversations enliven, so to speak, the everyday social commerce of Sora villages because they involve the things that matter most in life—promises, disputes, property, grudges, gossip, memories. Judgment and "redemption" in a silent afterlife must seem a thin alternative to negotiating wrongs with aggrieved spirits called forth almost daily and on command. The Sora confront their world and its challenges not by acquiring a propositional faith and then reshaping personal inner resources until they conform to it but by addressing problematic relationships in a public forum that includes the argumentative presence of those who are newly dead. Says Vitebsky, "It is through this play between their interior and exterior properties that Memories are able to be both deeply intimate and publicly negotiable. A sonum is my Memory of someone I have loved (or not, as the case may be); it is also someone who can turn in conversation to address any one of a dozen assembled rememberers in a manner specific to each of them and at the same time common to all; in addition, it is someone who resides in a feature of the public landscape" (1993: 201). Beyond the shaman's skill and the sonum's persistence, however, what makes a Memory's presence so compelling is that "you are forced to act out in public your mutual relationship and to coordinate this with other people's similar relationships" (202).[7]

There is something important that the Sora are doing with their Memories that is apparent once we get beyond the Western notion that belief is a private moral good, a "faith" that some people have and others do not. We need not accept uncritically Sora expectations that the newly dead want to be aggressive conversationalists, since that too is a culture-bound category, but it hints at possibilities that the traditional Western model does not. Cultural theorist and philosopher Michel de Certeau proposes that "what we do when we believe" (the title of his essay on this subject) is more important than what we *think* we believe, because belief is always embedded in a social formation. It must, therefore, be more than inner assent to an idea or a rhetoric of theological propositions. Belief, he says, is part of a moral economy of exchange wherein the partners are unequal and gifts and debts circulate in a network of mutual recognition. As with any kind of contract, each side has expectations of the other, makes promises, demands returns, extends credit, and looks toward completion of the agreement, sometimes very, very far in the future. Belief is the ideology of that relationship, an action that "occurs between the recognition of an alterity and the establishment of a contract" (1985: 192).

Whether in the mundane world of the living or the extramundane one of spirit, the key element of any contract is time: we all labor in the present to satisfy a debt so that in the future an advantage is gained, be it home ownership, graduation from college, or a crown of glory. In contracting with the gods, says de Certeau, "The 'believer' abandons a present advantage, or some of its claims, to give credit to a receiver. He hollows out a void in himself relative to the time of the other, and, in the interests he calculates, he creates a deficit whereby a future is introduced into the present" (193). We discover, through experience or conviction, that something is owed to a supernatural Other, and we bargain the terms of a moral or spiritual plan that will satisfy all parties and deliver a favorable future. Once that contract is made, all participants' actions are necessarily restrained as each side trusts the other to faithfully execute her, his or its part. But trust is also a point of vulnerability since it can be betrayed. To sustain trust, religious debtors must demonstrate good faith by what de Certeau calls "expectational practice," actions that show active and ongoing commitment to the bargain. All human contracts are complicated, those with supernatural entities especially so. There may be subclauses that changing circumstances require us to renegotiate, and believers who once bargained for a near-term healing may suddenly find their postmortem future more at contractual risk. So they renew or expand their pledge: the widow's mite, a pilgrimage, sacrifice of a goat, a promise to find lost nose rings. De Certeau's point is that whenever we contract with powers residing at the edge of imagination, expectational practices *are* our beliefs, since they presume "an alterity" capable of cosmic action. When belief is only a verbal affirmation, as an assent to a creed, "it ceases to mesh with some contractual practice. To posit the question: 'Do I believe it?' is already to leave the field of belief and take it as an intellectual object independent of the act that affirms it as a relationship. Belief is no longer anything but a stating when it ceases to be a relational engaging" (196). Belief, he would have it, is an action; declaring it is only rehearsal.

MODERN SOULS

De Certeau's linkage of belief and faith to the idea of contract is a striking insight, and it foregrounds something implicit in much of Western thought, something which has been obscured, especially since the Enlightenment and by the ascendancy of rationalist ways of knowing. The notion that souls are engaged in some kind of exchange between their possessor and creator is certainly there, especially in the doctrine of purgatory and, perhaps as telling, in the hundreds if not thousands of cartoon punchlines spoken at the Pearly Gates. But ideas and arguments about what these souls are made of and where they reside within us, where they come from originally, and their all-important journey to a permanent "soulscape" have taken primacy.[8] The range of afterlife beliefs in cultures historical and present is astounding, suggesting that no person, people, or religion has a special claim on the truth of the matter (Zaleski and Zaleski 2000).

The Old English *sawol* is ancestor to the modern *soul*, its first written appearances in the Beowulf saga, A.D. 825, and in an English Psalter. Historically, *soul* has had multiple meanings, including, says the Oxford English Dictionary, the vital force in plants and animals, the basis of thought and action, conscience, rationality and sensibility (both as feeling and as reasonableness), the source of emotions, and the essential part or property of something. For Euro-Americans generally, suggest Jill Furst and Leslie McKeever (1995), Western souls have historically included three distinctive features. Initially, there is that which animates our bodies and keeps them running as warm, biological things. A soul is an aspect of our physicality, our material selves, and when we die it is no more. That was the view of Aristotle in his *De Anima*; souls are intrinsic to all living things, plants, and animals, and are located in a specific organ, sometimes the lungs, often the heart (our romantic attribution of emotion to the heart preserves this idea), or, in the case of thinking and willing (*psyche*), in the brain. For pagan Greeks but also for many Christians, including medieval European scholars and physicians who read Aristotle, the physicality of the soul was obvious. Their materialist view was challenged and ultimately eclipsed by Thomas Aquinas in the thirteenth century, however, when he revived an idea from Plato that the soul's existence is not dependent on flesh at all. Souls are independent of bodies, although at birth they come with bodies as original equipment. Their existence parallels our animated fleshiness, and at death they leave and return to an eternal realm, no longer dependent on matter for their existence. Not only that, Aquinas held that there can be but one soul per body and that it cannot be recycled through future bodies as claimed in some other religions. At death, the singular soul is all that remains of us and it will undergo whatever punishment or rewards we have earned for ourselves. Soul/body dualism was essential to Aquinas's teaching and became the declared position of medieval Christendom.[9]

Second, souls are individually distinctive, so that after leaving their bodily container they are still cognizant of themselves and recognizable as the unique persons they once were. The modern expectation that we will be reunited with deceased family members and even pets is dependent on this idea. Historian Carolyn Walker Bynum (1992, 1995) has described the importance of themes of bodily fragmentation, dissolution, and reassemblage in theological discussions of resurrection from the beginnings of Christianity up through medieval times. One difficult issue was knowing which properties of the material self survive death. Gender? Race? Disfigurement? Youth? Another concerned how these properties will make us recognizably ourselves in a hereafter. The apostle Paul's solution in 1 Corinthians 15, his agricultural metaphor of radical transformation, left open the question of what our postresurrection bodies will be like; it was left to Augustine to make the matter more explicit.[10] He held that after death we are reassembled as intact persons, and whatever gruesome things may have happened to us during life or in time spent rotting in a grave will be overcome since ultimately our bodies are beautiful and acceptable to God. Flesh, for all its failings, is essential to our personhood, including our personhood in heaven. Even under the most extreme circumstances, as in dying by fire or being eaten by wild animals, all our bits and pieces will be reunited in spiritual glory. "And though [one's flesh] had been absolutely annihilated, so that no part of its substance remained in any secret spot of nature, the Almighty could restore it by such means as He saw fit" (Augustine, quoted in Bynum 1995: 104).

Given that the body is in some fashion coresident with God in eternity, Augustine approved the care and attention given the dying and the corpse. This was consistent with the blooming Christian cult of relics. That cult fostered belief not only in the corporeal incorruptibility of those who were saintly but also in the spiritual potency of even their smallest body parts, fueling the traffic in relics that operated in Europe for centuries and, in a smaller measure, still does (Brown 1981). A single lock of hair or a finger was capable of producing miracles, despite separation from the original owner, and "the more the martyr's parts were spread throughout the Mediterranean world, the more he or she came to be seen as housed within the fragment" (Bynum 1995: 105–6). The rest of us are "housed" in our body parts too, but, lacking the high virtue of saints and martyrs, we must wait out reconstitution until the end of time, appearing then in the familiar form we know ourselves to be. That view has never really gone out of fashion and persists in popular heavenly representations of the dead resting on clouds, experiencing flight, beholding spectacles, and enjoying the music of the spheres.

A third distinctive feature of Western notions of the soul is its capacity for communication. "Because it is insubstantial, it hears the whispered messages of beings beyond the natural world" (Furst 1995: 4). Communicating with the dead is not a modern or even a particularly Western idea, and it has important precedents in the Judeo-Christian tradition. In the biblical Old Testament, for example, traffic with the dead as well as with supernatural beings was possible but usually illicit or at least dangerous, something Saul discovered when he secretly consulted a conjuror, a woman at Endor, and asked her to fetch up the ghost of Samuel (see 1 Samuel 28 for the unpleasant consequences). Jacob and Job exposed themselves to danger by engaging supernaturals directly and whatever theological insights interpreters subsequently drew from those stories, the fact remains that their experiences were understood in their time as real possibilities. Apparently, less risk was perceived by medieval religious authorities who meddled quite openly in the processes of the afterlife. They operated what may have been the largest, longest running, and most profitable system of spiritual manipulation ever devised. The doctrine of purgatory, hugely popular from the twelfth to the sixteenth centuries, brought enormous wealth into the medieval church in exchange for masses alleged to speed the souls of the recently deceased toward heaven. An object of bitter attack by Protestants, neither the economics nor the theological rationale of purgatory could be sustained forever, and in its place came a more benign, efficient way of relating to the dead. That plan called for bypassing threatening supernaturals and greedy bishops altogether and visiting the dead directly, a technique promoted by the eighteenth-century aristocrat, engineer, biologist, and metallurgist Emanuel Swedenborg. He gets credit for proposing the first distinctly modern view of the afterlife. *Heaven and Its Wonders and Hell* (1965), first published in 1758, broke with the medieval past and laid out notions of the afterlife that are with us still.

MODERN SOULS, MODERN AFTERLIVES

In Swedenborg's view, communication between the natural and supernatural is not difficult since the dead exist in a world parallel to our own, separated only by a thin, porous veil. Spiritual travel across that boundary is easily done and Swedenborg himself made the trip many times, writing extensively about what he saw. Heaven, he said, is a world essentially like our own, only better. It is not a place of "rest" or, in the older medieval view, nonstop adoration of the Divine. It is an active place and in its distinctive way a material one, where the newly dead are not always aware that they are really dead since they have entered a realm similar to the one left behind. The celestial world consists of four layers, beginning with a spirit place that is really the doorway to all else. It is followed by a "natural" heaven occupied by "natural" angels, then a spiritual heaven wherein human social life has achieved perfection, and finally a celestial heaven where the original paradise has been recreated for us. There we all become angels and, in that fourth and highest realm, naked ones at that. Nakedness is associated with innocence and wisdom, and our task in heaven is to grow in wisdom so that our exterior, naked selves become a pure revelation of refined inner selves. Like mortals, angels experience mood swings and their interests change, thus their ascent through various gradations of innocence is as diverse as the life experiences of living people now.

Among the most intriguing (and humanizing) aspects of Swedenborg's views on heaven are those on love and marriage and how heaven generally replicates the class system of the world he knew. Love literally makes the world go 'round, both this world and the next, and in heaven we are all destined to have a celestial partner who may or may not be the person we are with now. "Marriage in heaven is a conjunction of two into one mind. . . . So in heaven a married pair is spoken of, not as two, but as one angel" (1965: 243). The clear advantage to this is that what I want, you want too, since we share one celestial mind. He adds, "I have been told by the angels that so far as a married pair are so conjoined they are in marriage love, and also to the same extent intelligence, wisdom, and happiness, because Divine truth and Divine good which are the source of all intelligence, wisdom, and happiness, flow chiefly into marriage love . . . [which] is the very plane of Divine influx" (245). Marriage of minds (or by minds) assures that one's angel partner is fully compatible, thus souls do not marry outside their accustomed religion, social class, ethnic group, or national identity, since "two unlike and discordant kinds of good and truth cannot make two minds one; and in consequence the love of such does not have its origins in anything spiritual" (249). As on earth but more successfully, spirit marriages perpetuate known social groupings. And, as with earthly marriage, spiritual partners procreate. But in heaven they produce truth, not babies. In fact, the production of truth is the job of everyone, and each angel has a specific task that in its own way advances wisdom. "There are in heaven," Swedenborg says, "more functions and services and occupations than can be enumerated," and what distinguishes heavenly labor from that of this world is that in paradise all work is for the sheer love of doing so, as a contribution to the general good without thoughts of personal glory or gain (260). Swedenborg's heaven is not only layered and hierarchical, like the Europe of his day, but it houses reproducing angels and a rich division of labor, similar to what we experience here. Our joy in that afterlife will be doing perfectly what we do now, merged spiritually with a perfect mate, and all out of greater love and usefulness to others, the whole expressive of God's intentions for humankind.

McDannell and Lang (1988) identify four elements of the Swedenborgian afterlife that mark it as modern and as an ancestor to many popular beliefs of our own time. First, heaven is real, potentially within and certainly all about us. When we die, we enter it immediately without having to wait as moldering dust for a remote apocalyptic event when our parts will be reunited. Second, heaven is a sensate place with material dimensions and substances similar if not exactly like what we know now. We are assured that there will be something there that is recognizable, and that we will be recognized in it. What we will look like is not really important; it is who we are as persons and what made us useful and loveable human beings that will be manifest. Third, heaven is an active place. It has its grand, structural order, and we will have, in effect, a job description custom made for us. We will do many of the things we did in this life, only better and with greater satisfaction. Our spiritual journey, begun in this life, will continue and have no end. Finally, the love God has for us is expressed through human love, and the next stage of it will be unencumbered by physical attractiveness or the size of our bank account. We will love spiritually and in purity, just as God does.

Swedenborg was a prolific author, writing numerous books on natural science and philosophy, and, as a major intellectual in his day, he was buried with near-royal honors in the cathedral in Uppsala in 1772. A small but vigorous movement of "reading circles" soon emerged, including one in Philadelphia in 1784, and his theories were familiar to theologians, philosophers, literary people, and the educated lay public throughout the ensuing century. He was popular with the American transcendentalists, especially Ralph Waldo Emerson, and a small denomination, the Swedenborgian or New Church, continues to advance his teachings. Part of the appeal was the clarity and immediacy of his vision as well as the replacement of supernatural torments with love, especially human love, as a prominent feature of the afterlife. In an appreciative introduction to the 1965 edition of *Heaven and Its Wonders and Hell*, devotee Helen Keller wrote, "It was as if light came where there had been no light before, the intangible world became a shining certainty. . . . Heaven, as Swedenborg portrays it, is not a mere collection of radiant ideas, but a practical, livable world" (vi). Practical, yes, and also a world afloat on the optimism, assuredness, and self-confidence of the European Enlightenment in which Swedenborg was comfortably at home. His heaven is unmistakably anthropocentric, an extension of this life but without its imperfections, and hell is the bed we make for ourselves here.[11]

The benevolence of this inspiration has persisted, especially in American popular culture, but 250 years later the clarity of what he saw on the other side of the veil has, with a few exceptions, blurred. While many Americans imagine themselves bound for heaven, just what they will *do* when they get there is unclear. In a theocentric heaven one prays to, adores, and worships Deity, in spirit and in truth, now and forever, amen. Communion with the godhead is all. John Wesley, a contemporary of Swedenborg who wanted to meet him but never did, dismissed the latter's humanistic imagery as a distraction from that deep and unending intimacy with God that is the whole point of salvation. But Swedenborg wanted to do more than sit among celestial clouds strumming a harp and singing praises. He wanted to enjoy heaven and have us enjoy it much as he did, as an aristocrat used to strolling in fine gardens, cultivating good taste, and engaging others in high-minded dialogue. But that is not what his heaven has come to be in our own time. "By far the most persuasive element of the modern heaven for many contemporary Christians is the hope of meeting the family again" (McDannell and Lang 1988: 309). The rich detail and the busy spiritual agenda of the Swedeborgian afterlife has been replaced by joyous reunions with loved ones on the front porch of Paradise. The spirit of Swedenborg certainly lives, if not in the details then in how people will occupy themselves with all that time on our hands.[12]

Characterizing visions of the afterlife as theocentric (kingdomlike) and anthropocentric (humanistic) is useful if we are primarily interested in what people say they believe. More interesting is how ideation becomes praxis. For that purpose, the two major themes I have already introduced, Vitebsky's notion of social Memory and de Certeau's spiritual contract, are useful. In the remainder of this chapter, I look at two quite different instances of religious expression in America's pluralistic religious culture, not as a comprehensive review of either one but to consider how contract and memory operate to generate ways of managing relations with the dead. The first, with its explicit emphasis on contract, is the Church of Jesus Christ of Latter-day Saints. The second, where the negotiation of Memory predominates, comes from those who say they have had near-death or out-of-body experiences, have seen what awaits, and are generally confident about how things will turn out. I choose these two not because I think they are typical of how Americans generally imagine the afterlife, at least in the details. Neither is. Rather—and this is the key point—they are exemplars of two points on a scale between which many (I suspect most) Americans hover, one quite traditional and the other late modern in its "spiritual but not religious" emphasis. More important, I discuss them because they each mark their place on that scale with great clarity of vision, something most Americans lack on the afterlife issue. It is that precision which makes them useful illustrators of afterlife themes, portions of each shared in various ways by many Americans who are affiliated with neither. They are clear instances of what de Certeau calls "expectational practice," which is what I want to foreground.

CONTRACTING THE FUTURE

Mormon history began with the idea of a contract and with Joseph Smith's prayers for guidance through the competing claims of New England's proliferating churches and sects during the 1820s, a period of notable enthusiasm in American religious expression.[13] In a First Vision he was told that all extant creeds were an abomination to God, and throughout his life he received additional revelations confirming and sharpening that view, until he came to understand that a radical "restoration of all things" was required. (*Doctrine and Covenants* is a record of those revelations and was published in 1835, followed by later editions.) Soon he found others who also believed it was time for an ingathering of likeminded, dedicated people willing to be Latter-day Saints for the work of that restoration. One early advocate and compatriot, Parley P. Pratt, proclaimed it a time for "'NEW WINE' and 'NEW BOTTLES'— 'NEW LEAVEN' and a 'NEW LUMP,' 'A NEW COVENANT' and spirit; and may it roll on till we have a new heaven and a new earth, that we may dwell forever in the new Jerusalem, while old things pass away, and all things are made new, even so. Amen" (Hughes 2001: 31). The instrument of that "new covenant" was to be the Church of Jesus Christ of Latter-day Saints, a religious community of phenomenal growth since its founding less than two hundred years ago and "regarded by scholars as the first American-born world religion" (Eliason 2001: 2).

The history of the Latter-day Saints (LDS) and the sociology of their distinctive religious culture makes clear the contractual nature of their "covenant community." It begins with a dramatic and heroic origin story, one that parallels in some respects the biblical exodus with its themes of persecution, flight, wandering under a far-seeing and God-inspired leader, and, after many tribulations, settlement in a promised, or at least promising, land. There are also schism, martyrdom, a faithful and rugged core of believers determined to succeed, and, perhaps unique among foundational epics, extensive documentation of the struggle by a leadership elite and their followers in numerous autobiographies and diaries written during that time. Begun in the spiritual fervor of the 1820s, the Saints eventually settled into the mundane and necessary demands of frontier survival. Early on they established themselves by founding banks and businesses, running schools and newspapers, planning cities, and creatively applying the best technology of the day to the challenges of irrigation and farming in an unfamiliar environment. They meticulously organized colonies throughout the mountain West and aggressively recruited new members from England, Scandinavia, and Germany. In this they were guided by a number of rules and practices to which most everyone assented: clear, hierarchical management and decision making; communal responsibilities, including extensive donation of labor and personal assets to the common good; a work ethic of self-sufficiency and neighborly welfare; marriage within the community combined with a full and exclusive social life to make sure that that happened; and an emphasis on education and literacy, giving central place to the Church's sacred texts and publications. In this life and in that of the world to come, hard work and communalism were the operating principles. Finally, the covenant with deity included the dream of a political kingdom to be called Deseret, based in Salt Lake City and encompassing huge tracts of the territorial West well beyond the current boundaries of Utah.

Several expectational practices are key to the Saints' relationship to their covenant. They include the populating of an elaborate heavenly or "celestial" soulscape, marriage as necessary and preparatory to attaining "glory" in the afterlife, and the use of genealogy as a linking device between mortal and eternal realms. Each illustrates de Certeau's view of belief as a complex and integrated set of procedures for satisfying contractual obligations of cosmic proportions. The universe this covenant established is magisterial and hierarchical, reminiscent in some ways of that of Swedenborg.

In LDS theology, God's plan of salvation offers eternal life to all who undergo a time of physical presence on earth and use that opportunity to prepare themselves for the heavenly joys of "exaltation" promised after death. We began our existence, however, not here but in a premortal realm, as spirit children, the offspring of a specific heavenly father and mother. That is our "first estate," the one from which we cannot progress in spiritual maturity because we have yet to be tested. That is why we are brought into the mortal world, a "second estate," where earthly parents give us the opportunity to grow in faith and to demonstrate a willingness to follow God's commandments. Because we are free agents, we can accept or reject the spiritual opportunities and moral challenges of earthly life, but our moral achievements in this world will be the measure of the joys to be had in the next. Facing temptations and tests, we know we fall short of God's expectations, yet when death arrives we can be confident we will be resurrected into the world of spirit because Jesus has prepared the way through his crucifixion. Despite an assured resurrection, however, not everyone arrives at the same place. Heaven is an ordered, elaborately hierarchical realm with ranks of perfection including three major degrees of glory and finer gradations of blessing within each degree. We arrive, much as Swedenborg believed, at a level appropriate to how well we did on earth, and our task, once there, is to continue where we left off, by cultivating greater spiritual perfection. Clearly, some of us are going to have a longer, harder celestial road to travel than others, but Jesus' atonement assures that we have all eternity to work at it. Perhaps most distinctive is the Saints' view that with diligence everyone can become a god in their own right, a god with God, a god at the apex of their own celestial kingdom among the infinite celestial kingdoms in God's grand scheme. And like the celestial parents who gave us birth as premortal spirit children, we will create new child spirits ourselves, not once but forever, who will replicate our journey in their turn. While that image of heaven may seem unusual to some Christians, the LDS statement of *Doctrine and Covenants* is clear that our destiny is more than becoming like God; it is to become gods in our own right. "Then shall they be gods, because they have no end; therefore shall they be from everlasting to everlasting, because they continue; then shall they be above all, because all things are subject unto them. Then shall they be gods, because they have power, and the angels are subject unto them" (Ludlow 1992: 132:20).

Two things should be noted about this vision of paradise: its general structure as an endlessly replicated soulscape and the physicality of the souls occupying it. Joseph Smith's insight on these points came from his interpretation of several verses in Paul's first letter to the Corinthians (15: 39–41), which speaks of the distinctive "glory" of the various species of living things on earth and the unique glory of the moon, sun, and each of the stars. Smith saw there a description of a dynamic universe of unending stellar systems constantly created, aging, and dying away. This was more than one man's quirky reading of an arcane biblical text, however. It was part of his broader conception of the relationship of science and religion, a topic that engaged nineteenth-century naturalists and religious thinkers generally. For Smith, science and religion, rightly conceived, are one; and he was not threatened by the debates between science and religion that raged in America, then as now. God is the sole source of revealed truth, scriptural and natural, and both are divinely inspired; faith and reason coexist. Frederick James Pack, a psychology professor at Brigham Young College, offered a definitive statement on this in 1908, saying that the "unending strife between science and religion is very largely the result of this artificial classification of God's laws into the natural and the supernatural. . . . *The term supernatural should become obsolete at once.* . . . It is high time that all of God's laws are recognized as natural." Further, "No warfare exists between 'Mormonism' and true science" (Paul 1992: 31).[14]

If the supernatural is an extension of the natural, astronomical knowledge is a significant adjunct (although not revealed truth itself) to understanding God's grand design and what we can expect in our postmortal existence. Nineteenth and early twentieth-century Mormon scientists wrote extensively on the "plenitude" of the cosmos, how it is endlessly populated with stars, planets, and other sentient beings. This notion of a plurality of inhabited worlds is in fact an old idea, beginning almost with the emergence of modern science in the Enlightenment and more recently popularized by Carl Sagan. Smith accepted astronomical pluralism and added that the moral character of the various worlds differ, being hierarchically ranked on a scale of goodness, with our earth the least worthy of the bunch. Similarly, the structure of the celestial afterlife is ranked by "degrees of glory." Based on John 14:2 ("In my Father's house there are many dwelling places"), those who die "are not placed in a monolithic state called heaven. In the resurrection of the body, they are assigned to different degrees of glory commensurate with the law they have obeyed. There are three kingdoms of glory: the celestial, the terrestrial, and the telestial" (*Encyclopedia of Mormonism* 1992, 1: 367). The telestial, as the lowest, is inhabited by those who rejected the gospel message and lived lives unworthy of it. The second or terrestrial realm is of those who knew and even accepted the Christian message but failed to live out its expectations as they should have. Housed with them are all who were otherwise honorable but died not knowing the gospel at all, commonly people of "heathen nations." These second tier resurrected ones work at repentance and spiritual improvement. The third level is that of "celestial glory," a place where the spiritually perfected "shall dwell in the presence of God and his Christ forever and ever" (*Doctrine and Covenants* 76: 62). They are deserving because of their active faith, full repentance of sins, and baptism by immersion and laying on of hands. This third level is subdivided into its own degrees of glory, again along lines of differential spiritual accomplishment. As a finely calibrated and constructed system, heaven has a place for everyone according to how well they lived up to the spiritual contract put into play once they were transferred from their premortal to their earthly estate. Unlike the dualistic structure of heaven and hell that has been authoritative among traditional Christians for centuries, one where the newly dead are consigned to their just deserts forever, the Saints' vision is generous and open-ended. Hope and the potential for personal advancement infuse the entire cosmos, and with sincere effort each of us can become godlike.[15]

A hierarchical cosmos is not unusual in Western speculations on the moral structure of eternity, but the Mormon understanding of souls and the stuff of which they are made is distinctive. Souls are a special kind of matter. Smith repeatedly described God as a "distinct personage" and Jesus and the Holy Ghost as "distinct personages"; and we, like them, are godlike entities composed of the same natural elements. In this formulation, Smith was applying to spirit his understanding of discussions of matter and energy common among nineteenth-century scientists. He argued that matter cannot be created or destroyed since it is eternal but it can be organized and reorganized infinitely. What we call spirit is one of the permutations of material substance, a special kind that is highly refined and not easily perceived. "There is no such thing as immaterial matter. All spirit is matter, but it is more fine and pure, and can only be discerned by purer eyes; we cannot see it; but when our bodies are purified we shall see that it is all matter" (*Doctrine and Covenants* 131: 7–8).

If spirit really is matter, albeit a rarified form, that has consequences for us when we die. At death the body disintegrates, but it will be reassembled molecule by molecule in the afterlife and will assume its purer form. Brigham Young was explicit about this: the mortal stuff we are made of will not become food for worms. Each particle of us is "watched over and will be preserved until the resurrection, and at the sound of the trumpet of God every particle of our physical structures necessary to make our tabernacles [bodies] perfect will be assembled, to be rejoined with the spirit, every man in his order. Not one particle will be lost" (Davies 2000: 95). The mortal organization of our material selves will, of course, disappear, but the spiritual organization of our bodies will last through eternity. That being the case, the method of disposing of bodies has never been an issue for Latter-day Saints. By tradition, burial in the ground has been preferred but, unlike Catholics and some Protestants, Saints have not opposed cremation on doctrinal grounds. The first cremation in Salt Lake City took place in 1877 when the practice was both new in America and controversial (Davies 2000: 137). Since in the Mormon view matter is eternal and cannot be destroyed, it really makes no difference whether we slowly decompose below ground in a gilded box or are quickly transformed into smoke and ash in a crematory fire. And while the configuration of Smith's cosmology is certainly his own, the idea that we enter heaven as reassembled, intact bodies is at least as old as Augustine, who saw in the parable of the lost sheep a foreshadowing of that heavenly event (Bynum 1995: 99).

The second major feature of LDS expectational practice is marriage. Earthly marriage and childbearing is a solemn obligation because it is the necessary first step in moving souls from their premortal state toward a spiritually mature postmortal one. Once on earth, each person is free to make his or her own decisions on matters of faith and faithfulness, but it is the understanding of the Church that parents are the custodians of spirits in transition to a greater glory. *Doctrine and Covenants* clearly develops the importance and implications of this aspect of marriage:

> And again, verily I say unto you, if a man marry a wife by my word, which is my law, and by the new and everlasting covenant, and it is sealed unto them by the Holy Spirit of promise, by him who is anointed, unto whom I have appointed this power and the keys of this priesthood; and it shall be said unto them—Ye shall come forth in the first resurrection; and if it be after the first resurrection, in the next resurrection; and shall inherit thrones,

kingdoms, principalities, and powers, dominions, all heights and depths—
. . . it shall be done unto them in all things whatsoever my servant hath put
upon them, in time, and through all eternity; and shall be of full force when
they are out of the world. (132: 19)

Saints recognize, of course, that a number of practical questions and
moral conundrums follow from this doctrine. What happens to the spirits of
children who die in childbirth? Is contraception acceptable, and are there ever
circumstances that would make abortion medically as well as morally justi-
fied? And what of gay and lesbian members of the LDS community? If the
production of children is a sacramental act, are they doomed to a lesser place
in the afterlife? Beyond the question of offspring, their presence raises a more
esoteric but interesting question: do premortal spirits have gender? If they do,
what does that say about individuals who are transgendered, who feel they are
a female spirit born in a male body, for example? Could the LDS cosmos grant
equal place to loving, enduring earthly families created not by procreation but
simply by association, nurturance, and care for one another?

In LDS expectation, "families are forever," literally, and it is the family
unit as much as the individual which attains glory and salvation. Marriage
contracted in this life persists into the next, and access to the highest level of
the Celestial Kingdom is dependent in part on temple marriage. "Thus a person who lives a righteous life in mortality and who has entered into an eternal marriage may look forward to an association in the postmortal world with
a worthy spouse, and with those who were earthly children, fathers, mothers,
brothers, and sisters" (Duke 1992: 858). Marriage is not just for the benefit of
spouses but is an arrangement that assures eternal association with all of one's
biological descendants in each succeeding generation, without end. Marriage
and procreation move whole genealogical lines closer to their ultimate goal of
spiritual purity and godhead status. While in this life we give birth to earthly
children, in the next we will give birth to spiritual ones. Those who for medical or personal reasons do not have children now will get their chance then.
Families are for everyone, whether contracted now or later, because it is in
family that we experience the postmortal world. It is easy to see in this construction a rationale for plural marriage. While never the practice of the
majority of Saints and banned by the Church in 1890, it nevertheless assured
an abundance of physical and spiritual offspring immersed in a rich family
life, now and in eternity.[16]

The enumeration of ancestors is the third in the trio of LDS expectational
practices. Most Americans have at least a casual interest in knowing something of their family history, and genealogical research is an engaging hobby

for many. For Latter-day Saints it is a religious obligation. Proxy baptisms populate heaven with ancestors who were not able to know the gospels in their lifetime, giving them the chance to participate in God's plan of salvation along with the rest of their genealogical line. While this may seem unusual outside the Mormon community, the intent behind it is strikingly democratic and recognizably American. The idea is that heaven is open to all, none will be turned away or left behind, and everyone has another chance to become better. Proxy baptisms assure the complete reconstituting of whole families as far as they can be traced. Regrouped in heaven, everyone shares in its glory while moving toward exaltation in the presence of celestial parents, spouses, children, and grandchildren. Again the mantra, families are forever.[17]

The elaborate genealogical records assembled by the church make this massive induction of ancestors into heaven possible. To facilitate this project, the Family History Library in Salt Lake City was founded in 1894 and it is the largest library of its kind. Its databases include the Ancestral File, the Pedigree Resource File, the Vital Records Index, and the International Genealogical Index. Millions of names are stored there, and researchers in over forty countries supply new information constantly. Family History Centers, over 3,500 worldwide, are the branches of the library and are attached to temples where they offer computer facilities and expert advice to everyone, regardless of LDS membership. To store the accumulating data, construction began in 1958 on "the Vault," a multimillion-dollar chamber carved into Granite Mountain in the Wasatch Range, twenty miles southeast of Salt Lake City. The *Encyclopedia of Mormonism* describes the site as

> a massive excavation reaching 600 feet into the north side of the canyon. . . . The office and laboratory section sits beneath an overhang of about 300 feet of granite and houses shipping and receiving docks, microfilm processing and evaluation stations, and administrative offices. Under 700 feet of stone, the Vault proper is situated farther back in the mountain behind the laboratory section and consists of six chambers (each 190 feet long, 25 feet wide, and 25 feet high) which are accessed by one main entrance and two smaller passageways. Specially constructed Mosler doors weighing fourteen tons (at the main entrance) and nine tons (guarding the two smaller entrances) are designed to withstand a nuclear blast. In the six chambers, nature maintains constant humidity and temperature readings optimum for microfilm storage. (Baldridge 1992: 563)

A costly enterprise signifying devotion to a theological proposition unmatched in scope since the building of Gothic cathedrals in medieval Europe, the Vault is emblematic of something fundamental in the salvationist regimes of all the historic religions of Western culture—the power of the

Word, especially the written Word. All the major Western religions depend on a foundational document and its material presence as words on a page are proof of the deity's intent, the manifestation of a "covenant" or contract. In the LDS faith, secular birth and death records as well as homemade genealogies partake in that sacredness. They are instrumental to preparing a place in paradise for those who might otherwise miss out. Christianity has been a text and word-oriented set of practices almost from the beginning, but the LDS community has given that idea a dimension even an avid correspondent like St. Paul would have admired.

The genealogies of the Latter-day Saints, the central importance of marriage and procreation, and a complex spiritual geography of the afterlife are expectational practices that mark an important point on the spectrum of religious experience in contemporary American culture. The Latter-day Saints are not different from other "mainstream" denominations in their emphasis on belief as consent to a contractual relationship between the individual and community, the individual and deity. They use a theological language of contract that would be familiar in many denominations: Jesus *paid* with his life the *debt* owed God by all who are sinners, who cannot be *redeemed* solely on their own account, and whose salvation was *purchased* through His body, blood and triumphant resurrection. Contracts of various kinds bind individuals to families and community and in a covenant community the bargain invokes the notion of a chosen people with special obligations: to the unborn, who as premortals depend on the living for advancement to the next stage of their spiritual growth; to those born too long ago to know the gospel but who can have their chance through proxy baptisms; and to those still living who do not know the LDS message but will learn of it through energetic missionizing. The rewards for keeping this demanding covenant do not end with death or even resurrection but continue beyond in "exaltation" to godhood itself.

There is embedded as well in this grand vision an additional element, less well known within the Mormon community (but familiar to a number of LDS historians), with implications for the Saints' contractual understanding of belief and of the afterlife. In *The American Religion* (1992), Harold Bloom has said that "The God of Joseph Smith is a daring revival of the God of some of the Kabbalists and Gnostics, prophetic sages who, like Smith himself, asserted that they had returned to the true religion of Yahweh or Jehova" (99). Bloom is not the only one to have noticed this. In 1994 Lance S. Owens published a lengthy essay on "Joseph Smith and Kabbalah: The Occult Connection" in *Dialogue, A Journal of Mormon Thought*. That same year, John L. Brooke's widely discussed *The Refiner's Fire* (1994) appeared.[18] Both developed the theme of a "hidden" history of the life of Joseph Smith, hidden not in the sense that it was secret (it was not) but that it lies on the periphery of current LDS orthodoxy. Smith had investigated older European Kabbalah traditions, themselves traceable to a complex swirl of medieval Jewish mysticism, early seventeenth-century Rosicrucian speculations, ancient alchemical practices, and the enduring influence of Swedenborg. These intellectual and esoteric currents were familiar to most educated people of Smith's time. He would have learned of them through his involvement with Masonry but his most important contact may have been Alexander Neibaur, a Polish Jew who joined Smith's church and became Smith's confidant and tutor in Hebrew. Neibaur came to Nauvoo with his books, including a copy of the *Zohar*, the foundational statement of Kabbalah, a document Smith must certainly have studied, since his notion of the plurality of gods comes from the *Zohar*'s exegesis of Genesis. Brooke argues, as do Bloom and Owens, that Smith was indeed something new and unusual in the American religious landscape of the early nineteenth century. More than a charismatic leader or a rural theologian, he was prophetic in the grand sense. He made connections where others did not see them and called into being a unique, covenant community that would live out his insights. Says Brooke,

> He had established a theology of the conjunction—the unification—of the living and the dead, of men and women, of material and spiritual, all united in a "new and everlasting covenant" over which he would preside as king and god. In these circumstances the conventional boundary between purity and danger, right and wrong, law and revolution simply melted away . . . visualized as [a] meta-alchemical experience running from opposition to union, an experience shaped and driven by the personality of Joseph Smith. (1994: 281)[19]

Indebted as he may have been to these Gnostic sources, Smith's vision of the afterlife remained distinctive in an important way, especially when compared to Swedenborg's, with which Smith was probably familiar. Swedenborg's heaven is one of individually achieved spiritual improvement, the soul busily working its way toward higher levels of spiritual maturity. Mormon doctrine replicates that idea in a general sense, certainly in its teleological directionality, but it adds a complicating factor. Wherever one arrives in the LDS afterlife, he or she is there, in part, because of favors dispensed by others, especially spiritual procreators/ancestors who brought one into a first estate, and earthly parents who made the journey of the second estate possible. We are, of course, responsible for the choices we individually make in this life. But beyond that, we are indebted to those who gave us a start, nurtured us along, and we are obligated to those (possibly multitudinous) generations we will sire when we become spiritual ancestors ourselves. That network of contractual obligations runs wide and deep, for we attain godhood status only within and beholden to cosmic genealogies extending through eternity. That is hardly a Gnostic heaven of individualistic striving and achievement. It is instead a cosmos of patron-client relationships. Patronage and clientage, even of the loving and familial sort, is an expressly contractual model with obligations and in-house loyalties constituting the system's operational style. LDS heaven is no Swedenborgian or New Age kingdom of free-spirited high achievers but one of family loyalists tied to lineage godheads; less an open class system of spiritual enterprise than one of multiple, embedded genealogical pyramids headed by spiritual ancestors of varying rank. Looked at it this way, Swedenborg's model is the more democratic and individualistic, the LDS one self-contained along anthropologically familiar clan and lineage lines. My guess is that this difference is due in part to Swedenborg's privileged position as a well-off Enlightenment gentleman who could indulge his desires without hindrance, compared to Joseph Smith's lifelong struggle to build a community of loyalists in a country that was less than tolerant of him and his doctrines.

If the LDS contract with ancestors and descendants, the past and the future, seems extravagant and demanding, perhaps that is because many twenty-first century moderns have a different view of what the afterlife promises. The Saints carry on the historical legacy of an explicitly theocentric eternity, reserved for those faithful to its covenant demands. The community so created places duty and obligation above personal preference and expects adherence to principles within a well-defined institutional framework. By contrast, the contemporary and much less encumbered option is that of direct, personal, extra-institutional spirituality with little in the way of contract or obligation, something akin to Robert Bellah's "expressive individualism" (1986). I turn now to an instance of that, one that shares the Saints' view that heaven is where we truly belong but with expectational practices radically different, centered on Memory, in Vitebsky's sense, rather than contract. And like the Saints, this gathering of believers is more traditionally American than they or their critics perceive. They are individuals who say they have died once already, toured a bit of the afterlife, and for good reason came back to tell us about it. They think we should all be optimists.

REMEMBERING THE FUTURE

Not everyone dies as did Betty Eadie but enough do to make it something of a contemporary movement, albeit a small one. As many as 14 percent of healthy, non-drug-using Americans may have had a near-death experience, an NDE, although the reliability of that number is unknown (Morse 1994:57). Eadie was a thirty-one-year-old mother when in 1973 she died in her hospital bed following a hysterectomy. It was not, she says, the first time she had had sensations of leaving her body; at the age of four, in a hospital with whooping cough, she arose and floated in the air, gazing down at her lifeless body after a doctor proclaimed her "lost" and covered her head with a sheet. In 1973, however, she did more than float. There was "a surge of energy. It was almost as if I felt a pop or release inside me, and my spirit was suddenly drawn out through my chest and pulled upward, as if by a giant magnet. . . . I turned and saw a body lying on the bed. . . . And then I recognized that it was my own" (Eadie 1992: 29). Literally disembodied, Eadie left the room through a closed window, traveling effortlessly at great speed to her home, where she paused to watch her husband and children in the living room. At that point she discovered one of the great secrets of the cosmos, that her children were not really hers but were spirits in their own right who, like herself, originally came to the material world from somewhere else with "an intelligence that was developed before their lives on earth" (34–35).

Eadie's journey to the afterlife began the moment she left her body and her family and entered another realm altogether. Quietly, three men appeared beside her as she arrived, looking like monks in their brown robes and braided gold belts. She sensed that they loved her deeply and had been with her even before her earthly existence, and they assured her that everything would be alright. Soon she was in a dark tunnel filled with other beings, human and animal, all moving toward of point of light that radiated an irresistible sense of love. Arriving at the source of the light, she partially merged with it and realized that she was in the presence of Jesus Christ. "Gently, he opened his arms and let me stand back far enough to look into his eyes, and he said, 'Your death was premature, it is not yet your time.' No words ever spoken have penetrated me more than these" (1992: 42). A second great truth then became known: everyone has a mission in their earthly life, everything that happens does so for some good reason, and underlying it all is a spiritual law of love that embraces each of us unconditionally. Hence the title of her book, *Embraced by the Light* (1992), a publishing phenomenon that rode the top of the *New York Times* best-seller list for four years.

Eadie's story is compelling not simply for the popular interest it aroused but for her personal history and her presence as the unofficial queen of a movement. She was born of a Scotch-Irish father and a Sioux mother, who divorced and sent their six children to a Catholic boarding school. Later, Eadie attended a Methodist school where, as in her Catholic experience, she tells us she was taught that Indians are heathens, unworthy of God, and probably doomed to damnation. As she matured, she spent time in other denominations, including the Lutherans, Baptists, Mormons, and the Salvation Army.[20] Since the publication of *Embraced by the Light*, however, she has branched out, becoming something of a spiritual entrepreneur. A slight, soft-spoken, and engaging person, she travels with her husband to numerous speaking events where she sells copies of her books and video tapes. She has her "official" Web site (embracedbythelight.com), a newsletter, and is popular with the members of IANDS, the International Association for Near-Death Studies, for whom she is an occasional keynote speaker. Equally important, she has been endorsed by a scientifically impeccable medical researcher, Dr. Melvin Morse, who wrote the Foreword to her best-selling book and has a notable research and publication history of his own, based on his work with dying children. Credit Eadie with launching something of a popular national conversation about the nature of dying, what we will find in the afterlife, and what we ought to be doing to prepare for it. Among those in the self-help and self-improvement industry, Eadie and her imitators (Sylvia Browne and John Edward, for example) occupy a prominent place.

Eadie, however, is only the figurehead for a phenomenon that others have explored in more rigorous ways. A model that has become the canonical NDE, one against which NDE experiencers often compare their own deathly encounters, was first developed by Raymond Moody, an academic philosopher and practicing physician. He published his clinical findings in *Life After Life* in 1975 and reissued the book in 2001, after having sold 13 million copies. As is typical of pioneers in any field of inquiry, he set out to develop a typology that would cover the range of near-death experiences his patients described. Over a period of years, he collected 150 cases, from which he devised a 15–step model of the typical features of a near-death experience. Far less flamboyant than Eadie and mindful of the strictures of scientific inquiry, he cautions that his model is only an abstraction, a composite of many stories. Nevertheless, there are recurring elements that run through each of them, beginning with an awareness that one is dead. That is followed by a sense of profound peace with no evident pain, even when death results from trauma as serious as a long fall or battle wounds. This momentary sense of pleasantness is interrupted, however, by loud noises that some say are disturbing and others find musical and beatific. Concurrent with these sounds is the sensation of entering a dark tunnel and of moving at high speed. Others may be in the tunnel as well, including animals, and some have said it is truly frightening, although for many it is peaceful and engaging. The experience of separation from one's body is especially dramatic, and Moody devotes more space to this phase of NDE than any other. People commonly "see" themselves crushed beneath a car or, like Eadie, expired on a hospital bed, as they hover just above their own corpse. Moody quotes a patient who died instantly in a high-speed collision: "Then, I was sort of floating about five feet above the street, about five yards away from the car, I'd say, and I heard the echo of the crash dying away. I saw people come running up and crowding around the car, and I saw my friend get out of the car, obviously in shock. I could see my own body in the wreckage among all those people, and could see them trying to get it out. My legs were all twisted and there was blood all over the place" (2001: 27).

The newly deceased have varying reactions to such a scene. Some find it interesting but sad, others are noncommittal, and many are baffled by what they are supposed to do about it. "What next?" they wonder, gazing at their remains. Moody speculates that they have yet to fully realize what has happened, or they simply look on in curiosity as medics and doctors rush about. Yet these newly dead are not bodiless. Many report they have taken on a new form, one Moody calls a "spiritual body [that is] nonetheless *something*, impossible to describe though it may be" (36). People sense they still have a shape, an upward-facing side and a bottom side, for instance, even when they have lost limbs at their death. They describe themselves as cloudlike, misty, colored, or transparent. They are often frustrated because the living can neither see nor hear them and when they try to speak to tell medical personnel that everything is really alright they cannot be heard. Spirit bodies are experienced as weightless and unconstrained by physical barriers. They move right through doors and walls. They believe they can see and think more clearly and can pick up thoughts from the living by some mechanism of direct transfer. And they report loneliness as they become aware that they do not and cannot share the social world of the living anymore.

This spiritual angst is temporary, for the suddenly dead are met by one or more helpful spirit beings whose job it is to escort them someplace else. They are not usually known by the deceased, although a few say they believe them to be guardian angels who have always been with them. As they are gently escorted away, a distant, beckoning light appears, often emanating from a single figure. The experience of the Light and "the being in the Light" is the center piece of many NDE accounts. The Light is of unusual but not blinding brilliance, described as "warm" and "pure love," and the being standing in it is usually recognizable. That entity, says Moody, "has a very definite personality. The love and the warmth which emanate from this being to the dying person are utterly beyond words, and he feels completely surround by it and taken up in it, completely at ease and accepted in the presence of this being" (49). While the experience of a powerful, seemingly magnetic light is common, the being recognized within it is dependent on the individual's religious background and prior cultural experience. Whoever or whatever it is, it communicates with the newly arrived not in spoken words but by thought transference. This first contact initiates a life review. One of Moody's respondents told him, "The voice asked me a question: 'Is it worth it?' And what it meant was, did the kind of life I had been leading up to that point seem worth-while to me then, knowing what I then knew" (52). The review is not a condemnation or judgment, not the folk image of St. Peter consulting a ledger at the entrance to heaven. Moody thinks his patients describe a learning experience where they were asked to ponder all they had done and then consider whether they were satisfied with it. The point of this gentle conversation, they said, was to clarify what they had learned or not yet learned about loving others. Significantly, this discussion is Moody's second longest in his account, a point to which I will return. For the newly dead, the life review is intensely visual and even colorful, memorable in the sense that every aspect of one's existence is revealed and recalled, inspiring satisfaction but also sadness over things that might have been done differently. Throughout, the being in the Light asks the deceased to reflect on how well and how fully he or she loved others. If there is pain or condemnation, it comes from the dead themselves, not the being in the Light.

Obviously, some do not stay, or rather are not allowed to stay, in this realm of bliss. They say that during a tour of heaven they reached some kind of border or limit and were told they could not go farther because to do so meant never going back. Their life review revealed earthly tasks yet to be done, and the being in the Light told them their "time" had not yet come. Some were turned back early while others were allowed a fuller glimpse of paradise. This may be much of the popular fascination with Eadie's account. She seems to have been allowed the full tour and describes lush, glowing landscapes of flowers, streams, and gardens. She visited a vast library where all knowledge is stored, where she "realized that this is a library of the mind. By simply reflecting on a topic, as I had earlier in Christ's presence, all knowledge on that topic came to me" (1994: 76). Like others, Eadie says that the entire experience was "ineffable," beyond description, and as a spirit she knew and saw all things—all knowledge, all time and space, all realities—making earthly life seem constricted and dull by contrast. In some accounts, those who died reconnected with predeceased family and friends. In Eadie's case, she was met by a large greeting party "wearing soft pastel gowns," spirits she had known in her pre-earthly existence and who were holding something of a graduation party for her arrival at her new home. For those sent back to earth, however, reentry into one's original body is less glorious and even unpleasant, like putting on damp, muddy clothes after a clean shower. Returnees commonly say they left the spirit world reluctantly and only because they had an obligation to complete their assigned tasks here, the whole reason for living at all. They came back to complete a mission before dying again.

The remaining elements of Moody's typology concern postdeath adaptations. Grieving friends and family find the recovered patient's story hard to believe and likely to have been provoked by strong medications or hallucinations. The effects of an NDE on survivors are well documented (Alvarado 2000) and they include introversion, a preference for solitary activities, reordered priorities, an inclination toward service to others, and sadness and even depression at the inability of others to accept what has happened to them. Despite these challenges, however, experiencers do not appear to suffer from serious psychiatric disorders resulting from their experience. Psychiatrist Bruce Greyson (2001) has compared the posttraumatic stress symptoms of experiencers with those of people who had had a near-fatal crisis but not an NDE. He found in both groups intrusive and disruptive memories of the traumatic event, but the experiencers did not show significant levels of socially disabling recall. They were not psychiatric cases as defined by the DSM-IV and were not in any pejorative sense "crazy."

The medical literature on near-death experiences is, if not large, at least ample. One can find there sophisticated research and discussions of medical typologies of NDEs, the phenomenology of near-death, near-death in cardiac patients, out-of-hospital care and quality-of-life issues, changes in personal values and scales for measuring the nature and intensity of the experience, comparisons with paranormal and psychiatric conditions, and clinical care and counseling guidelines. In addition, there are debates and editorial commentaries on possible causes and what larger truths (if any) they suggest. One of the most active researchers in this area is Greyson who, more than most, has established the legitimacy of the NDE as a topic of medical interest.[21] Like him, those who contribute to this professional discussion are highly credentialed researchers who write for peer-reviewed journals and take their subject seriously. Their publications show the precision and careful qualification expected of sober, scientific reporting, and they avoid the flamboyance of post-Eadie popularizers whose books occupy the self-help sections of chain bookstores. But one who straddles that boundary, a physician whose career has been built on rigorous, scientific study of dying children, is pediatrician Melvin Morse. Extrapolating from his research with young patients, he argues that not only is the near-death event a normal part of dying but that a huge cosmic truth stands behind it. Morse is not shy about advancing his case.

Much if not most of the literature on out-of-body and near-death experience is anecdotal, certainly that of the popularizing, confessional variety. To overcome that limitation, Morse selected two samples from his critically ill patients, those whose illness had a high likelihood of death and those with a life-threatening illness but at lower risk. Of the twenty-six children in the high mortality risk sample, twenty-two later described memories of being clinically dead. As children, their stories were not as elaborate as those of adults, yet they included familiar NDE imagery. One six-year-old, for example, said "It was weird. I thought I was floating out of my body. And I could see a light. There were a lot of good things in it" (Morse 1994: 67). Morse gave his young survivors paper and crayons and asked them to draw what they remembered seeing. Many produced images that included light, rainbows, deceased grandparents, and pets. Some drew doctors and nurses working over a failed body, seen from a viewpoint near the ceiling. Because children have had less time to learn the more complex views of death held by adults, what they had to say or draw about their NDEs was necessarily limited. Yet "their fragments, taken together, give us an understanding of a core NDE, strikingly similar to those previously described in adults" (68). Their experiences were real-time events, independent of medications and, Morse believes, independent of adult models. He concludes, "This evidence clearly suggests that NDEs in fact occur when they are subjectively perceived as occurring, at the point of death. As such, they must represent the best objective evidence of what it is like to die, regardless of which neurotransmitters or anatomic structures mediate the experience. They are as real as any other human experience, as real as math or language" (70).

Are Morse's conclusions believable, and are those of Greyson and other physicians? By contemporary standards of biomedical research, the definitive work to date is that of Van Lommel et al. (2001), a team that conducted a large, prospective study of NDEs in several Dutch hospitals. They tracked 344 resuscitated cardiac patients and compared the 62 (18 percent) who said they had had an NDE to a control group of those who did not. An NDE was defined as any "reported memory of all impressions during a special state of consciousness" including the features typically described by Moody (2001) and others. Patients were interviewed as early in their recovery as feasible and all were interviewed two more times, two years and then eight years later, to measure life changes. Experiencers and nonexperiencers were compared, and the data confirmed that a reported NDE was associated with life-transforming effects. But what caused the NDE in those patients who claimed one? The study ruled out the effects of medications or of psychopathology but left open another interesting possibility. Lommel affirms the reality of NDEs and states that in the absence of any other testable theory, "the concept that consciousness and memories are localized in the brain should be discussed. How could a clear consciousness outside one's body be experienced at the moment the brain no longer functions during a period of clinical death with flat EEG [electroencephalogram]? . . . NDE pushes at the limits of medical ideas about the range of human consciousness and the mind-brain relation" (2001: 2043). Based on the most rigorous, controlled research on NDEs yet, and published for that reason in the prestigious medical journal *The Lancet*, his advice to future researchers is a huge challenge: in any future biomedical studies of NDEs and out-of-body phenomena, "the theory and background of transcendence should be included as a part of an explanatory framework" because without that the study cannot be considered complete (2044). Note the word he uses —transcendence. That has never set easily with the empirically minded. Van Lommel says now it must.

On the strength of these and other medical findings, Morse is willing to make an unusual and daring leap toward van Lommel's recommendation. Memory, he argues, does not reside solely between our ears. Perhaps the short-term kind does, but long-term memory, as when we recall the dead and actually speak with them, or when we experience a departure from our physical selves, requires something else. He postulates that somewhere outside our bodies there is a "universal memory," a cosmic repository of energy flows and wavelike patterns permeating both matter and time. A natural phenomenon that is around us and in us, it is consciously engaged by many people as they die. As neurological structures, our brains are awash in these currents, and at moments of dire threat, they can and sometimes do connect with that cosmic source. The specific organ making the connection is the right temporal lobe, what Morse calls God's home within us. The right lobe is a transmitter and receiver, making all past memories (those of past lives, the common NDE sensation of perceiving all knowledge of all things, and the truth about ghosts) accessible.

> We tap into this universal memory in the same way that a radio receives radio waves. And, just as the air around us is filled with radio and cell phone waves, it is also filled with thought and memory from people and events, both past and present. When tapping into this memory field, the right temporal lobe

acts as a receiver because it is at times calibrated to receive memory that
exists in the universal memory bank. (2000: 86)[22]

Morse's account, like an eschatology, is rich with a language of distinctive
supernatural properties: holographic visions, the simultaneous occurrence of
all times and places, a universal mind, spiritual participation, and healing
through engagement with an embracing Love behind all things. Nor is he the
only physician to speak of death and the afterlife this way. He is joined by P.
M. H. Atwater, a widely read and highly regarded voice within the NDE community, who has had three NDEs herself and carries the transcendent vision
one very large step farther. Like Eadie, Atwater has her own Web site (www.
cinemind.com/atwater) and a host of popular publications, not least of which
is a coauthored book on NDEs in the well-known "Idiot's Guide" series. (I
mention this title not to ridicule but to point to how far beyond cult status
NDE publications have come in just a few years.) Her specialties include
future memory, what she calls "brain shift," hellish NDEs, the levels of the
afterlife, and living forever. Morse endorses many of her findings, and I want
to look briefly at what she says about dying children because it is with them
that she sees something new emerging.

"Brain shift," according to Atwater, is the engine that drives human evolution. (Charles Darwin might demur.) "*Among adult experiencers, I regard a
brain/spirit shift as a growth event*—a sudden, unexpected twist in life"; but
"*Among child experiencers, I regard a brain/spirit shift as an evolutionary event*—
for, regardless of how others are affected by a child's near-death scenario, the
second birth the child seems to undergo reorders or 'seeds' the youngster in
ways that are exceptional to regular behavior development" (2003: 13, 14,
emphasis in original). For Atwater, many of these child experiencers herald
the next stage of human evolution. They are an emerging human type, "imag-
iners" and "creative intuitives," who are "gifted" with higher IQs, less interested in money and consumerist living, and sensitive to esoteric knowledge.
Their personal style in human relationships is characterized by reconciliation
and forgiveness, not power. Yet they are determined to make social changes,
will be persistent in doing so, and are adept at mastering the modern technology which will enable them to achieve their goals. At times they may seem
troublesome to family and friends, but that is because they are attempting to
live a vision of resurrection, not because they were damaged by trauma. Their
NDEs, rightly understood, are the gateways to a new way of living. The initial
experience, for example, with its tunnel sensations and contact with a being
in the Light, is simply their introduction to alternative ways of perceiving reality. When these children have hellish NDEs, something Atwater was inter-

ested in when others were looking only for a blessed event, they confront the lies and deceptions that bedevil us all. The more common positive NDEs also teach: life itself is the greatest gift, and it can and will be enjoyed forever. The full, in-depth, world-exploring experience which those such as Eadie enjoyed is "an encounter with oneness and the collective whole of human kind; enlightenment" (183). It is the ultimate revelation. All NDEs, Atwater emphasizes, are natural, normal phenomena. They have their characteristic properties subject to scientific scrutiny and validation just like anything else. Where others speak of "faith," she sees an empirical challenge, citing as her inspiration Teilhard de Chardin, paleontologist, moral philosopher, and Jesuit, who she says taught that scientific research is the highest form of adoration. Rightly applied, it will reveal *the* fundamental truth of childhood NDEs—that an inspired "race" (her term) is growing up, unrecognized, all around. In a nod to the LDS vision, she cites Psalm 82:6 ("I have said, ye are gods") to declare "that we are gods in the making and that we are ever growing in spirit" (169). The next stage of human evolution is emerging, and, almost biblically, the little children are leading.

How are we to interpret the claims made for NDEs by scientifically minded researchers, popularizers, and those who say they have had the experience? One way, and not the only one, is to examine them as narratives, verbal accounts one step removed from the event itself. I do not doubt the reality of the trauma or the subsequent life-changing experience that inspires these accounts. But narrative is a second layer of understanding, a re-creation, and here the full apparatus of culture comes into play as the only means of conveying to the rest of us what the experiencer says happened. Giving close attention to the descriptive language Moody, Morse, Atwater and others use is, I believe, critical to understanding something of what the near-death experience is and, equally important, why as narratives they are not as unfamiliar or strange as they might initially seem. I suspect that what many experiencers have to say about an after-death existence dramatizes what many Americans, including those familiar with traditional denominational theologies, already hope for and believe but lack the evidentiary claims to justify.

AN INSPIRED ORTHODOXY

There is more to an NDE than what a typology such as Moody's, the visionary tale of Eadie, or the spiritual physiology of Morse suggest. In at least three ways, NDE narratives magnify some quite conventional elements of contemporary American death beliefs. I identify them as synchronicity, intimacy, and teleology. Each is packaged with a distinctive set of metaphors and dramatic imagery that clearly locates them on the "heaven as personal home" side of a contrast with the model of heaven as a contractual kingdom favored by the Latter-day Saints.[23] First, "synchronicity," considered by most experiencers to be a fundamental operating feature of the cosmos. Statements made by respondents include the following:

> People say that when we die we are "gone but not forgotten" but I know we are not gone. Death is just a presence elsewhere.

> I saw creation through God's eyes and saw everything is perfect. I know that I knew this before.

> On the anniversary of her [a child's] death, I saw a butterfly fly up and knew she was near. Everything, you know, is connected.

The theme here is that all events, times, and places are interconnected and present because invisible realms of reality intersect with our own at every moment. During a near-death experience, we access this larger reality, experiencing simultaneously events originating in all parts of it. Of course, as rational, earthbound creatures, we cannot know that, but while dying we enter into that ultimate reality and perceive its vastness. Experiencers often speak of synchronicity in visual terms, characterizing the cosmos they saw as a hologram. Once we are aware of our connectedness to it, we simultaneously participate in multiple planes of reality not unlike the three-dimensional visual effect of a two dimensional holographic image. The contrast between "dead or alive," the foil for the first respondent's statement quoted above, is to experiencers an example of earthbound, two-dimensional thinking. While the religiously pious may say that behind the visible universe is the mystery of God, and atheists insist that what we see is all there is, experiencers counter that wavelike energy circulates continuously among multiple holographic planes and that at death we are simply reformulated in another of its many dimensions. Ghosts, hauntings, and angels are manifestations of movement throughout this holographic system, and their reality and occasional presence should not surprise us. Nor should the condition of being "out of the body," viewing one's dying remains from above the operating table, be surprising. We can simultaneously be here and there because that is how the universe normally functions.

Synchronicity underlies the belief of many experiencers that there are no accidents, there is no randomness. Everything happens for some good reason, and events that we imagine occurred in the far past or may happen in the far future are, in some sense, around us at every moment. Many experiencers are comfortable with telepathy, precognition, dream stories, ghosts, and guardian angels because they are evidence of intrusions from the larger reality that envelopes us. When it breaks through as a presence, as Orsi says it sometimes does, it is a comfort, not a shock, as in the statement linking a dead child's spirit to a butterfly. And sometimes synchronicity is the basis of "in" jokes, as when a conference speaker once complained that experiencers' meetings never start as scheduled because everybody's watch has a different time. The remark brought hearty laughs, but some of the newcomers did not get it. Time and place are meaningless once you have died and seen in a moment the wonders of a synchronous universe where all that was and is happens, transparent and instantly accessible.

A second element in these narratives is their emphasis on intimacy, again a play on the "home" side of a contrast between home and celestial kingdom. The synchronous universe may be a kind of kingdom, but it is neither the royal architecture portrayed in Ezekiel (40–48) nor that of Christmas carols announcing ranks of heralding angels and heavenly hosts. It is personal and affectionate, focused on the hopes of the dying individual rather than the grandeur of the heavenly landscape.

> I didn't experience the tunnel, just The Light. It was more than a physical sensation. It is engulfing, warm, total.

> I could see my body sitting slumped on the edge of the chair below me as I became surrounded by a warm, bright, summer sunshine sort of light. It felt warm. I was so happy in it. The experience felt just so wonderful. I can not find words adequate to express my joy. (www.nderg.org case #176)

> I can positively affirm that being bathed in The Light on the other side of death *is more than life changing*. The light is the very essence, the heart and soul, the all consuming consummation of ecstatic ecstasy. . . . You can no longer believe in God, for belief implies doubt. There is no more doubt. None. You now *know* God. And you know that you know. And you're never the same again. (Atwater 1994: 154, on her own experience)

Most NDE accounts mention a powerful light, one far more powerful than mere physical energy. It appears first as a distant speck but grows larger with an unearthly brilliance that, oddly, does not blind the viewer to whatever else is in the scene. Artwork created by Morse's dying children often include rainbows and bright streams of radiant light. Some experiencers describe the light as simply pure love, a brilliant, expanding, engulfing presence which they intuitively understand as total, supportive love. Many also describe a being or beings in the Light, someone they approach who speaks to them not in words but with thoughts. Moody quotes a respondent: "The first thing he said to me was, that he kind of asked me if I was ready to die, or what I had done with my life that I wanted to show him." (2001: 51). Communications between beings in the Light and the arriving soul are rarely judgmental, always kindly, and lead the newly dead to reflect on what they have done in their life and if it was what they really wanted for themselves. Some say they felt remorse for things they had done or said but almost none said they were "judged" except by themselves. Some had negative and frightening NDEs, one in seven according to Atwater (1994: 41), but accounts of descent into a fiery hell were rare. She says the depictions of hell she heard were of a cold and gloomy place, sometimes with terrifying images, but these were not really visits to hell but psychic cleansing of the self prior to entry into the intimacy of the Light.

An emerging interest among some NDE activists that is related to this theme of love, light, and intimacy are the near-death accounts of people from non-Western or non-Christian communities. In their local as well as national meetings, experiencers acknowledge that they have few if any accounts from those who are Muslim or Jewish, or even African American. At a national gathering in 2001, a Japanese physician told of his attempts to collect Japanese NDEs and how frustrating it was because few people wanted to talk about it. He did not know much about the being in the Light, or if there was one in Japanese NDEs. This might be of interest to an anthropologist such as Lawrence Epstein (1990), who has described the terrifying journeys of Tibetan monks to the land of the dead, or to sociologist Allan Kellehear (1993, 1996), who found only hints of NDEs in Chinese and Indian sources. But the seeming ethnocentrism of Jesus-like beings reported by American experiencers does not seem to be a problem for them. I think that is because whether or not the being in the Light is Jesus (and many say it is), the real point is that the being is a proxy for universal Love with a capital L. The concept of all-embracing Love is just loose enough that any idiosyncratic or cultural manifestations can fit inside. Some say the synchronicity of the cosmos is designed to accommodate just that kind of variation, presenting a culturally appropriate face to each new arrival at the entrance to eternity.

The experiencer's universe is not only holographic and infused with a light of total, unqualified love; it is also teleological. Not a teleology reminiscent of older theologies with their hierarchical universe governed by an all-seeing deity but one that is purposeful in a personal and immediate sense. At some point in their near-death experience, experiencers arrive at a border—a river, a wall, or some kind of obstruction. They are explicitly told that they cannot proceed because their work on earth is not yet done and heaven is not ready to receive them. One of Moody's respondents, a woman who in death was on a ship crossing a body of water to where deceased family members waited, said, "the ship almost reached the far shore, but just before it did, it turned around and started back" (2001: 67). Typically, returnees say they came back for some good reason:

> We are all here to do an assignment of love. It is programmed in us at birth, our assigned memory.

> Everyone has an assignment in life. It is like I am a drop of water that evaporates and then rains again, its all part of a bigger cycle.

> I returned because I accepted my assignment. I walk the labryinth at Grace Cathedral. I am building a bridge between the traditional church and other spiritual modalities.

Physical reentry is not always pleasant, but social and psychological reentry can be more difficult, especially when family and friends cannot accept what experiencers say they saw. So they remain silent, holding their spiritual journey as a private treasure. Many take up the "assignment" they say they were sent back to complete: raise children, care for an ailing spouse or parent, provide some useful service to needy persons in the community. They are explicit that they no longer fear death, do not need to, and that there are things to be done in the time they have left. These they do, typically in a quiet yet purposeful way. I have asked experiencers if there is anything special they want at their funeral or as a grave marker when they die again. Many are uninterested in that. Why erect a stone to memorialize a past they have died to once already? Finishing the assignment chosen individually just for them is all the memory they want to leave, the story they want to carry to their next encounter with the Light.

THE NDE AS A POSTMODERN EVENT

How can we characterize this distinctly late twentieth- and early twenty-first-century configuration of death and afterlife imagery—synchronicity, holography, and teleology—that is so reassuring to people who have experienced something extraordinary? I do not doubt the terror, or the wonder, of what experiencers say happened to them. But in thinking about their after-the-fact narratives of events they say are unique and extraordinary, I think something can be seen there that is familiar, peculiarly American, and distinctly postmodern. Their accounts build with the same materials many Americans use to shape their afterlife beliefs without benefit of an NDE.

Modern deaths take place in a world far different from the religiously driven medieval one described by Ariès. Particularly with religious belief, in the last half century we have begun to see "the eclipse of eternity," as sociologist

Tony Walter calls it, a "shift in twentieth-century theology from seeing eternal life in life after death to quality of life now" (1996: 90). We create meaning where we can, with recollection and completion of "unfinished business" at home or in a hospice with family and friends. With the decline of gods and their heavens and hells, the meaning of a death comes instead from within us and from those who know and care about us.

Social theorist Anthony Giddens, in a discussion of the problematics of love, marriage, and fidelity in the postmodern world, hints at something that may be operating at the end of life as well. He proposes that until the twentieth century, marital relationships existed largely for having children, building an estate, controlling and transmitting property, and negotiating alliances between family units, functions more for ensuring the orderly continuation of the social world than for promoting personal happiness. The idea that we would enter intimate, domestic relationships strictly for their own sake, for the love, romance, or pleasure they can provide *qua* relationships, and only for as long as that proves to be compelling for us, is something historically new. "The term 'relationship,' meaning a close and continuing emotional bond to another, has only come into general usage relatively recently . . . we can introduce the term *pure relationship* to refer to this phenomenon" (1992: 58). The rise of the pure relationship amounts to a fundamental "restructuring of intimacy," as he calls it, and it has a number of features. Two that dovetail with NDEs are the primacy of the personal in evaluating experience and the recreated self as a product of individual rather than communal agency. Agency and self-reconstruction infuse NDE narratives. The images of the Light and of beings who stand in the Light signify that pure relationship – total, unalloyed, transforming intimacy without mediation by language or culture. Once we contact the Light, there is no confusion or misunderstanding about what is to happen: the goal of mortal living is eternal life shared with deceased friends and relatives, a life we will enjoy in perfect harmony forever. The ultimate ground of all pure relationships, heaven is a vision of trust that must be an enormous comfort to those who once felt they were lost to this life forever.

Clearly, experiencers have known something profound and for them the power of it cannot be doubted. But what, finally, does it mean? To what kind of reality does it point? Philosopher Christopher Cherry notes that to be clinically "dead" means an absence of brain activity, a flat EEG; in his eerie phrase, "electro-cerebral silence" (1995: 156). Individuals thought by that criteria to be dead have been resuscitated and sometimes they give classic, full-scale NDE accounts. If and when that happens, Cherry says, it would be "an instance of *mental* activity without its alleged universal causal correlate, *brain* activity. . . . I very strongly suspect that what distinguished authentic (paradigmatic) near-death experiences from other varieties of experience is that they, uniquely, *are* unaccompanied by brain activity" (156).

The "un-" in his "unaccompanied" will be a challenge for those committed to biological reductionist explanations of end-of-life visions, generated so they allege, by oxygen deprivation, powerful drugs, or the failing brain's struggle to make sense of degraded information. But if Cherry's suggestion is true, that some of our mental processes continue not inside but outside our brains, then where is that happening? To answer that, he makes a distinction between "experience hereafter" and an "experience of a hereafter." The latter is what we usually think of as that far shore where we will live on forever. Those who die but return bring us the good news that it really is there. But an NDE, says Cherry, is not really about that. It is only an "experience hereafter," mental activity apparently independent of our bodies. Many and maybe most of us, he believes, are capable of literally jumping out of our skins and momentarily connecting with a consciousness external to ourselves. But that need not be the gateway to something dazzlingly wonderful "up there." It is just and only itself, an amazing moment we may experience before we truly are no more. A lucky few have made it back from there, probably due to technology, but like the rest of us, they are on borrowed time. The lesson is not that there is no heaven to go to, or that there is, but that Mind in some very large sense may be everywhere, and only in our conceit do we confine it to the space between our ears. Consciousness in this cosmic sense is not dependent on organic brains and may not be unique to our species either. To learn that humbling truth, if a truth is what it is, may be all the information we can extract from a verified NDE.

Heavens and afterlives come in all shapes and sizes and on the spectrum of vernacular belief I postulate two contrasting points around which a great deal of cultural material clusters. The Latter-day Saints are exemplars of a more theocratic cluster, distinctive among contemporary Christians in that their views are more detailed and explicit. They, of course, present a vision based on Mormon history but they rely on themes other Americans know and share. Heaven is like the royal courts known from antiquity and well described in the Old Testament book of Ezekiel: grandiose, hierarchical, ruled by a central deity surrounded by hosts of lesser but important beings, a place that is gated, well lit, and available in varying degrees to those who have earned the right to be there. Justice is meted out in mysterious and not so mysterious ways, and the inhabitants occupy themselves with continuous praise to their god and for their good luck in being able to do so. Like all earthly kingdoms past and present, the kingdom of heaven proclaims its omnipotence and eternalness.

For the survivors of near-death experiences, heaven is less a royal palace than a domestic relocation, but it has its compelling imagery as well. I have focused on experiencers because, like the Saints, they dramatize in a graphic and explicit way cultural themes widely known and voiced by many other Americans. And like the Saints, they bring their own peculiarities to a narrative substrate that is contemporary and widespread, especially among those who describe themselves as more spiritual than religious, as pilgrims on a quest, or simply as shoppers in the denominational marketplace. For this group, personal experience, not creeds or contractual obligations, establishes truth, and the afterlife seen by experiencers is a big improvement over what we have now. It is boundless and colorful, freethinking and freely available, welcoming and nonjudgmental, purified of the strategizing and manipulating that afflicts ordinary human relations. It is infused with the Light of perfect Love. Like the Saints, experiencers see themselves connected to worlds beyond the morally impoverished one we live in now, and they too testify to something many Americans tell the pollsters they believe despite having less compelling evidence: that there really is something waiting for us. By contract or by dramatic encounter, we discover what Jonathan Sacks calls "the charisma of eternity made real in the here-and-now" (2003: 158).

5   PASSING IT ON

THE IDEA THAT CHILDREN know so little about death that they need a book to understand it is a modern conceit.[1] It seems improbable that a hundred years ago, when America was predominantly agricultural, anyone would have offered a book on death to farm children whose chores included beheading and plucking chickens. Nor is it likely that books would be needed for children in nineteenth-century immigrant ghettos where, packed in tenements, they regularly saw lives shortened by crime, tuberculosis, and sweatshops. Using books to teach children about death requires an audience with the interest and time for reading and a need to learn about things normally remote from everyday experience. The modern culture of childhood emerged in just such a setting, that of the urban middle class of the nineteenth century (Ariès 1962; Kline 1998; Zelizer 1985). In the protective suburban households that have since become the North American standard, death is not even an occasional visitor. People die in nursing homes, hospitals, and hospices. When they die unexpectedly, from accidents, violence, or premature illness, the suddenness of it is overwhelming and seemingly inexplicable. At these times, for children who know little of death and have no experience with it, books are informative and perhaps even comforting.

Children's literature, of course, incorporates the views on death held by the adults who write, purchase, and read the material. It replicates, often in explicit form, the ideology of a particular period or social class. Little Eva's deathbed scene in Harriet Beecher Stowe's *Uncle Tom's Cabin* (1852) is famous for its melodramatic sentimentality and romanticized Victorian linkage of childhood innocence to spiritual mysteries. As photography became more widespread in the latter part of that century, post-mortem portraits were common and deceased children, carefully posed and always dressed in their finest, were memorialized in photos for parlor display (Ruby 1995). No one felt that to be unseemly. Beginning early in the twentieth century, however, when the middle class was becoming well established and the management of death shifted from home to hospital, encounters with death were less common and children were thought to need "protection" from its grim realities. Even as late as 1952, when E. B. White published his children's classic *Charlotte's Web*, some reviewers criticized the book as inappropriate for young readers because of his thematic use of death in the story.

More recently, however, "this tendency has begun to be reversed, and children's books now contain topics that were previously taboo, including feelings, divorce, sex, and even death" (Lamars 1995: 153). Because these topics are potentially traumatic, for children as well as adults, the term "bibliotherapy" came into use in the 1950s to promote the notion that books can have restorative and therapeutic effects (Bernstein 1983). For example, child "readers may do several things: identify with others whose experiences are similar, release emotional feelings as a result of this identification, and gain insights into their own experiences" (Guy 1993: 32). Insights, release, and identity are, of course, age-dependent. Some have claimed that very young children have limited ideas about death and do not realize that it is permanent and final. By age five to seven, they know that a corpse is inanimate and will remain that way. That this fate comes to all living things is not apparent until age nine or ten. Others argue that adults rarely know with much certainty what children feel or understand about death because they rarely discuss it with them (Bluebond-Langner 1978; Ellis and Stump 2000). Whatever the truth of these assertions, clearly the authors of children's books calibrate their story lines to what they believe is age-appropriate for young readers, and publishers promote their books to specific age groups.

But children's books do more than promote identification with characters and insight into their predicaments. They transmit the larger society's ideological construction of death and teach culturally shaped scripts, the shared set of expectations and practices that guide behavior and expressions of sentiment. What is appropriate behavior and what constitutes a critical event is, of course, historically and culturally contingent. There is nothing "natural," for example, about a funeral or crying for a loss. These are learned, constructed activities whose performative attributes vary enormously from culture to culture and within cultures. Like any text, cultural scripts are public, learnable, and available for everyone to "read" and interpret as their situation demands. D'Andrade has used the term "schemas" to describe the motivational or internalized aspects of cultural texts, a schema being "an interpretation which is frequent, well organized, memorable, which can be made from minimal cues" and which functions as both goal and guide for behavior (D'Andrade and Strauss 1992: 29).

Books, of course, can do all that. But there is something else that underlines my attention to children and what they read. Robert Orsi has demonstrated in his research on American Catholicism that children themselves can be thought of as a "privileged medium" through which adults express their deepest understandings of the nature of the universe and the human place in it. Adults, of course, teach children their culture's script lines, from how to handle money to how to choose a mate, but in matters of death, grieving, and honoring memory there is more to it than intergenerational transmission.

> Children signal the vulnerability and contingency of a particular religious world and of religion itself, and in exchanges between adults and children about sacred matters the religious world is in play. On no other occasion except perhaps in times of physical pain and loss is the fictive quality of religion—the fact that religious meanings are made and sustained by humans—so intimately and unavoidably apprehended as when adults attempt to realize the meaningfulness of their religious worlds in their children. (2005: 77)

Change Orsi's "religious world" to any contemporary American variant—spirituality, family honor and standing, respect for nature, sacrifice for others or for country, agnosticism, atheism—and the statement still stands. In their minds and bodies, children are made bearers of what adults believe to be of lasting importance. Through them and with them, adults make their own expectations visible, the sacred having material presence in the behavior and demeanor of a child.[2] Books are powerful vehicles for accomplishing that, even in a culture of television excess and computer distraction because, like bereavement cards, books are purchased by adults who think them aesthetically and intellectually "suitable," to be presented on specific occasions and useful for initiating adult-child interaction in a sustained way. But they are not the only things children can see, handle, and ponder.

READING BONES

My comment on children growing up on nineteenth-century farms or in big-city slums, not needing books to learn about death, would apply to most children living in the world today. They live in the rural areas and crowded cities of developing countries where literacy is low and the deaths of people and animals are not concealed. Loring Danforth's (1982) ethnographic study of death rituals in northern Greece offers an instance of that. His book ends with a photoessay of village funerals made by photographer Alexander Tsiaras. The pictures, Danforth says, are not just illustrations for his text but "an independently conceived visual commentary" (viii) on how rural Greek communities ritualize death. Tsiaras photographs make an apt comparison with the North American children's stories I review below.

Children appear in many of Tsiaras's black-and-white plates as mourners, acolytes, and funeral participants. In Plate 21, for example, an Orthodox priest and three older women are formally posed in front of a brick wall, bells and small candles in their hands. Father Andrew is about to incense a grave and recite a prayer from the Orthodox liturgy, so the wailing has temporarily stopped and it is a quiet, solemn moment. Behind the wall are three boys, their heads above the top, one about to hop over and drop into the cemetery directly behind the priest and elderly women. Plate 26 shows five girls, about ages seven to ten, standing casually with arms crossed and hands on hips, intently watching an exhumation in the grave below. Several feet away, two teenagers lean against a rock wall, somberly watching the adults and contemplating the work of digging up a man buried seven years earlier. The diggers in the grave and the retinue with them are all older women dressed in black, leaning over the loose soil and staring into it as though looking for something lost. What are these rural Greek children up to, peeking over the cemetery wall and hovering above an open grave?

As Danforth describes it, the exhumation and deposition of a villager's bones in an ossuary is a public event. Typically, people die at home, where they are watched carefully, since the manner of dying—the appearance of serenity, the ease of the soul's departure in a last, brief exhalation—is an indicator of one's moral condition. In preparation for the funeral, the body is washed and dressed in clean clothes. The feet are tied together and the chin bound up with cloth, eyes are closed, and the lower half of the body is wrapped in a white shroud. Hands are crossed over the chest and a candle placed between them to pose the corpse in the reception area of the house. Visitors leave coins on the deceased's chest and kiss the forehead before processing through the streets to the Orthodox church and then on to the cemetery. There the coffin is lowered into a shallow grave with the lid open. An officiating priest pours red wine (and sometimes olive oil and water as well) over the dressed corpse, spilling it in the shape of a cross. The lid is then shut and the grave filled in. For the next five years, the family will host a series of memorial services, and women closely related to the dead may visit the grave daily to lament, pray, and tidy up the site. These ministrations are critical for moving the soul along a circuitous and perilous journey toward heaven and for assuring forgiveness of sins before entry into paradise. That process can take years, and bereavement is not fully over until the deceased is safely and assuredly in heaven.

An exhumation some years after burial is necessary to confirm that this spiritual goal has been attained. At one witnessed by Danforth, that of a young woman killed some years earlier in a car accident, loud laments were the backdrop for the men and women of her family as they began digging with shovels into her grave. When a change in the color of the soil indicated they had arrived at the decomposed coffin, the laments became louder and more intense. The mother of the deceased began working with a hoe, looking first for the skull and then the ribs and long bones. People in the crowd of mourners shouted advice as she labored in the hole: "more to the right" and "find the skull first" and "don't break anything" (Danforth 1982: 19). Scraping away soil with her hands alone, she finally felt her daughter's skull, stopped to cross herself, and then gently pulled it from the ground.

> Irini [the mother] cradled her daughter's skull in her arms, crying and sobbing uncontrollably. . . . She held [daughter] Eleni's skull to her cheek, embracing it much as she would embrace Eleni were she still alive. Finally she placed more paper money on the skull and wrapped another kerchief around it, a kerchief which had been embroidered by Eleni as part of her dowry. Irini kissed the skull and touched it to her forehead three times before she handed it to Maria, who did the same. Irini and Maria embraced the skull together for several minutes, shrieking and wailing. Then they handed it across the open grave to Eleni's father, who greeted his daughter's skull as had the others before him. It was then passed down the side of the grave to be greeted by sisters, brothers, cousins, and others. (19–20)

It was important for the children in Tsiaras's photographs to witness all this directly. It is a cultural script they must learn so that as adults they can do the same for others, perhaps many times, and it will be done for them someday too. They are not spared seeing their own future in the little stack of bones carefully scooped from the earth and laid out on a clean cloth next to the grave.

Eleni's skull and bones are then displayed and "read" by old women known to be experts in the craft. Those that are mottled and stained indicate a soul in trouble, one not yet in paradise and needing more prayers and ceremonies to help it gain a heavenly place. Bones that emerge from the ground well bleached are evidence of a successful transition, proof not only of the moral quality of their former owner but of the faithful spiritual attentions of family and church through a long period of bereavement. But no bone reading produces simple yes or no answers to these cosmic questions. Readings are opportunities for rich, lively, and gossipy commentary on the life of the deceased, the moral standing of the family, the spiritual health of the community, and the futility of things of the flesh. No one is immune to these elderly women's scrutiny and judgments. In one of Tsiaras's images, one of them holds an earth-colored skull in both hands and stares straight into the camera. The text says she addressed the photographer forthrightly: "Some day you'll see the remains of your mother and father exhumed this way. Some day you'll be exhumed, then you'll look like this too" (Plate 30). Like the curious and observant children standing above the grave, Tsiaras is drawn into the scene and made part of it; no stance of social science or photojournalistic distancing, or of childhood innocence either, is allowed. The lessons are too important for that.

Danforth's ethnography and the striking photography accompanying it are an anthropology of direct experience, foregrounding the stark physicality of death; the villager's elaborate and strenuous ritualization of it; the theology of an engaged, dirt-under-the-fingernails response; and ultimately the theodicy that gives each death its distinctive meaning. Theodicy, a class of theological ruminations on the hidden meaning of misfortune and evil, including the evil of death, is a pervasive feature of all the larger "world" religions (Bowker 1991), and it is common to localized belief systems as well. In theodicies, we are not abandoned by the gods to suffer alone, because there is always some larger purpose behind what is endured, even when it cannot be perceived. In fact, the gods may have meant it to be this way so that, as Geertz aptly put it, the religious problem is "not how to avoid suffering but how to suffer, how to make of physical pain, personal loss, worldly defeat, or the helpless contemplation of other's agony something bearable, supportable—something, as we say, sufferable" (1973: 104). Kleinman makes of theodicy a device for critical social analysis, calling for an anthropology of "social suffering," the dissection of modern discourses and practices of pain to reveal how they connect us to "everything that really matters" (Kleinman, Das, and Lock 1997: 315). For the Greek children observing their covillagers' funerals and exhumations, the script for what "really matters" includes communal mourning and lamentations, long periods of penitential bereavement, an elaborate and historically rich ontology of the nature of the universe and the place of individual lives within it, an ancient and familiar tradition of ritual practice, and direct experience of what everyone's fate will be. Seeing the dusty, discolored skulls of co-villagers kissed and cradled with much love must be powerful and unforgettable.

READING BOOKS

In contemporary North American culture, children's learning about death is very different. First, any particular instance of death—that of a sibling, parent, or pet—is felt to be an "inappropriate" intrusion into childhood experience. Death transgresses the firm line separating the adult world with its responsibilities and labors from that of children with their brief and precious freedom. In an almost Rousseauian way, Americans imagine childhood as a time of spontaneous and natural goodness, parents and educators responsible for raising children in a way that shields them from the unpleasantness that adults often know. Traditionally, that has meant that children should be sheltered from funereal weeping, open-casket viewing, and interment rites. Current fashion reverses that and now urges their inclusion, interestingly, for about the same reason: to protect children from their worst imaginings so that, like adults, they may experience a smoother recovery and final "closure."[3] To that pedagogical end, many children's books on death include an introductory page or flyleaf inscription addressed to adult purchasers and readers, advising how best to use the book to meet the bereaved child's psychological needs. Says one author who is also a physician: "As parents we want desperately to protect our children from that pain, but we cannot. What we can do is help them get through it. . . . This builds a stronger, more secure sense of self, which is one of the gains that can grow from the loss" (Holden 1989). As bibliotherapy, a book is to help a child "get through it" so he or she can resume the educational tasks and character-forming play preparatory to entrance into the adult world.

Second, teaching children about death is difficult because adults themselves are not of one mind on the subject. Public as well as private discourse about death is multivocal, contradictory, diffuse, and often opaque. What little consensus does exist centers on two rhetorically important issues, the need to "work through" and "resolve" grief in a reasonable length of time, and an expectation that the bereaved will find "closure" and "get on" with life. Widely proclaimed in popular literature and television talk show confessionals, these vaguely conceived tasks usually beg the question: just what is "grief work?" What is "closure?" How do we know it when we see it? Television's Mr. (Fred) Rogers, in an introductory statement to the adult purchasers of his title *When a Pet Dies* (1988), says simply that with a book "we try to fill the empty space that was created in us by the loss," and, "As for what happens *after* death, I believe that's best discussed in light of each family's traditions and beliefs." But what does Mr. Rogers's verb "to fill" refer to here? What should we be using as "fill"? What family traditions and beliefs are to be invoked? Authors provide solutions, transmitting to children what they think parents have difficulty say-ing themselves.

It is only in the last twenty years or so that authors of children's books have sought to "decontaminate," as Timothy Moore and Reet Mae (1987) put it, the topic of death. They surveyed both children and youth fiction to measure the extent to which adult stereotypes associated with death were replicated in mate-rial for younger readers. "Books are one source of vicarious socialization," they suggest, and despite the pervasiveness of television, books can be particularly involving since children commonly read them repeatedly and relate the sto-ries to their own experience (1987: 54). They ask, therefore: "Does current children's literature portray realistic grieving patterns and appropriate grief resolution, or do the books depict grief being repressed, denied, or absent altogether?" (55). Whatever Moore and Mae mean by "realistic" and "appro-priate," they found in a sample of 49 books substantial replication of adult viewpoints and adult stereotypes. For example, displays of grief were often gendered, with stoic, task-centered males heroically carrying on their accus-tomed duties, while females took on expanded nurturing functions. Women were far more likely to express their grief and to cry openly. In many of the books, the long-term impact of death on survivors was not mentioned, and grief was "resolved" within a short time. Many stories included mourning rit-uals, although fully a quarter did not, and few books had any suggestion that death might have transcendent implications. Moore and Mae concluded that in the books reviewed in 1987 there was "little to dispel the myth that death and its consequences are remote, fanciful events," while in a few the discus-sion of death was so blunt and even fearsome that "Factual rather than fic-tional accounts may be better suited to helping children come to grips with death" (61). Another critic who read over 80 children's books complained that he "was dismayed by how many demonstrated minimal empathy for the psy-chological world of the child. Many of the books were one dimensional, superficial, and embarrassingly contrived" (Garber 1995: 221).

These criticisms were of books published in the 1980s and 1990s. In the current crop, however, the psychological poverty and stereotypes reviewers found then are less evident. A different set of themes has taken hold, a markedly different kind of scripting. Contemporary North Americans are nominally religious, consistently telling pollsters they believe in God and have never doubted God's presence. Fully a third claim to have had an important life-changing religious experience (Cimino and Lattin 1998), and "spiritual-ity" is ubiquitous, even if church attendance is not. But this piety rarely shows up in books intended to explain death to troubled children. With the exception of one subgenre of children's books, those from religious publishing houses, these intellectual and emotional puzzles associated with death are solved using other, less avowedly supernatural resources.

STORY TIME

In the world of children's book publishing, there are currently about forty titles explicitly concerned with death.[4] To interpret what is offered in this literature, I followed two procedures. First, I looked at the communities represented in the stories. That is one indication of their intended audience, the type of readers authors believe will find their stories meaningful. My second and more important concern was how the stories handled five key areas of American death practices, ones I judge to be systematically problematic. They are (1) the occasion of a death and the announcement of bad news; (2) expressions of grief and the duration of bereavement; (3) ritualization, including the funeral or memorial service, display of the body, and final disposal; and (4) memory and the search for finality or "closure." I also looked at (5) what the stories present as a metanarrative of death, the larger symbolic or ontological message that adult authors (and presumably adult readers) want children to understand.[5]

Generally, these stories are inventive and very much a fun read. These are not morbid books. They include a kindly badger who has an out-of-body experience; children who amuse themselves with a game of "capture the flag" in a darkened casket display room; dinosaurs solemnly marching to a cemetery to bury a pet hamster; a chocolate chip cookie surreptitiously left inside a casket; and a visually dramatic voyage of a ship sailing into eternity. One comes with a sing-along CD. The artwork is frequently sumptuous. These are mass-market books and sacred traditions are hardly mentioned; the few references to heaven are bracketed with qualifiers and explicit doubts are expressed by adult characters. Hope for realities beyond the earthly is underplayed in otherwise generous discussions of the emotions that death inspires. Older Freudian views of "grief work" that include separation and substitution are not entirely absent, although it is clear they are being replaced by newer orthodoxies related to articulating and sustaining memories.

Pet deaths are common in these books. Animals are named and included in domestic life, making them part of the moral order and, as something more than livestock, entitled to full funeral honors. Doctors are rare in children's death books, except for veterinarians, who are always kind and gentle. Children in these stories go through the same range of emotions and experiences that might accompany a human death, and, after a time of grieving, a replacement pet often completes the story. Backyard burials that include head-stones and plant markers are common. While pet death is the focus, it is clear that the lessons learned are intended to be more general. In the introduction to his book, Mr. Rogers advises that "Since all living things die at one time or another, I trust that this First Experience book will be of service to you beyond the death of a pet" (1988). There is no doubt that that is the intent of *When Dinosaurs Die* (1996) and *Badger's Parting Gifts* (1984) as well. These stories are really about human families, cast as friendly reptiles and family-oriented forest dwellers, who live and die in caring, supporting communities just as people do.

FIVE SCRIPTS FOR YOUNG MOURNERS: BAD NEWS

The dying children in Myra Bluebond-Langner's 1978 ethnography of a hospital terminal ward knew when one of the other young patients died by watching how adults moved about the hallways and observing which rooms had closed doors. They were rarely told of deaths directly, either by adults or by other children on the floor. Even when a death is anticipated, conveying bad news to survivors and confirming its reality through the evidence of a corpse is the awkward, dramatic, and typical beginning of a death script. The "skill" of delivering bad news, not something doctors have been well known for, is now being cultivated as medical practitioners take more seriously their bedside manners with dying patients and families. The nuances of bearing bad news are occasionally discussed in the medical literature (Arnold et al. 1995). Physicians are generally advised to prepare patients and families well in advance so that there will be no "surprises," to assess each patient's understanding of what professional staff are telling them, and to convey upsetting information simply, honestly, and patiently, allowing time for people to express feelings and consider their options (Girgis 1995). In most of the children's books I reviewed, the onset of a character's decline is made clear so that an announcement is not a surprise. We are told in the second sentence of *Badger's Parting Gifts* (Varley 1984) that Badger has foreknowledge of his death. During his last days he watches the younger animals run and chase, and, "hoping to prepare them" so they will not be too sad, he tells them that he will soon be gone. In many of these stories death is something that happens to the old rather than the young, usually from chronic and lingering conditions, and something of a deathwatch may occur.

Even where death is sudden, sad news is normally told in a straightforward way and a plan of action is outlined. Familiar adult euphemisms—

"passed away," "no longer with us," "gone"—are rare. In *Saying Goodbye to Daddy* (Vigna 1991), Clare's father dies in a car accident, and her grandfather withdraws her from school at midday. At home she is frightened when she sees her mother crying, but "Mother and Grandfather took her into their circle"—they are shown sitting on the living room couch together—and the father's death and some details of the accident are described. In several stories, the proof of bad news is extended to touching the corpse at the funeral home. In *Saying Good-bye to Grandma*, the main character accompanies her parents to the viewing. "I tried not to look at her face, but I couldn't help it. There was powder on her cheeks, more than she usually wore," says the child matter-of-factly. "She looked the same as always." She asks someone for permission to touch. "He nodded, and I touched Grandma's hand, wishing I could wake her up. I wished that she could turn and smile and hold me the way she used to do. Her hand was cold" (1988: 24). This more contemporary "bad news" approach and interaction with the corpse replaces older preferences for "sparing" children exposure to the specifics of death. Abruptness is unusual, and what clearly is not present in these stories is the "closed awareness context" and "ritual drama of mutual pretense" that Glaser and Strauss (1965) documented as standard bedside manners nearly half a century ago, practices still common, I suspect, in some families.

FEELINGS

Once the reality of a death is established, the second component of the script line, appropriate grieving, is introduced, and characters are usually encouraged to express themselves. What is striking about the depictions of their emotional life at this moment of crisis, however, is its narrow range. While children's books are not intended to be scaled down "grief manuals," they nevertheless present their readers with models of suitable emotional expression. While a few books hardly mention emotions, most name and describe several. Crying, sadness, loneliness, and confusion are common features. One title, *It Must HURT a Lot: A Book About Death and Learning and Growing* (Sanford and Evans 1986), gives the emotional experience of grief something many other books do not—a somatized edge. In a few stories children do not feel like eating, or they retreat to a bedroom because they want to be alone. But here, Joshua knows grief viscerally after the neighbors accidentally back their car over his dog. "I HATE THEM" (large type in the original), he yells, and then cries himself to sleep. He feels isolated and snaps at others who offer to help. But gradually, "while thinking hard all by himself, he knew that some

BIG changes were happening inside him." The changes, however, shift quickly from the physical to the psychological—discovered insights, little truths about human behavior, the text listing each one inside a heart-shaped image printed in the lower corner of each page. They are "special secrets," and include statements such as "When I love lots I hurt lots" and "Good memories always stay." When he recalls that his friend Eric yelled at him because he cried, the heart tells us that Eric loved the puppy too and that "Everybody handles feelings in his own way." Each little maxim, six in all, is Joshua's retrospective appreciation of behavior he now understands in a new way. These insights accumulate, and "in time" he feels better. Toward story's end, we are told, "He was stronger now, and Muffin's death had helped him grow." In many of these stories, emotional pain leads to new and greater self-realization. Fred Rogers's book on pet death advises that "When a pet dies, we can grow to know that the love we shared is still alive in us and always will be."

While many of these books have an obvious debt to Kübler-Ross and rely on her conceptualization of grief, of equal interest is what they underplay or omit. Few move beyond sadness and anger to childhood fears or guilt. An exception is *Saying Goodbye to Daddy*, in which Clare is assured that, even though her father is dead, she will not be abandoned by her mother, who "expect[s] to live a long, long time, longer than you can imagine." Her anxieties about her own future are explicitly addressed. So too is her guilt; she is told that she did not "cause" her father's death through misbehavior or remarks made to him in anger. These are common worries among children, yet in their focus on grief as the emotional "work" of recovery, many stories overlook them. *When Dinosaurs Die* presents the most expansive view of childhood emotions, and it is, not coincidentally, the book that is most clearly multicultural. Numerous anthropomorphized dinosaurs are shown doing and saying lots of different things as part of a single scene. For example, a two-page spread bears the heading "What Does *Dead* Mean?" A short paragraph gives the simple, no-nonsense account one would expect from a kindly adult, explaining that the heart and breathing stop, the brain does not work, and the person no longer moves. That is fine as an adult response, but the dino children, who are playing in a field and have discovered a dead bird, express it in their own ways: "Bang, bang, you're dead"; "Let me see"; "Is she sleeping?" and "She feels all stiff and cold." When the schoolmates of Nora Saurus are asked what they want to do when she returns to class after a funeral, they reply, "We could hug her"; "Should we say I'm sorry?" "I don't know what to do"; "Still be her friend"; and "I don't want to talk about it." In discussing their feelings, the dino children dream of a dead playmate, talk of being chased by ghosts, and pray that a dead father might be returned alive. An angry girl tosses away her blocks and asserts that it is not true that grandma is dead, while her nonchalant brother replies, "She is, too." The simplicity of the story line is made complex by the multiplicity of characters and the variability of their responses.

This diversity of expression is unusual, however, for in so many other titles, where the action takes place in smaller groups and in isolated families, no suggestion is made that there are diverse ways of responding to loss. Whether this is desirable or not, it is relevant in terms of what might be called post-Kübler-Ross theories of grief; for example, Attig's (1996) thesis that grief is really about relearning to live with the deceased in a new way, and Walter's (1999a) view that grief is expressed and "resolved" in intensive, intimate discussions with others who knew the deceased in their own, distinctive ways. In these models the linearity implied by Kübler-Ross's stages is replaced by a collage of partial and even contradictory images, communally shared, that generate a new and more complex narrative that survivors use to reimagine and rebuild their relationship with a lost love, friend or acquaintance. The dino children experience this newer way of expressing feelings.

FUNERALS AND THE AFTERLIFE

The same criticism, that many of these stories present few options, can be made of the funerals and, especially, the metanarratives of death that go with them. As the third element in the script, funerals and memorial services are depicted briefly and generically. Backyard burials are for pets, mainline churches and funeral establishment chapels for people. Attendance by children is encouraged, not mandatory, and formal services generally get less page space than do receptions. One less-than-enthusiastic child says, "We are going to church for Uncle Phil. She [mother] says it's important for us to all come together to show respect and say good-bye" (Pellegrino 1999). That is advice that, with slight modification, could be given to a child on any Sunday morning when breakfast, television, or the comic pages seem like more interesting options. Perhaps one reason funerals are so uninspiring in these books is that those so briefly portrayed touch on such a narrow spectrum of American religious life. We do not see any New Orleans jazz funerals, military funerals, Jewish or Islamic funerals, or idiosyncratic "designer" ceremonies of the kind many people are now choosing. Funerals exist in human cultures for many reasons, for comforting the bereaved and asserting the worth of life despite the inevitability of death, for expressing hope through ritual practice and gesture, for guiding the dead to their permanent abode with other spirits and ancestors, and for communal affirmation of transcendent realities. The narrative space given to funerals is slight in these books, and the ultimate fate of the deceased is the thinnest part of the territory; two-thirds make no mention of the eschatological prospects of the individual who died. The subject of heaven as conventionally (and vaguely) understood and the transformative nature of death are rare topics, even at the funerals. Perhaps the most explicit reference in these mass-market books to anything traditionally religious is in Jane Thomas's *Saying Good-bye to Grandma*, where Suzie says, "We all stood up to sing, 'Amazing Grace, How Sweet the Sound,' Grandma's favorite hymn." In other stories, mention of heaven is given more as a token of reassurance than as an idea to be explored. For Clare, the topic comes up on the way back from the cemetery when she asks where people go when they die. "'I don't know for sure,' Grandfather said. 'The minister says Daddy's in heaven. But whatever people believe in, the memory of how someone lived stays on after that person has died'" (Vigna 1991). By contrast, the dinosaurs have a lot more to say. They offer ten solutions, which include but go well beyond memories—to honest doubt ("Mom's soul is with God, but I'm not sure"), organ transplants, resurrection, South Asian cycles of rebirth, and a simple "Huh?" An editorial aside suggests, "If you have questions about it, ask your family or your religious leader" (Brown and Brown 1996), although on the evidence of these stories, families and religious leaders do not have much to say either.[6]

It may be inappropriate to ask young children to think about their own end, or to wonder what ultimately happens to us. Many adults do not consider questions like that appropriate for themselves either. But at least for those already dead, if not for us the living, these stories offer two solutions to what endures, a cult of memory and the adoration of nature.

MEMORY WORK

Throughout these books, a common response to death is stockpiling memories, the fourth element in the script. In *Goodbye Max*, a boy and his friend recall all the things Max the dog once did at various stops along the boy's paper route. In another story, grade-schoolers recall the activities a fellow student enjoyed, and put them into letters to his parents. In *Saying Goodbye to Daddy*, Clare's mother opens her dead husband's wallet and spreads out the contents for the grieving girl. Each item is precious and a memory of an occasion together. One of the more elaborate accounts is *Badger's Parting Gifts*, the gifts being the many good memories he leaves behind. Badger dies just as winter covers the earth, but when spring arrives the animals gather to talk about his life among them. They recall he taught Mole how to cut out a chain of paper moles from a folded sheet. He helped Frog improve his ice-skating skills and showed Fox how to make a Windsor knot in his tie. Brown and Brown's dinosaurs once again outclass everyone, with no less than fifteen "Ways to Remember Someone." All this memory building is, of course, in the service of life, helping friends through grief and suffering and offering a way of talking about pain. Even when we are not thinking about the dead, the dinosaurs remind us, that "is not forgetting the one you love; it just means you are doing other things. Hurray for life!"

While "memory" as a psychological process certainly has much to do with memorialization, that view of it is limited; mental "surfing" is not all that memory is about. There is an interesting and vigorous literature by historians, social scientists, and cultural studies specialists on what is variously called "public memory" and "cultural memory." This work has focused on topics as diverse as landscapes, monuments and memorials, parades, tourism, concentration camps, pioneer settlements, calendars, and ethnic celebrations (Ben-Amos and Weissberg 1999; Bodnar 1992; Gillis 1994). In her work on the "political lives of dead bodies" in the reconstruction of postsocialist eastern Europe, Katherine Verdery (1999) looks at what she sees as the critical components of a cult of memory: "kinship, spirits, ancestor worship, and the circulation of cultural treasures. Rather than speak of legitimacy, I speak of reordering the meaningful universe. I present the politics of corpses as being less about legitimating new governments (though it can be that, too) than about cosmologies and practices relating the living and the dead" (1999: 26). It is exactly Verdery's "reordering of the meaningful universe" by realigning relationships between the living and the dead as a cultural (and even political) project that is pertinent here.

A death almost always brings a family and loved ones together to jointly grieve, commemorate, and, as is now said, "share" the loss. But deaths are also times of anger and frustration, when family factions and old grudges threaten to disrupt appearances of solidarity and mutual caring. Families are minicultures in their own right, enclosed and guarded worlds with their own histories, folklore, cast of legendary characters, and conflicts. A death threatens surface integrity and mutual goodwill precisely at the time when it is most needed. Executive decisions about funerals and costs have to be made on short notice; property and goods carrying powerful sentimental attachments must be divided, their ownership negotiated; subtle relations of authority and standing among the players may be at play, recriminations not unheard of.

There is no reason children should be involved in matters of this sort, although they sometimes are, and no reason that children's books should dwell on the problems of adults. But what they do dwell on clearly contrasts with the shadowy backroom scenes of family politics that children often sense. The stories emphasize a fiction, one central to the cult of memory already present in adult formulations. It is an idealized and unidimensional portrait of the deceased, someone without warts or error, preserved in redacted memory through photographs, annual visits to a gravesite, and, in these children's books, numerous scenes of reverie in pastoral settings. Funeral props and performance reinforce the image: the embalmed corpse fashioned through chemistry and heavy cosmetics as a posed sleeper; the body on display a "memory picture" for the gaze of visitors; family photographs and personal possessions bearing witness to the life interests of the deceased; eulogies spoken anecdotally, how we would like the dead to be whatever their shortcomings may have been. A purified memory of the deceased—their hobbies and favorite foods, kindness toward others, their everlasting love for us—is the only immortality these books acknowledge. It may be the only kind that can be pondered. These stories make that lesson clear.

APPROPRIATING NATURE

Memory is linked to one other rhetorical device, the final element of my five-part script. Again, Badger's departure from this life is helpful. Snug in his tree-trunk home, he writes a letter to his friends and then falls asleep in a comfortable chair by the fire. In a dream state, he senses that he is moving down a long tunnel, and because his weak legs are suddenly strong, he tosses aside his old walking stick. "Badger moved swiftly, running faster and faster through the long passageway, until his paws no longer touched the earth. He felt himself turning end over end, tumbling and falling, but nothing hurt. He felt free. It was if he had fallen out of his body" (Varley 1984). And, he had. The illustrations make clear that Badger's grand exit is an out-of-body experience not that different from those described in the previous chapter. In many near-death accounts, the dying person leaves ordinary time and encounters a powerful spiritual force, often personified by recognizable religious figures such as Jesus or angels. In Badger's case, however, we are not told to what distant place the tunnel takes him. The account of his dying simply stops. But that is no matter, for the author does not intend to pursue a discussion of heaven and its precincts. Turn the page, and there is young Mole, wandering out to the hillside where he and Badger were last together. "'Thank you, Badger,' he said softly, believing that Badger would hear him. And . . . somehow . . . Badger did." Thus the story ends, with an image of Mole on the green hillside, looking up into an expansive, cloud-flecked sky.

A "trailing off into nature" motif is common to many of these stories, the plot lines and artwork directly linking death to a sentimentalized view of nature. Two of the three books bearing the imprimatur of the American Psychological Association (APA) are entirely about plants and animals, the natural world revealed in lush and brilliant imagery. In one, *The Three Birds* (Van den Berg 1994), the mother of a family of birds dies and the baby bird asks where she is now. Father explains that "She is living in the sun." He elaborates: "It is warm there, and she can fly again." The infant wants to join her, but father says it is not possible. "Only a bird that can no longer fly in our world can live in the sun." The two fly off into a winter sky, "to look for the warmth, you and I." *The Goodbye Boat* (Joslin 1998) is a minimalist presentation of dramatic art and almost no words. An older woman boards an arklike ship and sails away toward the horizon, leaving her young friends behind. They wave, wonder, and then cry as the ship gets smaller and smaller, disappearing into a gray seascape. In their dreams they imagine that "it's surely sailing somewhere new," and indeed it is. On the last page, the ship nears a sunny shore with trees and a dove, the unnamed older woman still standing before the sails. The colors have changed too, the earlier spreads of North Atlantic oceanic gray transformed into warmer, tropical tones of brown, orange, and yellow. Nature "answers" the children's questions about our ultimate repose, not specifically but in generalized and visually rich terms. One Amazon.com customer/reviewer said of this title, "Much to talk about, much to ponder." What specifically is to be pondered, she did not say. But there are clues.[7]

It is not a stretch, given the history of American cemeteries—the "rural cemetery movement" of the early nineteenth century (Sloane 1991); the placement of post-Civil War military cemeteries in pastoral settings (Laderman 1996; Wills 1992); and their evolution into commercial "memorial parks" of the Forest Lawn variety—to think of the natural world as a powerful element in contemporary death imagery. But it is not nature in wild exuberance, obedient to the laws of ecological succession. Death is coupled instead with a contained nature subdued by landscape architects, teams of gardeners, mowing machines, pesticides, local building codes, and the whims of trustees. Winding paths amid ponds and pocket glens are not "natural" so much as congenial to a view of the natural world as our last, best respite from the unpleasant urban spaces Americans generally disdain. In children's stories, nature is boundless, friendly, and embracing, artistically rendered as a peaceful and comforting presence. What we are to ponder is a sentimentalized, sacralized nature as the realm "to which we go" once we die. The spirits of dead relatives and pets haunt these stories, not in fearful, ghostly ways but in their association with agreeable flora, sunshine, and summerlike weather patterns. Nature inspires memory, and in cloudscapes, seascapes, and distant panoramas we are invited to seek the newly dead who mysteriously reside there. The idea of grand natural vistas, a nineteenth-century trope of scenic painters such as Thomas Moran (whose massive canvases inspired the national park system) and repeated since on countless calendars and postcards, comes to the rescue of the dead who, in our reveries, have an agreeable place to go.

Purified memory and sentimentalized nature, the last two features of the script, function as what Clive Seale (1998) aptly calls "resurrective practices," contemporary enactments of Sahlins's salvational ethos. As familiar narrative devices, they assure us that the "normal" world we experience does in its mysterious ways continue, acting as a "defence against ontological insecurity" (205) and the frightening possibility of once-and-for-all extinction. This is an important point, for it recognizes that language is more than a means of transmitting information. In telling tales, we verbally repair the broken world a death creates, reincorporating the dead by means of a tamed nature we can control and understand. Nature is abundantly populated with the dead in Buscaglia's popular *The Fall of Freddie the Leaf* (1982) and Mills's *Gentle Willow* (1993), the latter carrying the APA imprimatur. In Naomi Judd's *Guardian Angels* (2000), homesteading grandparents Elijah and Fanny (Judd's own great-great-grandparents) appear as great cumulous clouds, plowing and scattering seed through the sky above their fields, barn, and Kentucky farm house. As resurrective practices these accounts are simplistic secular alternatives to traditional theologies, their literalism perhaps off-putting to some. But they are not just that. I suspect they give children (and many adults) reassurance that they have not been abandoned. Seale argues that bereavement counseling and pastoral care are "a type of performative ritual in which people are offered the opportunity to write themselves into a dominant cultural script, resulting in the reward of secure membership in an imagined community" (1998: 196). Children, and probably many of the adults who sit with them over a book, can "read" themselves into a communal script that works for them. Perhaps remembered badgers and anthropomorphized clouds are really about protection from abandonment, which is not an unworthy goal for a children's book.[8]

A (SOMEWHAT) DISSENTING VIEW

The stories in the books considered so far share a number of themes. Funeral ceremonies are "boring" and psychologically remote, eulogies are neither mentioned nor remembered, and trips to cemeteries are infrequent. There is hardly an acknowledgment that outside the world of these tales, as most adults know, the newly bereaved are busy with funeral arrangements, body disposal decisions, travel plans, well-wishers with *their* professions of grief, pro forma bereavement cards to be read, and well-intended casseroles to be graciously accepted. Understandably, young children are not involved, since they do not make the important family decisions. Yet in foregrounding emotions as the only pertinent concern at the time of a death, very little is said (or taught) about suffering except that it is private, restricted to interior monologues and confidential conversations with a priest, counselor, or close friend. The best endings these stories offer are those many adults hold out for themselves, depositing the dead in the mind's clutter of memories and finding solace in contemplating their presence in clouds, hills, stars, or some "better place."

In a small number of children's books, however, something else is on offer —an explicit eschatology revealing God's plan for human pain and anxiety. Sectarian children's books do not redeem the fearsomeness of death with happy memories, worthy legacies, or romanticized nature. They go straight to a spatial, visual, aural, and kinetic Kingdom of Heaven. Heaven is confidently portrayed as a wondrous realm much like the present but, just as Swedenborg proposed, scrubbed clean of earthly ills.

Religiously inspired titles are a distinct minority on the shelves of mass-market bookstores, but they form a vigorous if small genre. Nor are they as monolithic as some might think. Kathleen Bostrom, a children's author with a master's degree from Princeton Theological Seminary, has three titles in her publisher's "Little Blessings" series. *What About Heaven?* (2000) is explicit not only about the accoutrements of the afterlife but about the biblical rationale for each. The book opens with a series of questions that a very young child might ask, followed by easily understood answers. These answers are repeated later in the book, accompanied by biblical verses that provide scriptural justification. For example, several children (with their cat, dolls, and toys) riding in a small car ask: "Is heaven a place that is near or that's far? Can I get to heaven by boat or by car?" Two children looking at stars answer the question: "Though heaven's a place that you can't see from here, It says in the Bible that heaven is near." Four who are swimming in the ocean reply, "You don't need to know how to fly or to swim. The way is with Jesus, believing in him." Biblical authorization for the spatial nearness of heaven is drawn from Matthew 3:2, "Turn from your sins and turn to God, because the kingdom of heaven is near." Not only is heaven nearby and accessible through Jesus alone, it is perpetually in full daylight (Revelation 21:25, "Its gates never close at the end of day because there is no night"), and everyone has their own private room (John 14:2, "There are many rooms in my Father's home, and I am going to prepare a place for you"). As for the residents, their bodies have changed into something perfect and new. No one gets sick, earthly wounds are healed, and clothes are permanently clean (Revelation 3:5, "All who are victorious will be clothed in white"). Food is readily available, the animals do not fight or bite, and "Everyone there will be able to talk, To sing and to dance, and to run and to walk" (2000: 33). Millions of angels perpetually float and sing above pavements of gold, crystalline rivers, mountains like jewels, and ripe fruit trees. "Heaven is wonderful, don't you agree? It's simply the best place we ever could be!" (2 Cor 4:18, "The joys to come will last forever"). For Bostrom, the place of the dead is colorful, social, and active; as familiar, fun, and safe as a backyard sandbox.

Larry Libby's *Someday Heaven* (1993) is more circumspect, probably because it is directed to those slightly older ("For Children of All Ages"). Again, the question of heaven's location is important, and it is addressed at the start, but with more explanation than mere citation of biblical chapter and verse. Heaven is *up*, that is certain. God looks *down* on us, Jacob dreamed of a stairway that went *up*, and Jesus also went *up* into heaven: "He rose higher and higher in the air—like a balloon that floats so high in the wind that it looks like a tiny silver pin stuck in the wide blue" (3). Heaven is a real place but probably not, says Libby, in a remote corner of the galaxy or anywhere within the natural world. So he says, but his book's artwork carries a different message. Heaven has vast, vaguely twelfth-century Gothic cathedral archways and corridors, the streets are golden, and the architecture of the buildings is distinctly first-century Mediterranean. Light is conveniently and continuously radiated; life among the dead is intensely social, with new arrivals continuously greeted by well-wishers; and everyone can fly just like the angels since heaven has atmosphere enabling lift. "What could be more fun than burrowing through a cloud or chasing a rainbow or just floating lazily through the air on your stomach and watching the birds play tag below you? What could be more fun than that? We'll just have to wait and find out, won't we?" (31). Birds? Aerial games of tag? Meteorological formations? While Libby is cautious to say that the Bible can be vague about these diversions, he is sure that heaven is much like life here, only more fun. His purpose "isn't to detail angelic anatomies or describe heavenly architecture and landscaping" (although he does that abundantly and with exuberance) but to "help us set our hearts" on our future home and generate the longing to be there someday (44).

Not all religious titles attempt a literalist rendering of biblical imagery. One instance is Naomi Judd's *Guardian Angels* (2000), a story that is also a song sung by Judd on an accompanying CD. In the Foreword, she writes, "Do you believe in Guardian Angels? I surely do. Since I was a child, I've had the unmistakable sensation of being lovingly watched over, protected, and guided by one of God's celestial messengers." She adds that she has found over three hundred biblical verses referring to them. In the song and story, a young girl finds a century-old photograph of her great-grandparents, people she never met, and she notices that their eyes are identical to her own. On a visit to the ancestral Kentucky farm, she senses (as does Judd) that these pioneering ancestors are still present, as guardian angels. And indeed they are. Long dead Elijah and Fanny keep appearing in the cumulous clouds above the barn and behind the farmhouse, looking very much like sturdy, hard-working nine-teenth-century farm folk. Even after the unnamed girl returns home to her brownstone in the city, they follow her in spirit and likeness, their photograph placed on her nightstand. She senses her connection through history, family tradition, and memory. While biblical imagery is an important backdrop to all of this, it is not really the point. Judd's concern, like that of many spiritually oriented Americans, is continuity with family history and participation in a domestic community which, as it happens, is a celestial one as well. Her title moves away from more traditional sectarian imagery.

Sandy Eisenberg Sasso's *For Heaven's Sake* (1999) brings the ancient escha-tological concerns of faith communities out of the clouds and back firmly to earth. Heaven is not a remote (or even nearby) sacred landscape but some-thing intrinsic within each of us, here and now. The top of the preface page quotes a Hasidic legend about a Rabbi visiting paradise. Pleased to see so many scholars studying and teaching, he comments on the wonder of it all. But, an angel tells him, he is not really in paradise. Paradise is within the scholars and teachers. It is within us all, right now. A small headline at the bottom of the same page declares in boldface, "For People of All Faiths, All Backgrounds." This story is going to be ecumenical.

"Isaiah loved blueberries," it begins, and the boy's unrelieved passion for them is evident on his face and hands. Throughout the day, he is subject to adult admonitions which always begin, "For heaven's sake, Isaiah . . . "; but each mild scolding leads to a serious metaphysical puzzlement. What is this heaven people keep referring to? He asks his father (heaven is much like the taste of brownies), an uncle (it is above the clouds), his older sister (it is not there so do not worry about it), and mother (who refers him to grandmother). Grandmother is more savvy than the rest and knows to teach by example. So the two of them visit a soup kitchen where she and grandfather once volunteered and a library where stories are being read to appreciative children. Back home, bowls of blueberries with whipped cream are waiting, and Isaiah is advised that heaven was in those places, in the people who were helping others. For this pleasant and instructive day Isaiah gives grandmother a very blueberryish kiss. "Grandma, I think Grandpa is in heaven and heaven is also in you." Isaiah brings us back to memory, human love, and a spot in our hearts for those who are gone. It is a perfect, postmodern solution.[9]

So what is the moral of these stories, and of my excursion into the small body of children's literature that concerns itself with death? Clearly, one goal is to uncover in an unlikely place what adults do and believe, what is problematic for them, and what they think important to pass on to grieving children. Adults' dependence on a book for helping their children is telling, and probably a sign of adult uneasiness in the matter. They rely on "experts" to tell them what to do and say, and the experts accommodate them, usually in the Foreword, with its advisory hints and encouraging tone. But there is more to it than heartfelt reading and a calming story.

I have argued that in late modernity, Americans are not inclined to describe themselves as "religious" in the sense of denominational affiliation, but do think of themselves as privately "spiritual." By the polls, a god who is accessed spiritually has never been more popular. Why, then, is there so little enthusiasm for God as so named in these mass market children's books? Most do not engage religion in its more traditional, liturgical sense, their authors and publishers apparently feeling it is not of great interest to potential purchasers. I think this can be explained by recalling an older philosophical concept, theodicy, first systematically developed by the seventeenth-century German philosopher and mathematician Gottfried Leibniz. Theodicies are explanations of why a perfect god created a world where pain and suffering persist despite the Creator's good intentions and omnipotent power. They are commonly associated with long running religious traditions wherein collective memory has been institutionalized and is dramatized by a supporting ritual apparatus. A formalized apologetics of misfortune is part of the package. But the American children described in these books are exposed to a very different program, one that could be labeled, only somewhat facetiously, a "meodicy" rather than a theodicy. Contemporary children's authors are seemingly wary of suggesting that death might imply something more, in a cosmic sense, than pain and loss—except, perhaps, when they invoke nature. Transcendence is not a word they use. Their stories reflect the larger cultural shift away from formal religious participation and the evolved metanarratives associated with ancient traditions. For those who are "spiritual" outside these frameworks, what remains as a touchstone of understanding is the perceived needs of the suffering self. Most of the children's books considered here are a rendering of this late twentieth-century style, replacing the resurrective solutions and elaborate theodicies of the past with free-form spirituality.[10]

6 IN OUR HEARTS FOREVER

WHAT DOES IT MEAN to memorialize those who have died? Lincoln's famous eulogy for the dead at Gettysburg was spare, somber, and modest: "We cannot dedicate—we cannot consecrate—we cannot hallow this ground. The brave men, living and dead, who struggled here, have consecrated it, far above our poor power to add or detract" (Wills 1992: 61). But his sense of the carnage, with its appeal to God and history, is not the current fashion. Most no longer think of death as an occasion for memorializing in Lincoln's sweeping, transcendent sense. The preference now is to "celebrate a life," because that seems more personal, meaningful, even upbeat. There are some creative ways to do that.

Eternally loyal Green Bay Packer fans, for example, can order a green and gold casket from a Wisconsin manufacturer. His promotional letter, on a bright yellow sheet and addressed to "Dear Fan," ends with a cheerful, "We wish you a successful season and hope to hear from you soon." [1] More celestial possibilities are available at the International Star Registry at www.misschildren.org. They will name a star after the departed, and their "star kit" ($116) shows survivors where to find it in the sky. Much more dramatic, Angels Flight (www.angels-flight.net) will load Fourth of July rockets with cremains for "a final image of your loved one you will cherish forever." Prices begin at more than $3,000 and include appropriate music and a yacht ride to the watery "service site." In northern California, well-published inspirational guru Salli Rasberry and coauthor Carole Rae Watanabe (2001) are creative in a different way. They treat memorialization as an art form and offer workshops on coffin and urn painting. Participants create personalized body disposal containers, useful for the time being as furniture or for flower displays. Rasberry followed her own advice and created a "coffin garden" in her back-yard, where she is making preparations for herself.

> I am designing a coffin made from willow branches formed in the shape of a swan, as I want to be propped up during my memorial ceremony with those big wings enfolding me. Before my time comes, I hope to use my cof-fin as a rocking chair in the garden so I am attaching wheels to move it from place to place. I will lie in my swan beneath a lattice-work bower covered with flowers in hues of blues, pink, and purples gathered that morning from the garden. . . . After the ceremony I will be wrapped up in a beautiful woven shroud, which we enjoy now as a table covering, and cremated. (2001: 96–97)[2]

Less frothy, survivors of the Colorado Columbine high school killings wrote personal messages on the coffins of classmates, shown on the front page of the *New York Times* (April 25, 1999). One message is quoted in the caption: "Honey, you are everything a mother could ever ask the Lord for in a daugh-ter. I love you so much!!! Mom." Personalized in much the same poignant way, spontaneous roadside memorials proliferate at the sites of fatal car acci-dents. While state highway departments generally prefer simple markers with warnings about drunk driving, family and friends occasionally construct elab-orate, makeshift displays of flowers and mementos, virtual minishrines to the deceased. And for those who cannot get enough of celebrating lives, even while on vacation, there are several choices. Scott Stanton's *Tombstone Tourist* (1998) is a travel guide to the last resting spots of celebrity artists, actors, authors, and musicians, from Acuff to Zappa, people you might think had already had their fifteen minutes of fame. Patricia Brooks's *Where the Bodies Are* (2002) is a state-by-state guide to those she says were "rich, famous and interesting." George Gershwin and Malcolm X are in New York, Ernest Hemingway in Idaho, Roger Maris in North Dakota, and in New Mexico you will find Billy the Kid, Kit Carson, and D. H. Lawrence.

How can we begin to characterize this enthusiastic, sometimes quirky variety of commemorative practices, as diverse as "ecoburials" in unmarked forest plots, paeans to dead pets on the Internet, or the call to NPR's over-the-top auto mechanics, Click and Clack, from a listener wanting to know if it would be alright to put her father's ashes in the gas tank of his beloved Chevrolet? (The answer was no, they will clog the fuel lines. Put them in the ash tray where they belong.) The Vietnam Memorial in Washington, D.C., where personal mementos left at the base of the wall now fill a government warehouse, provides a clue to interpreting this exuberance.

As is well known, Maya Lin's winning design for a Vietnam Memorial was controversial from the beginning. Some described it as a "black gash" in the earth, an image of shame and humiliation, while others claimed that a woman, a mere student who is a Chinese American lacking direct experience of the war, could not know how veterans of that unpopular struggle wanted their sacrifice recognized. Nevertheless, the monument was built as Lin conceived it and is now the most frequently visited memorial in the nation's capital, drawing as many as twenty thousand people per day. It is open at all times, and many come at night for their time of reflection. There is even an annual pilgrimage of motorcycling vets, beginning on the West coast and ending at the wall (Michaelowski and Dubisch 2001). More than a memorial, the place is a national shrine.[3]

Marita Sturken (1997) describes the wall as a gigantic screen onto which visitors project their feelings about the war and the war dead. Its polished black surface reflects an image of the beholder, filtered through the 58,196 names inscribed there. Names alone are listed, in the order in which people died, without designations of rank, service, affiliation, or hometown, details that would distract from the singularity of each life. There are no visual images to suggest race, ethnicity, or religion; the message is simply that these dead are individuals, not representatives of their service units or their communities. Walking onto the grounds, one gently descends along 250 feet of black wall toward a central apex before rising at the far end, a small, somber journey past a mind-numbing array of names. The last is itself something of an imponderable: someone had to be the final casualty, but being number 58,196 is no consolation. At the center, twelve feet below ground level, the noise of nearby traffic is muffled and there are few distractions. The smooth reflectiveness of the wall invites physical contact, by touching with a finger or a hand, making a rubbing with paper and pencil, or posing for a snapshot, all these actions serving as embodied connections to a controversial time of disastrous national policies, manipulative political leadership, and unacceptable human costs. This is not a triumphalist monument. Most remarkable, however, is its accumulation of personal objects left along the base, more than forty thousand at the time Sturken wrote, and far more now. They are as varied as personal letters, toys, dog tags, clothing, poems, combat boots, photographs, war medals, MIA/POW bracelets, bullet casings, flowers, liquor, religious icons, and at least one Harley-Davidson motorcycle. (There have been two suicides as well.[4]) Originally treated by the National Park Service as lost and abandoned property, now everything is sorted, classified, and stored, elevated to the status of national artifacts. (See Thomas Allan's *Offerings at the Wall* (1995) for photographs of things left there.) For Sturken, these objects-as-relics constitute "talismans of redemption, guilt, loss, and anger" (1997: 78), tokens of pain and nostalgia left anonymously on behalf of someone named on the black marble. Many allude to issues beyond Vietnam: abortion, gay rights, AIDS, the first Gulf War, and the war in Iraq. Leaving objects is a way of connecting personal and family history to a national epic, however tragic it was. But the offerings suggest something else that sets this memorial apart from others on the Mall.

Memorials generally can be thought of as pedagogical devices, the powerful ones instructive on some singular, well-made point. The two arms of Lin's design point directly to the Washington and Lincoln monuments, the former a giant monolith suggestive of little more than the name of a near-mythic ancestor, the latter a stone eulogy, its occupant ensconced as though a god in a Greek temple. Jefferson's by the tidal basin references Enlightenment liberalism and rationality in its classical, Romanesque style. Impressive as they are, each is a government-issue monument, its official meaning proclaimed in visitor pamphlets, agency Web sites, souvenir booklets, post cards, and knickknacks available on-site. At the Vietnam wall, however, more than authorized pieties are on offer. The unplanned flood of personalized items, their significance known only to each donor, is what Sturkin calls "an inventive social practice" and a "politics of remembering" (1997: 259). Unlike other national monuments, this one invites visitor participation in an ambiguous and contested moral space where the humiliation of a failed war and questions about its extravagant human cost are still engaged, and where individual hopes of "closure" and resolution eclipse abstractions about national honor and patriotism. This awkward juxtaposition of competing sensibilities, the vernacular and the nationalistic, defines the spirit of the place, as people quietly discuss the effects of the war on their lives, their memories of those named, and what it all means to them individually. This semiprivate, unofficial engagement with the past, which is transformed into a tragic myth-time and deployed for commentary on the present, is the kind of memory work that interests Sturkin and others who examine the contemporary significance of public monuments (Gillis 1994). As vernacular expression of memory has become more common in the public realm, it reveals how memory and memorialization operate in private family settings as well.[5]

MEMORY WORK

Memory, as conventionally understood, is both subjective (internal, private rumination and recall) and objective (past events and objects such as photos that reference them). This notion of memory rests on two assumptions. First, that it is a "natural" part of us, like eyes or ears, and as long as we are healthy, it will pull up stored information about previous experience. Memory can "fail" with age and disease, but that too marks it as part of our normative, biological inheritance, just one more body part that can malfunction as we age. The second assumption concerns its location. In contemporary folk imagery, memory is in "the mind," although what "mind" is and how it is connected to organic brain functioning is hardly clear. As a body function, memory is commonly characterized as a container wherein a lifetime of images, thoughts, and experiences are archived. That mental stuff is part of our individuality, along with our tastes in music or dress, an idiosyncratic lode of information tucked away in the mind, the ultimate in private property. This storage-container model, of course, is a bit of folk imagery, nothing that comes from neuroscience. Its sources are some very old Greek and Enlightenment theories of mind, themselves the common sense of their times. The assumptions behind them then were much the same as they are now: the mind is a space like a dark closet and memories are stored objects to be retrieved at will; when brought out into the light, they look much the same as when first put away. As intuitively obvious as that seemed to ancient Greeks, to sixteenth-century European intellectuals, and to most of us now, memory can be conceptualized as something more than storage capacity.

First, recollections and reminiscences can be approached as statements of perspective rather than after-the-fact mental replays, memory serving less as a catalog of how things were "back then" than as a commentary on how "back then looks to us now" days, weeks, years later. As perspective rather than recall, memories are rarely veridical because, as Michael Lambek argues, they are essentially narratives which are incomplete and highly mediated by subsequent experience, "the view of there from over here" but at a "situated distance" (1996: 242). Whether recounted among friends gathered at a celebratory meal or subvocalized in mumblings at a graveside, they are imaginative re-creations, providing a current take on what past events mean in the present.

Second, as narrative re-creations they draw their imagery, power, and believability both from details of the remembered past and from the everyday idioms in which they are recounted. Idioms are stock features of any culture, the commonly held images and thoughts available to everyone who participates in a shared language and tradition. They constitute what the historian of memory Maurice Halbwachs (1992) calls "collective memory." To create memories, we dip into that communal source, expressing ourselves in the images, symbols, and metaphors of the public realm without which we could not articulate what we experience in either the past or the present. Third, memory as narrative is a distillation of experience, in some sense its "purification." In the privacy of what is called mind, we constantly and skillfully censor and forget, embellish and enlarge, creating a particular version of the past that has usefulness in the present. Purification can make glorious an experience that was humbling, or mitigate some horror that was otherwise senseless, in what Lambek evocatively calls the "transformation of pain into art" (1996: 248). Finally, and especially pertinent to matters of death, memories are about the future, or more accurately, the anticipated future. We revisit and revise, purifying the past to bring it in line with hopes for the future. That too has its uses.

Through the artifice of memory we create, in Benedict Anderson's (1991) well-known phrase, "imagined communities"—places past, present, and future —that we inhabit, if only in the mind. This is a more active and creative process than mere recall. Taken as a whole, memory is really a species of storytelling, one that is artful, strategic, and oriented toward both past and future. That makes it sociological as well as psychological. It is, says Lambek, about "assertions of continuity on the part of subjects and claims about the significance of past experience. Such tacit assertions and claims, based as much on cumulative wisdom and moral vision as on individual interest, form a kind of moral practice" (1996: 248). Memory as "moral practice" is strongly associated with the imagery of death and the customs of a small community on the fringes of the globalizing world illustrate how memory as a social phenomenon works.

BONES OF MEMORY

Inner Mani is a remote, desiccated, and impoverished region of southern Greece. Its historical isolation is due to a mountain range separating it from the mainland to the north, and a bouldery, windswept southern coastline once vulnerable to piracy. Scattered among the rocky slopes are Maniat villages, each one a labyrinth of narrow streets and tightly clustered houses; a central Orthodox church; and one or more two-story towers. The towers are used as houses but once had defensive significance, when Inner Mani was a region of blood feuds and revenge killings among antagonistic patrilineal clans. They are still important, but only as symbols of the faded power of the clans that built them, having been safe places to hide while enemies in their own towers plotted counterstrikes.

Mani rituals of memorialization now focus on more conventional deaths and are, along with the olive harvest, the major public events of village life.

Anthropologist C. Nadia Seremetakis, who calls herself a "dutiful ethnographer," has worked in this region for a decade, much of it "attending and actively participating in two or three mortuary events per week. Even while on short trips to Athens, I would be expected to attend death rites in the city or back in Mani" (1991: 7–8). She has kinship ties to the area, is fluent in the dialect, and writes of a world she knows intimately. I will consider here just one feature of Mani memorialization, although it is part of a larger complex of death-related practices. Secondary burial, common in other parts of Greece as well, is a lengthy ritual process which generates a "second body" of death, as Seremetakis puts it, one that follows the first after all flesh has dissolved. Additionally, there are dramatic lament performances which are vivid public expressions of grief. Both secondary burial and sung laments are female activities, characterized by a distinctive discourse expressive of women's power and solidarity. They are vernacular practices, conducted outside the purview of the Orthodox Church and its male priests, who, while tolerant, consider laments marginal to church rites for the dead.

As the Mani see it, the period separating the first, or mortal, body from its defleshed spiritual one is more important than the date on a death certificate. The latter is not the end of life but the beginning of a transformation, starting with the wake and ending three or even five years later, when the deceased's bones are exhumed, carefully examined, and placed in an ossuary. Death is not an event but a lengthy and clearly demarcated ritual process for installing the dead-in-waiting in the afterlife. It begins when the deceased, dressed in his or her best, is placed in a wooden coffin and taken by procession from home to the church funeral and on to a cemetery for burial. There the casket is placed directly in the ground or in a small cement vault with a cover (the "door" mentioned in the passage below) and a headstone placed just above it. The grave is shallow, and for good reason. Some time later, as many as three or even five years, it is opened so the bones can be removed, cleaned, and "read" through divination. Traditionally, older women who were family members exhumed the bones, but more recently others have been hired when relatives are not available. For those who undertake this necessary task, it is stressful, especially the first time out. One respondent described for Seremetakis her first exhumation.

> First of all, I had armed myself with self control and strength because I didn't know what I would face. I hadn't done an exhumation before. . . . "Sofia," I said, "You'll go down first, I can't." The coffin had disintegrated, it was only the skeleton [whispering]. Something like a mummy. So immediately you recover from the first chill and go to work. . . . First of all we took the head,

the skull. We placed the bones in a pail as we took them out, one by one. . . .
We cleaned the big ones, the spine, ribs, everything. Then we put in the [still
intact] socks the two feet up to the knee, to catch all the tiny bones, and we
lost none. . . . We did the same for the hands. . . . Imagine, I want now to go
exhume my father myself. I now know what I am going to face. (1991: 181,
183; brackets in original)

In this passage from Seremetakis's field notes, the speaker refers twice to
"facing" the deceased. But what is faced is hardly the pose of sleep so carefully arranged by American embalmers. In a phrase, Seremetakis evokes a
Mani sense of memorial aesthetics starkly different from our own: "erased
facades of a residual identity" (1991: 220). Exposed and naked bones, fresh
from the earth and bereft of their owner's flesh, are the deceased's "second
body," a decayed and bony portion of the self still in transit to the afterlife.
Every bit of bone is searched out, washed, and displayed in preparation for a
reading, a moment of high drama for the family and village friends who
attend. "Both color and odor reveal the moral past of the dead" (1991: 192),
and signs of impurity—blackened bones, bits of flesh—are examined by older
women skilled at interpreting spots and blemishes. In small village communities, where memories of those now dead are readily recalled, a reading is
something of a judicial pronouncement by the diviner, those gathered form-
ing a jury eager to hear of the moral condition of the deceased. The bones are
then packed into a box and carried off to a shed, unceremoniously left with
all the other little boxes that have accumulated over the years. If the reading
went well, the work of mourning is over and the dead are at peace. If it is
doubtful, masses will be said to help move the deceased along in his or her
difficult journey toward a final rest.

This drama of exhumation is part of a Mani ethos in which even olive
trees have a part. Death and olive harvests are the two great "ingathering"
events, defining what it is to be Mani and female. They explicitly link one to
family, ancestry, and place. Like graves and lament performances, olive trees
are sites for storing emotions and memories. Historically, both men and
women worked in the wheat fields and olive groves. Men did the heavier
work of clearing land, hauling stones, and plowing, although women often
did these things as well. Now men migrate to urban centers and foreign countries to work in the modern market economy, sometimes taking their families
with them. Depopulation has been a trend for half a century. Women who
remain continue to labor on their land and in the groves, sites of precious
connection to ancestors who also labored there, assuring the family's future.
Each olive grove bears, it is said, the "signature" of its founder and all who

subsequently worked it. Seremetakis observes that "the memory of shared substance is concerned with material components, with tangible tracks" (1991: 217); olive trees, laments, and exhumed bones are all tracks that make vivid the reality of death's separations.

How different the Mani configuration of death is from those of the urban centers of industrial Europe and North America. It begins with years of patient grave tending, followed by a communal exhumation and divination, the living in partnership with the dead. Death's "tangible tracks" are unambiguous—processionals, special funeral foods, grave tending, mottled bones, determined diviners—the whole a robust liturgy of the personal made cosmic, and no woman in Mani is ever "at a loss" for what to say. Memory as moral practice invokes olive trees, land ownership, the gendered division of labor, ancestors likened to the architecture of the house, and the moral standing of the dead in their home village at the time of death, all interpreted in dry bones by women skilled in reading their blemishes. That familiar American artifact, a store-bought card declaring "there are no words to describe our sadness," would be incomprehensible in this context.[6]

THE CULT OF MEMORY

In Mani, the bereaved are clearly concerned with moving the dead toward a remote paradise, their death rituals the exhausting, dramatic work of getting them there. Memorialization among North Americans makes quite a different point. There is less interest in cosmic migration, at least among the Protestant majority, since that seems to happen more or less automatically. And graphic depictions of the afterlife do not have the cachet they once did; it is unclear what the dead find when they arrive at their final destination. So North Americans do the next best thing: they "celebrate a life." Ceremonial appreciation and brief expressions of sympathy to family and friends need not be burdened with theological overtones, nor does a "celebration" have anything to do with moving the dead toward an indeterminate heaven. Rather, as the obituaries and bereavement cards often say, the dead live on "in our hearts and minds." Eulogies, laments, hagiographies, grave markers, epitaphs, statues, roadside memorials, spontaneous accumulations of flowers at crime scenes, and elaborate postings in cyberspace make that statement in various ways, committing the dead to living memory rather than a locale beyond the natural world. The focus is on what the dead did with their lives, their interests and peculiarities, and how survivors "shared" that life with them. Memory as moral practice is both the selectively remembered past and the imaginative redacting of a relationship, generating what I would call a "cult of memory." It is a distinctly postmodern idiom, the dead granted the only kind of immortality they (and we) can be sure of, namely, abiding remembrance in the hearts of survivors. A variety of material props and domestic rituals work toward that end, and they are notable for their creativity and vigor, occurring as they often do outside the purview of commercial funeral companies and religious authorities. In the remainder of this chapter, I focus on several features of this cult of memory, including obituaries, the trend toward spontaneous and personalized memorialization, and the growing role of cyberspace in "celebrating" the dead. Obituaries are the logical place to start since, for most of us, "an obituary is the final public notice of an existence" (Hume 2000: 152). It is also where survivors begin reconstructing a disrupted relationship.[7]

Obituaries, like eulogies, are an old literary genre and Janice Hume's study of almost 5,000 of them published in American newspapers tracks the shifting interests of obituary writers and readers from 1818 to 1930, an exercise that opens, she says, "small windows" onto the values associated with life and death in earlier times. "Newspaper obituaries are a recognized forum for telling stories of the deaths of individuals as well as for legitimizing those stories for a mass audience" (2000: 16). Legitimizing is the key idea here. Obituaries are more than personal statements; they are literary miniatures that chronicle a life and valorize the values associated with it. They are as much teaching and learning devices as the advertisements and news stories packaged with them, providing information easily scanned and mentally digested along with the morning coffee. Because they are the products of "certain principles of selection, emphasis, and presentation concerning death and the values of a particular life" (23), we could think of them as shards of prevailing cultural ideology. Editors and obituary writers may not have thought of them that way, but, notes Hume, "because of their commemorative nature, [obituaries] gave newspapers the opportunity to promote virtue" (147) and grant public acknowledgement to some lives while ignoring others. Some examples illustrate that, and by beginning with older ones, the distinctiveness of current formulas will be obvious.[8]

An obituary must be selective, compressing into a few paragraphs only the information the author considers salient. Obituaries are also selective in that some people will have one and others will not. In the early 1800s, for example, women accounted for only a quarter of the published obituaries in Hume's sample. Excluded men were those without prominence in military or political endeavors. Nonwhites were rare, and Native Americans were written up only if they had had a relationship with whites such as befriending settlers, as allies in combat, or partners in negotiating settlements and treaties. Typically, men who got an obituary were praised for gallantry, boldness, devotion to duty, and zeal for a cause, values appropriate to the warrior and political class of a country newly separated from colonial overseers. By the 1850s, however, obituaries began to describe men as educated, industrious, competent, respectable, and mannerly, the attributes of leaders of an industrializing economy whose concerns were management of labor and resources, workplace values rather than those of the battlefield or frontier. In addition, obituary writers of the period thought it appropriate to comment on things we now consider private: the monetary worth of a man's estate or his personal piety. As now, a good show of bravery at the end of life was appreciated but was expressed in the elaborate prose favored by Victorians. No one today pens anything like this obituary written for young James Oldham, age twenty-six, which appeared in the *New Orleans Picayune* on August 2, 1855:

> 'Twas but yesterday we greeted him in all the pride of manhood; now he sleeps in eternal night. The hand that in life had often grasped in friendship his many friends, is now clenched with the last conflict; the eye that so often irradiated his intellectual countenance, is now rayless in its indented socket; and the warm gushing heart, that was "open as day to melting charity," is forever hushed 'neath the humid cerements of the tomb. (65)

Narrative lines for women in the nineteenth century were different. A woman's commitment to Christianity led the list of celebrated attributes, and religious devotion was routinely followed by the values of the hearth—patience, obedience, resignation; a good woman was loving, charitable and, most important, dutiful and useful. Unlike the obituaries for men, those for women did not consider whether their subjects had political opinions, theologically distinct views, or an active public life. Although many women undoubtedly had such, these features were not broadcast in an obituary where family reputation and standing in the community was at issue. For example,

> In Cumberland, State of Maryland, on the 31st of December [1818], Mrs. Christina Miacha Magill, wife of Samuel Magill of that town [died]. . . . after an illness of two weeks, leaving an infant daughter of that age, the only living pledge of her affection for a fond husband. In purity of heart—intelligence of mind—mildness of disposition—and suavity of manners—she has left few superiors among her sex. (35)

The complications of childbirth, perhaps a factor in Ms. Magill's death, were always dangerous. But in this instance, what happened to the infant daughter? Even less noted in obituaries of the time were the deaths of children. Child death rates were high, with many children never living to their first birthday, and consequently their deaths were not newsworthy. On the occasions when a child's obituary was published, mention was made of the child's "promise" or fortitude in dying in an adult-like manner. Typically, a child's age at death was given in years, months, and days since, apparently, the exact length of an abbreviated life was of more interest to readers than anything else that could be said about them.

Obituary writers had a strong interest in religion, and for good reason. The 1830s were marked by the second Great Awakening (the first in the 1740s), a mass revival among Protestants at which revealed truth, emotional fervor, and purity of heart were dominant themes. In this context, family love and nurturing attentiveness were the conventional expressions of piety for women as well as common themes in their obituaries, often presented there in a style that was explicitly instructional. One Mary Vincent, for instance, died as "a beautiful illustration of the blessed principles of Christianity," and Eleanor Sprigg's obituary recommends that we be "led to reflection [on] the merits of the dead. . . . It forces us to know that, by the practice of virtue, we shall at length all be reunited in another and a better state of existence, never again to die or be separated" (45, 51). Augusta Morrison of Baltimore, described as "a most obedient daughter, affectionate sister, kind, gentle and amiable in her disposition," gave "every evidence that she was blessed with those christian graces that come only through our Lord and Saviour" (74). Morrison died at age nineteen, very much a "good death" as the Victorians understood it.

Similar sentiments were in vogue well into the twentieth century, not only in Baltimore but in the rural heartland as well. Historian Dawn Nickel has documented these in a study of care of the dying in western Canada (2005). For example, womanly virtues were central to the life of Millie Eith Sjorlund, who died in 1927 at Wetaskiwin, Alberta, at thirty-three. "She always greeted everyone alike with a pleasant greeting and cheering smile, a friend of all who knew her. Hers was a character of sterling excellence and she had the highest ideals of fine and clean womanhood. Always in such perfect good humor, even to the last, amid great sufferings, she had a light heart." The obituary adds that she was "deeply mourned by her husband and ten small children at home." Ten by age thirty-three—"great sufferings" indeed! Nickel notes that "the memorialization of a woman's virtue, in this example, may have been amplified or multiplied by the number of children she had!"[9]

During the early and middle years of the twentieth century, however, obituaries for women began to take a different tone. Men were still the subject of choice and women still described in relation to their husbands, as in the convention, also common on headstones, of listing men's names in full and treating women as dependents: "Mary, wife of. . . ." Nevertheless, women were increasingly named in their own right or depicted in terms other than religious. Some had taken up worthy causes ("Credit was given Miss Knowles for the reformation of many young women who had been sent to the institution"); others excelled in education ("a lecturer at Columbia University since 1910"); a few had bragging rights to prominent ancestors ("direct descendant of President James Madison's father and of John Hancock"), a move away from the previous emphasis on devotional piety (Hume 2000: 101, 114, 118). Philanthropy, political influence, prominence as a socialite, and descent from "pioneer stock" and settler families, all were acknowledged, and they showed that in the new world of twentieth-century consumerism women as well as men had secular interests beyond the household and were individuals in their own right. It is not surprising, given this trend, that contemporary practice has become more democratic and celebratory, featuring the achievements and distinctive attributes of both men and women, prominent and humble alike.[10] But one downside has been the abandonment of the florid prose once expected of a good obituary, which had been a little art form in itself, and its replacement by something more akin to a job résumé. In contemporary newspapers, the deceased's education, work activities, military service, volunteer interests, and clubs and affiliations are ticked off more or less in chronological order. Even where a life is portrayed as a series of achievements and triumphs, ending in a heroic struggle against a terrible disease, the grocery-list nature of current obituary writing is evident. It is an odd way to celebrate individualism, leaving the quirkiness of everyone washed pale in editorial blandness.

Who writes these obituaries? What conventions govern their production? Newspapers routinely publish stories on the lives of national and local worthies, but that is news coverage. Obituaries are different. They may be authored by family members or friends but are frequently written by newspaper staffers, often journalistic rookies or individuals near retirement preferring a low-stress assignment in the newsroom. They are paid notices, sold by the column inch, and each newspaper has its own format. The style sheet for the *Denver Post* is a good illustration.[11] It specifies that a proper obituary has, among other things, the deceased's name (first name used only in the first, introductory sentence), age, cause of death ("optional for the family"), eulogy comments ("such as *beloved husband or wonderful father of*"), place of death (optional), officiating funeral company, and time and place of the service. Additional information may include occupation, community involvement, hobbies, military service, marriage, survivors, religious affiliation, pallbearers, and suggestions for memorial contributions. Generally, says the *Post* style sheet, the obituary is one long paragraph, but should the family prefer, it can be broken into five smaller ones, and the contents of each is specified: name and vital statistics in the first, occupation and "significant biographical information" in the second, and so on. The style guide ends with a checklist printed all in capital letters, as if defying its own instructions to "Please draft obituary in your own words." If it all seems like canned writing, it is. One critic of grocery-list hagiography has commented that

> Most American newspapers treat obituaries more as a revenue source than as a literary opportunity. The obits in the [Dallas] *Morning News*, for instance, usually take up two pages, but a page and a half of this is occupied by paid obituaries, a gray expanse of pallid prose that, for the most part, sounds as if it had been written by a platoon of undertakers, which it generally is. (Singer 2002:28)

But that may be changing, due in part to the spunk of some British newspaper writers. In 1986, the *Daily Telegraph* hired one Hugh Massingberd as its obituary editor, and he quickly became the patron saint of inspired obituarists, as they call themselves. He emphasized a personal, candid approach, the foibles as well as the endearing qualities of the deceased getting full mention in somewhat longer essays. Stock phrases—"devoted and loving mother," "loyal employee who will be deeply missed"—were replaced by descriptions of real lives and events offered up in snappy, truthful prose. Devoted obituary readers, of which there are millions, must have appreciated the freshness of opening lines like this one: "David Robeson Morgan was a brilliant man whose future looked good, until he had a frontal lobotomy in 1947" (Singer 2002).[12] And it would be hard to miss the brutal candor of this: "The cancer emerged in his tongue, and the removal of a large section of this under surgery left a master of the quick riposte incapable, even with the aid of a plastic valve, of emitting much more than a series of honks and clicks" (Starck 2001).[13] Humor counts too. The *Daily Telegraph* obituary for Lord Oranmore, dead at the age of one hundred, described his penchant for raising hogs in the drawing room of his mansion. He hoped (erroneously, as it happened) that bacon from aristocratic pigs would bring a higher price. A prominent London restaurateur, according to the obituary, was once confronted by a customer holding a cockroach found in the washroom of his tony establishment. "'Madam,' he exclaimed after studying it closely, 'that cockroach is *dead*. All ours are alive.' He then apparently swallowed it, washing it down decorously with a glass of vintage Krug" (Conniff 2003: 89). And the writer of an obituary for Linda McCartney, wife of the Beatle, shucked all pretense of saying only nice things. "Short on glamour, divorced, a single parent and an American, she was to many a less attractive catch than McCartney's previous girlfriend, English actor Jane Asher. . . . [Linda] was derided for a lack of musical talent and an ugly singing voice" (Starck 2001). The creativity and sharp eye of the British writers, admittedly devoting much of their best work to the famous and infamous, quickly distinguished their efforts from the hack material churned out for American newspapers readers. While the American writers seem satisfied with a drab short listing of hobbies and volunteer work, the British obituarists look for something sharper, a "defining line, an insight into the heart and soul of the life" (Singer 2002) that illuminates as well as recalls.[14]

Recognizing that there might be an audience for this emerging trend, several Americans have begun promoting the British style. Carolyn Gilbert, a former high school English teacher, organized and convened the First Great Obituary Writers' Conference in 1999, a statewide gathering of Texas obituary enthusiasts. That quickly became a national, and then international, event; its seventh incarnation was held in Bath, England, in 2005. Gilbert's organization, the International Association of Obituarists, runs a Web site (www. obitpage.org), where she describes herself as "devoted to the idea that it is possible to address a serious subject—like obituaries—with reverence and a wicked sense of humor at the same time." Steve Miller, a New Jersey newspaperman, had the same idea when he founded *Goodbye! The Journal of Contemporary Obituaries* (http://www.goodbyemag.com/). His obituaries reach for the "defining line" British writers relish, plus some. For example, on Edward Gorey of gothic illustration fame: "In college [Harvard in the late 1940s] he developed and perfected his persona—long fur coats worn with tennis shoes, pierced ears, painted toenails, and other theatrical eccentricities that marked him for life as a distinctive but largely unrecognized type: the dandy-nerd." Or of singer John Denver, under the headline "Country Boy Kaput": "The Big Problem: too goddam cute. With John Denver there was first the hair. Then the o-so-cute granny glasses. Then the homey garb. The bashful nature. He was unthreatening in appearance, attitude, sound. Saccharin tunes lapped the scuppers of an aurally sedated audience that ended up shelling out hundreds of millions for a Rocky Mountain High that left only the tiniest of hangovers." And of the unfortunate Michael Yakubic, inventor of Saran Wrap. While out for a countryside stroll, he died of natural causes, his body falling into a creek, where it lay undisturbed for a full week. Wrote Miller, "Apparently, no embalming was necessary. The body somehow managed to stay crisp and fresh the entire time."

The intellectual horsepower behind this newer creativity comes from an Australian journalism professor, Nigel Starck, who crusades against what he calls "posthumous parallax," the "bending of life histories towards all that is light and wholesome, away from anything that might reflect unfavourably on the dead" (Starck 2001, 2005). In his war on banality, he takes on one of the most familiar clichés of eulogizers everywhere: thou shalt not speak critically of the dead. In an essay that has been influential in obituarist circles, "Capturing Life—Not Death: A Case for Burying the Posthumous Parallax," he recognizes that obituarists are sometimes in a dilemma. Should they go with euphemism, overlooking the unseemly or hidden, however large that was in some people's lives? AIDS, for example, was once a front in that war. In the early phases of public awareness it was rarely mentioned as the cause of death, a courtesy to families who did not want a public declaration that the deceased might have been gay. Was that truthful? Was it consistent with professional standards of accuracy? Did it serve the interests of a readership that was innocent of the medical horrors and prone to stereotyping and judging? "Both realism and euphemism punctuate this uneasy discourse," says Starck. "The reader is confronted by passages of vigorous illumination and by slabs of plodding recitation." Journalists should do better and readers ought to expect more. "I have found that the obituary can offer an eminently satisfying experience for the writer, the student, and the teacher of creative nonfiction. At its best, it demands elegance of expression and discipline of purpose, a gift for relating anecdote and a rigorous checking of fact, a sense of history and poetry, and a style of writing which should be at once engaging and authoritative" (2005).

One of the most lyrical obituaries I have read is that written by *Newsday* columnist Jimmy Breslin for his daughter Rosemary, an elegant example of the newer style in the genre. A list of her accomplishments, normally the sum of the standard obituary, is limited to the first short paragraph. The remainder is the death bed scene, Breslin, tacking between the labored breathing of his forty-seven-year-old daughter and several events from her life: rummaging through her mother's purse for ice cream money; watching her mother die; determinedly preparing scripts for the television series *NYPD Blue* despite the pain of tubes in her arms. Then the breathing stopped "before an onlooker with frightened eyes," Breslin's reference to himself. "The mother took her hand, and walked her away, as if to the first day of school" (June 20, 2004). No lengthy résumé. No easy sentimentality. Just the unadorned statement that a mother, herself long dead, quietly met their daughter and "walked her away" into mystery.

The newer, "high end" obituary writing—literate, engaging, honest—has arrived, but it is almost always limited to those whose lives were noteworthy. *The Last Word*, a collection of nearly a hundred obituaries from the *New York Times*, is subtitled *A Celebration of Unusual Lives*, and includes obituaries and news stories on the likes of Orville Redenbacher (popcorn king), Thomas Kuhn (philosopher of science), and William Shea (stadium namesake) (Siegel 1997). And *Times* writer Robert McG. Thomas, Jr., considered one of the best, has published *52 McGs* (2001), a collection of his favorites. While he often wrote obituaries of those well known, his collection is interesting for including others who were distinctive, or peculiar, in more modest ways. His McGs include the Reverend Louis Saunders, who officiated at the burial of Lee Harvey Oswald; Emil Sitka, a properly stiff character actor who took many of the pies and punches thrown by the Three Stooges; and Nguyen Ngoc Loan, the South Vietnamese cop infamously photographed in 1968 executing a Vietcong prisoner in the street.

What can ordinary folks do to break through the plodding slabs of gray text and grab a little of this ingenuity for themselves? They can write their own obituary ahead of time, an idea warmly endorsed by Gilbert. That way, they get the last word and can show some passion. One John Bunyan Carver began his by saying, "If you're reading this right now, I guess I'm dead. . . . I've got some bad news for you (beside the fact that I'm dead) . . . just as I always suspected, God is a Republican" (*Winston-Salem Journal*, September 9, 2002). Declining to comment on deity, Susan Lane wanted readers to know that she was "an unapologetic liberal and a delightful dinner and party guest. She was never a member of the NRA or the Republican Party" (*Richmond Times-Dispatch*, quoted in the *Seattle Post-Intelligencer*, January 14, 2004). And apparently, some newspaper writers keep a running obituary on themselves, updating it periodically with their latest accomplishments. Obituaries are popular features that are profitable for newspapers and entertaining for readers. But there are other ways the departed can have a final statement.[15]

GRAVEYARD GOODBYES

Walk through any cemetery and you will see that most markers say little about who is underneath them: a name, birth and death dates, maybe mention of a relationship or an affiliation. Gray slabs of text once again. But some stand out, even oddly so, proclaiming the individuality of their owner. Individualistic expression is rapidly becoming the norm, on headstones as well as in obituaries. The beginnings of this historical trajectory are evident in numerous New England village graveyards, some as from as far back as the 1600s and themselves transplants of customs favored by the Puritan faction of the Anglican Church in England. Their style was something of an innovation, since in medieval Europe most people were buried without visible markers at all. After the eleventh century, statements of identity began to appear on the monuments of local worthies. Typically, a name, profession, and date of death were inscribed, sometimes with an added memento mori, a line or two urging passersby to pray for the deceased and think about their own demise. Ariès (1981: 219) cites as an example, "Good people who pass this way, To God unceasingly please pray, For the soul of the body that lies below." Functioning as small broadsides to piety, the emphasis of these inscriptions was the soul and its salvation. What mattered was one's eternal fate, not who or what one was while living. But New Englanders saw it differently.

The first run of New England epitaphs identified only the elite of colonial society: governors, mayors, clergy, and merchants. But that was eventually democratized. Women's share of the epitaphs grew and the number of inscriptions in Latin diminished. Younger men, not just aged patriarchs, began to appear more frequently, and their memorials included both death and birth dates and places of origin. By the nineteenth century these minibiographies became more detailed and included information on longevity, apparently of heightened interest because it was often expressed in years, months, and days. Epitaphs for children began to appear in the late 1700s, as did inscribed remembrances for adolescent boys, girls, and young mothers. In these, the thematic interest was less the fortune of a soul than the details of a life, including place of origin, life span, occupation, marital status, and even cause of death. The purpose of the epitaph was changing, less concerned with recalling honors than with expressing family grief.

Early American epitaphs also gave prominence to the body and its decay. They announced, "Here lies the body of" or "the remains of." More space on monuments was given over to statements about the causes of death and about how the dying faced their suffering. Diseases and catastrophes were sometimes named, as was the virtuous courage shown by victims. But by 1800, attention was shifting away from bodies, bones, and disease to an invocation to memory instead. Thus, standardized prefaces like "To the memory of" and "Sacred to the memory of" became common. This was a significant theological shift, for there had been questions as to whether moldering remains awaited the call to resurrection, which was not expected until the end of time, or whether souls immediately went to heaven and found their salvation without the benefit of resurrection. The status and location of the dead were not entirely clear. Such issues, important to some people, were finessed by discarding references to suffering and decay on headstones and by recasting the grave as a site of "perpetual memory," one "sacred" to the memory of its inhabitant.

At the same time that souls were abandoning their bodies and graves, the look of the older markers was changing. The stereotypical New England death's-head, a gravestone motif with leering skull and attached wings, lost favor to cherubs, angels, clouds, and willow trees, with an almost cheery romanticism the older Puritans would not have appreciated (Deetz and Dethlefsen 1967). Whereas earlier epitaphs defined the dead in terms of abstract qualities of piety, family honor, and citizenship, newer memorials focussed on biography, career, and personal struggles. Increasingly, the dead were becoming individuals in their own right, regardless of their religiosity, the fate of the soul, or station in life. Children, in particular, began to populate cemeteries. Colonial children rarely had marked graves but by the nineteenth century cemeteries began filling up with headstones fashioned as a sleeping child, an empty bed or chair, miniature toys and images of lambs. They signaled two trends: the new place of children in memorial ritual and the naturalization of death, characterized as "slumber" rather than a moral condition.

In the nineteenth century, as urban and churchyard cemeteries became more crowded, unsightly, and hazardous to public water supplies, burials were moved to out-of-way rural areas. They also came under the control of the municipalities that built and operated them, a transformation known as the "rural cemetery movement" and "rooted in the assumption that the most appropriate place for death was a 'natural' setting—that is, one designed to simulate a pastoral landscape" (Laderman 1996: 69). Among the most prominent of these are Mount Auburn Cemetery in Cambridge, Massachusetts, and Green-Wood Cemetery in Brooklyn, New York, precursors to all modern American cemeteries, of which Forest Lawn in Los Angeles is probably the best known. They were, in effect, the first theme parks. Historian David Sloane writes that "As America became more urban, domestic horticulture also became a cherished cultural symbol. Americans closely identified domestic tranquility with agriculture and horticulture" (1991: 46). It made sense, then, that cemeteries should be products of the landscaper's art as well as utilitarian places of storage. As a kind of garden, the new cemetery was designed to induce a sense of the sublime while simultaneously isolating the place of the dead from that of the living. The cemetery offered a retreat from city noise and a time for relaxation and contemplation. Monuments were to be viewed as one strolled along curving paths, past pools, and through shadowed glades of groomed landscape where birds and breezes were the only sounds. Death, like

nature, was tamed in these new "memorial gardens," where human achievement and individual distinctiveness were showcased in stony, sometimes
gaudy "advertisements for myself" (to borrow a line from Norman Mailer). In
a democratizing America, where the entrepreneurial spirit inspired a newly
powerful middle class, memorials emphasized personal accomplishment, useful labor, and modern affiliations. Many, of course, continued with religious
iconography, but it shared space with images of nature, ethnicity, trades and
professions, voluntary associations, and abstract principles such as justice and
patriotism. As stone telegrams to the living, their messages express the personalities, desires, and relationships of those now gone.[16]

Of these, children's graves are often the most touching. They signal a premature death and usually link their occupants to themes of domesticity.
Nineteenth-century middle- and upper-class children, their appearance set in
stone, are depicted in their Sunday best along with a pet, book, or favorite toy.
A life-size Lulu Fellows, about age thirteen, sits in a comfortable chair in
Chicago's Graceland Cemetery in her long, modest dress with lace collar and
locket, holding an open book. She will always be someone's shy, inquisitive,
attentive daughter (J. Brown 1994: 161). Nearby sits Inez Clark, forever age
six, also impeccably dressed, but a very different child. She holds her stone
umbrella and looks out at the world, as though ready for adventure and travel.
She is no bookworm but someone eager for all the experience she never had.
The same could be said for Mandy Moore, who died a century later at the age
of seventeen, in Oklahoma City. We see not her visage but a granite grand
piano lid, upright and inscribed with a musical staff and a quote from Psalm
33:3: "Sing to him a new song; play skillfully, and shout for joy" (1994: 180).
In its vibrant, almost jazzy black-and-white contrasts, there is no doubt that
music is what she lived for. This use of objects—a book, umbrella, piano—in
the depiction of children is recent, a nineteenth-century invention. Small
empty beds and chairs, lambs, rocking horses, and idealized sleeping babes
point less to the personalities of the deceased than toward a new aesthetic, the
sentimentalized distancing of children, even in death, from the adult world.
Richard Meyer, who writes eloquently on the "voice" of American cemeteries,
observes that "the sculptural portrayals of children and their belongings
insured that they would remain ever a part of the goodness of the home
sphere, ever undisturbed and unchanging, and, most importantly, forever
innocents in a worldly world" (1992: 28). That same theme emerges, powerfully, in the current fashion of spontaneous roadside memorials.

Nineteenth-century adults were also memorialized in more personal
ways, their careers and adventures featured on headstones. Brown describes
the graves of two soldiers, one in Denver and the other in Chicago, who left

in granite their military hats, a bedroll, and an ammunition belt (1994: 196). William Tecumseh Sherman, buried in St. Louis, is less modest. Hero to the North and scourge to the Confederacy, his triumphal monument is flag draped with two shields and a military drum. Two arched spears recall his frontier life with Native Americans, and an acorn symbolizes strength (198). Less heroic, a panel on the Denver monument of a Mr. Schaeffer shows the inside of his workshop with its tools, a table, and wall charts. Obviously, a project is underway, but it is never going to be finished. "He died as he lived, believing in God and the great judgment day. Here rests a Woodman of the World" (203). The Woodmen of the World was a popular fraternal and patriotic organization in the first half of twentieth century, and Woodmen markers, often decorated with images of trees, are common in American cemeteries. Not quite "woodsy" but individualistic in its own way is the message left by Julian C. Skaggs of West Virginia, obviously a character during his sixty-eight years. His epitaph simply reads, "I made an ash of myself" (Meyer 1992: 91). "Themed" headstones like these could be cited indefinitely and are consistent with the emergence of themed memorial parks and gardens. Their message is a secular one, that human interests and affiliations take precedence in memory. Who one was and what one did is more interesting than the "better" or "happier" place one might be now.

Contemporary instances of memorial design make clear that this "presentation of self," as Erving Goffman once called it, is a vigorous trend. Of late, the style has moved well beyond work life, as designs have become increasingly individualistic and, frankly, more interesting. While there is not space here for comprehensiveness, a few examples are suggestive. London's Kensel Green Cemetery sports a very large and very British stone dart board. Who it is for is not clear, but in the *Guardian* photo (September 6, 2000), it is well decorated with flowers, bunting, trinkets and two champagne bottles. Slightly more pensive but still whimsical is the monument for Mitchell Moore. Seen in a *USA Today* shot (February 13, 1996), he stands by a life-size stone Wurlitzer jukebox, a classic of the 1950s, with the titles of his favorite rock-and-roll tunes engraved exactly where they would be on the real thing. The same *USA Today* page shows the headstone of "A Gay Vietnam Veteran" with his pointed message: "When I was in the military they gave me a medal for killing two men and a discharge for loving one." John J. Grimes went with a commercial rather than political motif, his etched photo flanked by the images of two cans with the Anheuser-Busch logo (*Seattle Times*, March 3, 1996). Finally, in one small town I discovered a young man's will on the back of his headstone. His wishes were clear. Among other things, "I give my vehicles and tools to my dad. I give my fishing things to my mom. I give my sister Chris my camping things. I love my dad and wish him a horse that wins. I love my mom and wish her a big fish. I love my sister. She is always for me to talk to and borrow money. To all my friends, especially my hunting partner, I leave anything they want. Just tell mom."

It is only a small step from headstone expressiveness inside the cemetery fence to a contemporary phenomenon seen by most everyone who drives a car: the spontaneous roadside memorial. My first encounter with this was many years ago on a steep, narrow road twisting through the mountains of central Idaho. When a fast moving logging truck appeared in the rearview mirror, the only sane maneuver was to pull over and let it by. I stopped near a small hand-painted sign, a balloon, and some children's toys fastened to a tree. Several years earlier, a ten-year-old girl, waiting there for a school bus, was killed by a truck and her father publicly announced his anguish to any who would stop and read his sign. Homemade memorials such as his are now common, the place where death struck apparently as important to memorialization as the grave. Many state highway departments post warnings at the sites of fatal accidents, from white crosses to small signs bearing the name of the deceased. Groups like Mothers Against Drunk Driving (MADD) have pushed hard for this, while, increasingly, bereaved survivors have acted on their own. Holly Everett (2002) has documented this form of memorialization, particularly in Texas and the Southwest, but it is widespread in North and South America and some other countries as well. Two things are significant about this as a distinctly modern, vernacular form of expression.

First, the materials used to create these memorials are often ephemeral; explicitly so. In their commonality, even banality, their use as public markers creates a moral space somewhere between the informality of home life and the cultivated formality of a cemetery. Personal goods and private hurt are put forward for public notice, specifically at a place not intended for that use. "As revealed by my informants' statements," writes Everett, "many aspects of unofficial memorial maintenance are further indicative of their interstitial nature, as their continued existence exhibits a combination of tacit civic support and active community involvement" (2002: 82). In the Austin, Texas, area of her research, she found memorial materials as diverse as plastic and real flowers, planter boxes, a trellis, ribbons, bows, a grapevine wreath, toys, miniature statuary, bricks, a lapel pin, necklace, photographs, a bungee cord, crucifixes, handpainted messages, part of an electrical pole fashioned as a cross with ceramic insulators and barbed wire, a football, and an existing fireplug that had been integrated into a display. On holidays and birthdays, decorations appropriate to the season are put out, evidence of continuing attention and maintenance. Readers can probably recall items they too have seen; some I recall are ballpoint pens, cigarette lighters, home-canned pickles, a bottle of hot sauce, piles of oyster shells, framed photographs, marbles, flags, pinwheels, wind chimes, coins, lipstick, candy, a marijuana cigarette, and handwritten poems. Even a grim looking Karl Marx is not immune—his imposing tomb in London's Highgate Cemetery was cluttered with Post-it notes at the time I was there.

Second, some spontaneous memorials evolve into minishrines where people stop and add their bit to the accumulating memorabilia. Local sheriffs are not always happy with this, as these shrines distract drivers and are dangerous to those wandering about the roadside. One controversial instance in my own area was that of a teenager, a popular football player in his small town high school, who died in an accident on a major highway. An enormous quantity of his personal and football paraphernalia was hung from trees at the shoulder of the road, where they attracted friends, townsfolk, and curious drivers who slowed to take it all in. Safety officials wanted it removed, and it eventually was, but not before the resistant family had its say in the newspapers and on local television news for a week running. The "right" of the family to grieve, as they and reporters played it, was pitted against a heartless county bureaucracy obsessed with traffic control. Most spontaneous memorials do not turn into media events, but neither was this an instance of something unusual. It was simply a local example of something familiar, post-Princess Di and post-9/11. At the scenes of tragedies, there is now a public expectation that something spontaneous and highly visible will appear. People want "something done" to honor those who died tragically, and they want to be part of it. This is not exactly new; the bodies of both Abraham Lincoln and Franklin D. Roosevelt were taken on long, final train rides that attracted thousands who stood along the tracks and waved as the rail cars sped by. What is new, however, are the large accumulations of flowers and personal mementos left at unlikely sites that become "hallowed" for just that reason: the memorial steel fence in Oklahoma City, in which mourners lodged all manner of mementos; the seeming acres of flowers piled as "tributes" along the sidewalks around Buckingham Palace; the spontaneous gatherings that occurred in every American city on the day the Twin Towers went down. Each is a "work of affecting presence" which seeks to sustain a dialogue with the dead, says anthropologist Robert Armstrong (quoted in Everett 2002: 80). We do not want them to be completely gone, and we want them to know we remember the small, familiar, incidental things that exemplified their specialness.[17]

Once the obituaries are written, the eulogies given, the headstone installed, and the bereavement cards read and stored away, survivors are expected to "get on with life" and return to their routines of job, school, and housework. That is best for them and, they are assured, it is what the dead "would have wanted." But for some, funeral formalities or a monument by the side of the road do not yield enough of an "affecting presence." Like the Mani with their grave tending and bone reading, they want something continuous and more direct. Fortunately, there is a modern venue for that, especially suited to vernacular enactments and far more lively than any cemetery or roadside display.

HEAVENLY HYPERLINKS

Cyberspace is an electronic democracy for all things terminal—funerals as commerce, consumer rights, death humor, gothic rumination, unlikely techniques of body disposal, and instant memorialization of the dead, whatever the species (human, canine, feline, and the occasional horse and bird). Simply because of its role as a shopping mall, there is much to be had on the Internet. Coffins can be purchased online, even on eBay. Large manufacturers such as Batesville have sites displaying what they sell: caskets, urns, and "memento chests" for storing cremated remains prior to scattering. They also have an online "Logo Store" with T-shirts, baseball caps, shot glasses, and model trucks just like the big rigs that deliver company products nationwide. On a smaller scale, Bert and Bud (vintagecoffins.com) are two casket craftsmen who offer custom-made containers as well as T-shirts and posters. Their products are promoted with the motto, "don't be caught dead without one."[18] The Trappist monks of New Melleray, Iowa, also handcraft modest but elegant caskets and urns (trappistcaskets.com). The latter are available in oak, walnut, and glazed ceramic, and there is even a "companion urn" that accommodates two. Less traditional funeral products that can be put to practical use now are available without waiting for the world to come. Urnmax.com sells a decorative clock-urn for less than $200 (no doubt a conversation piece as well as an heirloom-to-be), and the folks at casketfurniture.com offer "The Edison," a casket-phone booth, an art-deco casket-sofa said to be "the ultimate place of rest," and "The Osbournes," twin caskets equipped with large speakers ("Volume: Could Wake the Dead"). If something other than a container is required, The Cryonics Institute (cryonics.org) will put the customer into permanent cold storage, what they call "vitrification," until the fatal condition that caused death can be cured. Equally permanent, but without possibility of revival, is the "LifeGem" from lifegem.com. The company will manufacture "a certified, high-quality diamond created from the carbon of your loved one." Carbon is extracted from the deceased's cremains and put under high pressure and heat, the resulting "diamond" cut to your specifications. Each lifegem is unique and comes with the promise that "you have the most honorable memorial available." Their ad at one time featured a touching photograph of a smiling couple in an embrace with the tagline, "Take me along."[19]

Beyond commerce, but only slightly so, is a plethora of online advice and helpful services. Some sites address the practicalities of end-of-life decision making. (Enter "funeral planning" as a search term to find many of them.) Grief is also well covered. And on the memorialization front, there is help available for creating obituaries and eulogies that will be more than the hackneyed presentations they often are. Two sites offering this service are typical. PositiveEndings.com promotes what they call a "pre-bituary," a statement written by the living for publication when they are gone. As a pre-need service, PositiveEndings "writes your adventure the way you remember it. . . . A Positive Endings obituary helps us all better understand the unique contribution every life makes." The illustrative pre-bituaries have story lines less cramped than those in newspapers and contain an abundance of personal details. Tellingly, the site's founders prominently mention their business and marketing backgrounds, attributing their inspiration to a media researcher who "is considered the pioneer of generational studies . . . . specifically focusing on the Baby Boomer generation." Like all savvy marketeers, they know their demographics, and so their appeal is to like-minded individuals who want the eulogy they deliver to sound like a solid business presentation.[20]

LovingEulogies.com appeals more directly to the anxiety of those who dread any kind of speech making: "Asked to Deliver the Eulogy? Accept the Honor Knowing You Will Deliver a Loving Eulogy. . . . The Eulogy *You* Deliver Will Be the One They Talk About for Years to Come!" Two services are offered: custom and instant. For a custom eulogy, the site operators call the bereaved with a list of twenty-one questions from which they develop a personalized speech. Quickness of response is what the customer buys, at $29.95 for a twenty-four-hour turnaround and $99.95 for a six-hour one. Instant eulogies are available in the Thirty Template Pack ($19.95), which includes a writing guide, thirty funeral poems, and one hundred quotations "suitable for insertion." Site operator Jan Shepardson will even edit what you write. The Template Pack includes eulogies for specific categories of persons, including mother, father, wife, husband—those one would expect—and also neighbor, coworker, "father who reconciled with abandoned family," and, interestingly, "curmudgeon." This Web site has an unlikely endorsement—again suggestive of its demographics—from *Maxim* magazine (August 2004), better known for its features on sex, entertainment, and sports. LovingEulogies.com went eulogy-to-eulogy against two competitors to get the magazine's award in the custom speech category.[21]

More important as an expression of vernacular practice is the emergence of the online "virtual cemetery." Used as a search term, that phrase pulls in an assortment of sites—almost 200,000 on Google. Some are simply lists of burials and headstones, information gleaned from public records or compiled by local historical societies interested in preserving old cemeteries. Others are sites developed and used by genealogists, helpful for locating the burials of "lost" family members. Of interest here, however, are virtual cemeteries as extensions of print obituaries, venues where survivors post online memorials and where friends as well as the curious can visit and leave comments. (One, lastwishes.com, even enables the dead to talk back with prerecorded messages.) There are a number of these sites, some free and some not, which use an index or grid to help the user find a specific memorial. Judging by the number of visitor hits, they are very busy places.

Virtual Memorials (virtual-memorials.com), established in 1996 and featured on ABC News and CNN, is well known. Its operator, Sharon Mnich, is based in Atlanta, and at this writing her site had posted over 3,700 memorials along with all the e-mailed "Reflections" attached to each one. The reflections for any one individual can number into the hundreds, and the site gets over one million hits each day. Mnich's purpose in running this busy operation is clear. She wants visitors to spend time there with loved ones, to use it as a place of contemplation, and to create a record which will be of permanent value to descendents. It is to be "a place where future generations can learn about their ancestors long after original records, photographs and writings have been lost or destroyed." This idea came to Mnich when her parents died. Family members were scattered, and she needed a central place to store and make available the family history. An online genealogy seemed a good choice, but she wanted more than names on a family tree. As she puts it, the dash separating dates of birth and death on a headstone represents someone's life, and a life should not be hidden behind an anonymous mark. Her grandmother wrote stories, for fun rather than publication, and adding them to the online genealogy was a way to say something about her interests and, as it happened, was the beginning of virtual-memorials.com. Mnich now describes the project as a "grief resource," something far larger and more demanding than the family home page from which it originated.[22]

Creating a personalized space in a virtual cemetery is easy. Virtual Memorials, for example, accepts entries with an online form, e-mail, or by the postal service. Text-only memorials are free. A basic package priced at $35, however, includes one memorial page, one photograph, a thousand words of text, a "Reflections Page," where visitors leave comments, a visitor counter, a family e-mail link, special listing under "Recently Created Memorials" and three updates of the text without charge. The most elaborate package ($225) expands the choices to six pages, up to 15 photos, 3,500 words of text, a customized background, unlimited e-mail links to family and friends, a link to preferred charities or to the family home page, and up to twenty updates. More is charged for adding unlimited photos, text, music, and videos. Once a cyber-plot is purchased, there are no additional maintenance fees. There is an obvious appeal to memorializing this way, aside from costs that are competitive with newspaper obituaries. Online, much more can be said. "Our lives," says Mnich, "extend beyond the mere numbers on a tombstone. The Internet and its new technologies have given us the ability to preserve in colorful detail the chosen highlights of our lives as we have never been able to before." Virtual Memorials, like some others, is a full service site with a "support center" of grief resources, counseling, books, and end-of-life planning. So equipped, these sites are one-stop service centers for comfort and advice.

What does an established cybermemorial look like? At the time of this writing, that of Kelly Alison Bradley was one of three memorials on Virtual Memorial's home page. A student living in Houston, Ms. Bradley died in 1986 at eighteen, in a car accident. Her page shows many of the conventional features of obituary memorialization, as well as the possibilities of computer technology. It opens with her photo and a quote from an inspirational book, the latter making the point that angels are among us but often in disguise. An anonymous commentator then asks if Kelly Bradley was one of those angels, followed by a traditional obituary sentiment: "Kelly was bright, fun, and a constant inspiration! Her cheerfulness was contagious!! In her short life, Kelly shared love and laughter with us all!" Several click-on buttons floating above daisy wallpaper direct the reader to a biography, a gallery, and a selection of reflections. The biography page is in the traditional obituary style. She was active in high school chess and drama clubs, band, and the student council. She was a member of the National Honor Society. She liked reading, played softball, won numerous drama awards, and graduated Summa Cum Laude. Finally, the cause of death is noted and survivors are listed. The gallery contains six photos taken at different ages and the reflections page opens the site to visitors. One must enter a name, e-mail address, and location before posting a comment. Reflections are listed with the newest first, and for Kelly there are more than 300 (including one each in Swedish, Spanish, and Albanian).

Many are familiar expressions of sorrow and make general comments on what a fine person she must have been. Some are addressed to the family, some to Kelly herself, some to the world at large. A few comment on the attractiveness and meaningfulness of the site, but a striking number can best be described as narratives of shared grief. "I am sorry for your loss. I lost my nephew last July 11th in a terrible car accident and Sunday would have been his 18th birthday. . . . May God Bless You and help you get through your awful tragedy and let's believe that your daughter and my nephew are watching over us each day and would want us to live our life to the fullest as I know they did. Take Care!" But more is going on here than virtual visits and shared sympathy.

Mnich says she has regular contact with many of the families she lists. Some people check their posted memorial regularly, even several times a day, to read the newest reflections. Some users have discovered relatives they did not know they had. Many say that over a year or two they have learned new things about the deceased: activities they pursued or how they affected others when they were alive. Sometimes surprising revelations turn up, extending the story line of the dead into a continuing minisaga which makes them seem alive once again. Through the site's reflections, strangers have sometimes become acquaintances and then friends, remaining in e-mail contact on a regular basis. Mnich feels that men are especially attracted to the "techy" possibilities of virtual cemeteries and that they express the early stages of their grief by scanning in photos, music, and spoken messages. On death anniversaries they return to the site, updating it and adding new material. Teenagers' uses are more complex. Mnich believes many site visitors are teenagers who, she surmises, are more comfortable expressing themselves online than face to face. More than many adults, they are familiar with chat rooms and a mediated style of communication. She says memorials of those who died by suicide are heavily visited by teens, occasionally troubled ones contemplating their own suicide. They may post suicide notes with their birth and death dates, the latter just days or weeks in the future. When spotting these (she monitors but does not edit what goes onto the site), Mnich e-mails back, trying to get more information and asking how she can help. In addition, she has used e-mail to mobilize families who themselves have posted a suicide death on her site, and they in turn e-mail the distraught individual with words of support. All this behind-the-homepage communication makes the site more than just a list service or even a chat room. Literally "under the radar" of more traditional grief, counseling, or genealogical services, virtual cemeteries are unique places. At little cost, they store visual memories of the dead, convene an electronic community of family and strangers, and create opportunities for discovery, outreach, and reconciliation available to anyone with access to a computer.

Continuity and perpetuity, aspects of so-called perpetual care, are common themes in the funeral and cemetery business, and so they are for the operators of virtual cemeteries as well. Many advertise their sites as places of "permanent" memorialization, since cyberspace is presumed to be immune to the erosive effects of rain, freezing, earthquakes, vandalism, and bad cemetery management. But is that possible? Mnich says she wants to "provide a place where these cherished images will have a permanent home," but cybertechnology in itself does not guarantee that kind of stability. Since they market a service, virtual cemeteries have accounting and legal expenses, as do all nonprofit or corporate entities. Electric bills have to be paid and equipment serviced, repaired and replaced. Supervision is ongoing and labor intensive. And as with in-the-ground plots, purchases of today's cybergraves help cover the cost of maintaining those which came online earlier. Finally, there is the mortality of the operators themselves. Unless they have institutional support and can pass the site on to a reliable organization, the whole thing could die with them. Mnich says she is concerned about that and has contacted churches and even the Smithsonian as potential sponsors. She thinks the best prospect, however, might be hospices. If virtual cemeteries were made a component of hospice care, families as well as patients could be invited to use them "preneed" as an integrated part of end of life care. Whether that will happen is still not known.

Finally, virtual cemeteries for pets may be the ultimate in vernacular mourning, those sites as filled with memories and love as any for people. Mycemetery.com is a good example, promoting itself with a long list of awards from sources as diverse as *Cat Fancy Magazine* and Cool Pet Site of the Day. It was even honored with the Internet Roadkill Award. Like human sites, it invites brief commemorations, poems, and photographs. A donation for maintenance is requested, averaging $15, and like human memorials, those for pets are funny, sad, and touching, this portion of an ode posted for Blackie, for example:

> Here lies Blackie,
> Chased a car,
> Caught in the muffler,
> Dragged through the tar,
> Around the corner,
> Across the track,
> He might not be dead,
> But he never came back.

Or this sad postmortem apology to "Touche Turtle—R.I.P.":

> When I was a small child, I was given a Desert Tortoise as a pet. I loved him
> dearly and named him Touche Turtle after the famous Hanna-Barbera car-
> toon character. One day, I was shocked to find that Touche had dug himself
> into a burrow and had died. I was heartbroken, and was afraid to touch him
> for a couple of days, but I decided I had better be brave and give him a
> decent Christian burial. I put him in a cardboard box, dug a deep hole in the
> back yard and laid him to rest with a few improvised words and a bier of
> flowers from the garden. As time went by, I adjusted to the loss of my cher-
> ished pet, until several years later, when I discovered to my horror that
> Desert Tortoises hibernate through the Winter. I'm sorry Touche . . . where
> ever you are! Please forgive me![23]

Why have virtual cemeteries, memorials in pixels, become so popular?
There are multiple reasons, but one is clearly demographic. Twenty-first-century families are mobile and dispersed, and the boomers have adapted, even
if their parents have not. Keeping in touch by e-mail and digitalized distribution of photos of the grandchildren's latest art are logical preliminaries for
those inclined to go the next step and create online memorials. The technology is convenient and familiar and virtual cemeteries provide an easy-to-use
format, accessible to anyone. Recall Morrie, of Tuesdays fame, admonishing
Albom to visit his hillside grave so they could continue their conversation. He
promised to be there, listening. The Internet may work as something of a substitute for that kind of immediacy. In a striking essay entitled "From Cemeteries to Cyberspace: Identity and a Globally Technologised Age," Elizabeth
Grierson (2004) invokes the images of space and mapping to characterize
online memorialization. She contends it is something we do less to remind
ourselves that the dead were once alive than a strategic move to create a special, utopian place for them to be, one "which is absolutely final yet infinite
in its translatability" (2004: 3).[24] Cyberspace is, after all, a "space," and it can
be a utopian one as well as any other. Heaven, the classical utopia of the
Western imagination, has always been populated by beings unencumbered by
earth, air, fire, and water, emancipated from the infirmities mortals bear.
Appropriately, the texture of its cyber parallel is a weave of ones and zeros,
minimalist conceptual particles rushing along at the speed of light, which
offers a suitably modern conceit for canceling out the degradation of physicality and decay. Far better off than corpses isolated in moldering boxes in the
ground, the cyberdead can be summoned forth with the click of a mouse.
They can be addressed directly, and often are, as loving thoughts about them
are shot with electronic speed into the perfected ether they inhabit. No need
to consult the huge oil-and-canvas utopias of Renaissance painters or the stiff

statuary in every corner of Europe's cathedrals to guess what heavenly wonders the dead enjoy now. As a technology for imagination and hope, cyberspace puts the user in control, and with a keystroke re-creates a lost presence, albeit a faux one, as far as Orsi's spiritual presences go. When all this happens, says Grierson, "A heady utopianism abounds" (2004: 6).[25]

There are other things occurring as well. Operators such as Mnich engage their users, and users engage each other in other forums, the mobilization of e-mail inquiries to potentially suicidal teens being one example. Many postings invite comment; others simply share a painful experience. Some writers find a single point of coincidence—same age, same town, same kind of tragedy—and ask for more information about the deceased and how he or she lived. Inclusion of the dead in the conversation, as when addressing them directly, grants agency and expands transcendently the reach of a message. In her reflections pages, Kelly is addressed a number of times, albeit in conventional terms. "God made you an angel," is a common theme. One reader goes farther, implying that Kelly has returned in the form of someone else who was born at the moment she died. That may or may not be helpful, but it is offered in such compelling terms that even doubters would be touched by the writer's sincerity.[26] Critical comments, even hurtful ones, are rare but do appear and are usually condemned by a subsequent reader. Irrelevant rants appear and they are ignored. What seems significant in all this is that participants act as though they really are in a face-to-face community, imputing feelings much like their own to others visiting the site. The mood is explicitly confessional, with a sense that a community of caring, however ephemeral, really is out there.

Cyberspace is an explicitly and extravagantly visual medium, and that alone gives it religious potential. Historian David Morgan has written extensively on what he calls "visual piety," the uses of religious icons and images by believers. "What the image depicts and what the devout viewer thinks it means merges seamlessly into a compelling presence. . . . I propose, though, that we may recognize this power of naturalization in *any image* whose reception involves the magical sense of making the absent present. In fact, there is ample historical research to show that prints, paintings, drawings, and even accidental patterns can render for viewers the ontological presence of someone or something" (1998: 9). He argues further that image making and image receiving constitute a "world creating" activity, most likely to occur at critical junctures where the apparent stability of everyday reality is challenged. Whereas intellectuals and religious elites, especially in Western traditions, are likely to resort to textual and linguistic strategies for resolving conflict and contradiction, vernacular practice is heavily skewed toward the iconic. Online memorials, by Morgan's argument, can be understood as one expression of visual piety, one for reimagining the dead. They are venues that grant agency to the bereaved who interact with one another and, some apparently believe, with the deceased as well. Cyberspace is pixels and code only to the engineers; to users it can be a visual "every-space" inside and outside both time and mortality, democratically accessible from any keyboard anywhere.[27]

There is something beyond pixels, however, that is odd about this. Does it not seem an unseemly conjunction, this community of invisible strangers, thousands maybe, invited to observe a personal tragedy in a culture where death is normally thought a private, family matter? That peculiarity suggests an interesting point. If the dead do haunt in these late modern times, Web sites are one of the places they do it. Virtual cemeteries tell us something about ghosts.

Sociologist Avery Gordon (1997) examines what she calls "ghostly matters," but not in the usual way. Haunting, she says, has to do with violence, trauma, disappearance, and inappropriate absence, and how deaths such as these invade the present. The cases she examines are varied: the only woman in a group photograph, taken at a 1911 psychoanalytic congress, who vanishes from the formal histories of psychiatry; thousands of *desaparecidos* (the disappeared) abducted and never heard from again under Argentine military dictatorships beginning in the 1930s; African Americans in the South, one in particular, who killed her child in 1856 rather than allow the baby to grow up in slavery. Hauntings begin with removals and eliminations that are unexpected, unjust, and often associated with violence; inopportune exits with grievance still felt on both sides of eternity—"endings that are not over is what haunting is about" (1997: 139).

Manifestations of ghostliness occur widely, and they vary widely. In the medieval period of western Europe, the source of some North American ideas, the dead could reappear Lazarus-like as a resuscitated human, as a soul which, in old woodprints, appears as a small naked figure issuing from the mouth of the dying or as a phantom wearing a shroud (Schmitt 1998: 206). We are more likely now to imagine ghosts as they were in nineteenth-century literature, as an uncanny presence like Edgar Allan Poe's "The Raven," or as something from Hollywood's parade of monsters with back-from-the-grave attitude. But the shape of the apparition, dramatic or melodramatic, frightening or reassuring, is not the point: "The ghost is not simply a dead or missing person, but a social figure," writes Gordon. "If haunting describes how that which appears to be not there is often a seething presence, acting on and often meddling with taken-for-granted realities, the ghost is just the sign, or the empirical evidence if you like, that tells you a haunting is taking place" (1997: 8). Hauntings do occur, and they have their diagnostic features. They disrupt "the propriety and property lines that delimit a zone of activity or knowledge," exactly as happens with the distinctive and unexpected mixture of public and private on the Internet. They are also a symptom that something is out of place and gone, wrongly so. We the living may not be culpable, but a haunting reminds that restitution and reconciliation in some form is needed. Haunting is a very social thing and, perhaps, a thing of hope. Its hint of presence, uncanny or not, is a notice that "the ghost is alive, so to speak. We are in relation to it and it has designs on us such that we must reckon with it graciously, attempting to offer it a hospitable memory *out of a concern for justice.* Out of a concern for justice would be the only reason one would bother" (1997: 64). The Internet cemetery creates just such a venue of "hospitable memory" where the job of finding sense in pain is begun, all in the company of a curious and encouraging community of strangers. The dead, some write, know and appreciate that we do this for them. If that is so, then online users do more than perpetuate memories. They reconcile all parties to loss, enabling the living and the dead alike to go separate ways as best they can. That may be all the justice to be had, something the Sora knew already.

It is a novel premise, cyberspace as an engine of omnipresence bridging life and death, or at least presence and absence. But it also looks familiar, like another way to manage traditional hopes of reconciliation and safety—salvation of the old, reliable kind.[28]

MORAL PRACTICE

Michael Lambek's idea of memory as a moral practice is one way to interpret the multiple kinds of memorial expression discussed here. Recall that he sees memory and memorialization as a kind of *poiesis*, a term Aristotle used to describe inventive thought located somewhere between abstract contemplation (theorizing) and immersion in particulars (naturalistic reductionism). Poiesis has to do with "making" and "composing," hands-on work that reshapes the familiar in unexpected and surprising ways. Memorial poiesis is just that, a creative action that conjoins a number of things. First, it is recollection at a situated distance. People and events do not come to mind as a "how it really happened" rendering. Memory is rather the view of them and then, from here and now, the intervening time and subsequent experience modifying what is seen. We invent—and that is the key idea—a redacted version of who and what the deceased were. That makes memory the ultimate revisionist historian, "purifying" the past so as to better serve present realities. "Working through grief," as the cliché puts it, is that kind of purification, the poiesis of a new space where survivors can live with their memories. The Mani do this by reading bones and chanting laments. Americans magnify individual uniqueness and store it in their hearts and on the Internet for safekeeping.

Second, memorial poiesis is dependent on stock cultural imagery. The contrasting practices of Mani Greeks and contemporary Americans make that clear. The Mani preference is strikingly physical, visceral, and public. The newly dead are on display, at home and at the church and cemetery, wine splashed over them as they are laid in their shallow grave. Years later their bones are lovingly dug out by hand, washed, kissed, passed around, and wrapped. Funeral processions, wailing, and exhumation are village events. In its performative dimension, death is women's business, attached to them by essentialist interpretations of male and female difference. The contemporary American way of death could not be more different, at least for the white middle class whose preferences in this are dominant. Death is a family matter, and rules of privacy and respectful distance operate. Open-casket funerals are still permissible, but memorial services are more common, keeping the dead discreetly out of sight. Even when present, bodies are heavily cosmeticized, viewed mainly by family and friends in cloistered funeral company "viewing rooms." Obituaries are résumés; eulogies, succinct overviews with a bit of listener-friendly humor; and receptions, polite gatherings that conclude the formalities and send mourners and friends on their way. The dead are revisited on Memorial Day, when convenient, or on the Internet, where they appear as digitized icons. Hope is proclaimed not by a fearsome old woman pronouncing judgment while gripping a stained skull but by strangers whose good wishes are read in private solitude off a computer monitor.

Third, memory is future oriented. For the Mani, the eternal rest of a soul justifies the years of faithful grave tending and summary bone reading. There is an intensity about it, even a precision, that must be reassuring. The living are doing right by those they loved, and the same will someday be done for them. Nobody's immortal fate is left to chance. North American practice is future oriented as well. There are promises that "we will meet again," of "returning home." Sometimes these notions are religious, the dead joined by flights of angels as they ascend for an accounting of what they did "here below." But if the more secular imagery of some headstones is to be believed, the dead will spend eternity sailing into sunsets, flycasting in perpetual streams, or enjoying the books/music/sports/pets important to them while alive. Why do so many Americans favor that individualistic, idiosyncratic style? Because, I suspect, they are not sure souls really exist; if they did exist, they would be easier to talk about. A poiesis of memory is the modern substitue for the soul.

THE FUTURE OF DEATH

THE AMERICAN WAY OF DEATH, as Mitford described it in 1963, is not what it was then. Her broadside against the funeral industry raised an important consumer issue but hardly told the whole story. Nor does Kübler-Ross's depiction of dying a "good death" fit well with current realities. There is a larger pattern in contemporary dying, although it is not always visible to those who must deal with it. In the discussion of souls and soulscapes, I argued that images of a postmortem existence are not fantasies to which people irrationally cling when life is literally falling apart. In the details, they may be wonderfully fantastic, contemporary redactions of a long chain of slowly changing images and propositions. But as cultural artifacts, they are part of something reasonably coherent, possessing an underlying orderliness. To demonstrate that, I drew on the model proposed by Robert Hertz in his study of secondary burial in Indonesia and Kalimantan. He argued that any culture's death practices and beliefs, although seemingly a curious collection of rituals and beliefs and ideas, have an implicit logic. Its pattern is triangular, the three points of the system being the survivors, the corpse, and whatever place the dead are believed to go.

It was not, however, the three points of the model that interested him, but the connections between them. How do survivors relate to and treat the body? What of the person is left after death, and where does it reside once it has left the body? What do the living do with and for that lasting essence after the funeral and body disposal are past? If people can imagine and construct relations with one another while alive, it is not a great stretch that they would imagine continuing bonds with those who are dead. His key insight was that the treatment of the corpse reveals the rest of the system. Begin with the survivor/cadaver relationship, the base leg of the triangle, and the rest follows. In the remainder of this chapter, I want to briefly recall what Hertz's schema suggests about the American way of death and, in light of that, what the old concept of salvation has come to be at the beginning of a new millennium.[1]

One of the things Hertz recognized is that death is a process, not an event, despite medical and legal imperatives to give it a date and hour. The three dominant American models in that drama are represented by Joseph Cardinal Bernardin's principled, religious response of submission; Morrie Schwartz's notion of every man as a hero; and Bill Moyers's (and Thomas Youk's) search for control as a last act of selfhood. As models they are modern ars moriendi, signaling in their variety that magisterial theological metanarratives, be they from medieval Europe or from the Sora at the time Vitebsky was among them, can dominate only so long as the institutions and rituals that encode them are durable. In North America, times have changed, and salvation of the old kind has become optional. The emphasis now is on insight and coming to terms with the disappearing self. If one can have a "lifestyle," one can have a "deathstyle" too, each as important as the other.

The base of Hertz's triangular system is the treatment of the corpse, but in the American case we have to begin earlier. The stretched-out time of dying is a modern medical miracle that makes death different. We live longer, and when our time comes, death will more likely come from chronic rather than acute disease. This decline generates a preliminary social death, the long period of lingering made possible by ICUs, ventilators, and other medical regimes. The unfortunate Terri Schiavo is an extreme example but she is not alone. A largely invisible hospital and clinical population of people like her is growing, persons who may or may not be dead but whose bodies persist due to intensive care, resource investment, and familial determination. The ethics of modern medicine often prolong that condition. A parallel phenomenon, "anticipatory grief," has also come into being. Onlookers and survivors grieve a death prior to its occurrence, because they have forewarning. That may or may not be helpful for "resolving" grief later, but it does stretch out the engagement of the living with the dying. As a learning experience, it is a stark one. But medicine has a solution for that, too: palliative and hospice care, the hope and practice of dying without pain.

Once death arrives, more decisions must be made, and the choices are more varied than Mitford would have imagined. The range of products available suggests that death is as much a matter of taste and style as are fashions in footwear or handbags. One can interpret that as a result of the industry's strategy to defend itself; funeral services and gear are not something most consumers want to buy and, further, there is competition out there that is not going to go away. The ecoburial and home burial movements, while certainly small, challenge traditional commercial practices because they offer something many Americans appreciate—noncommercial choice at the end of life and emphasis on individuality, even quirky individuality, from burial in concrete fish havens on the ocean floor to dispersal in a rocket's red glare in the summer night's sky. Body display, headstones, obituaries, and online memorials all speak to the specialnesss of the one who died, a virtue proclaimed even for anonymous bodies buried at public expense.

The second leg of Hertz's model, the relation of the newly deceased to whatever awaits, is the weak one in American reckoning. Not much seems to go on there. There were debates in the distant past about what souls are, where in us they reside, and how quickly they get to where they are supposed to go once they leave. Prior to Swedenborg, souls were depicted as spirit entities, often children, with no discernable individuality. After his reformulation, they became us, with our distinctive attributes of gender, age, and personality. But where the soul goes, if anywhere, is now an open question, subject, of course, to personal preference. We have to shift to the third side of Hertz's model, how the living relate to the dead, to get a firmer fix on the released soul's new location. I have argued that the cult of memory is the dead's new home, effectively functioning as the modern form of saving grace. In the older, Freudian model, we were to do "grief work" to separate ourselves from the dead, to get them out of mind and memory, the better to "move on" toward "closure." The new model of grief work, called "continuing bonds," inverts that (Klass, Silverman and Nickman 1996; Goss and Klass 2005). The challenge is to learn to live with the dead in a new way, to find a space in our lives for theirs. Thus we "celebrate" a life, not just at the funeral but on anniversaries, in discussion with friends, and in small, private moments many years later. What Orsi called "images of presence" are the newer manifestations of older, more traditional realities. A grandparent's photograph on a night stand (Naomi Judd's song and story) or a report on the social and intellectual life of heaven (Betty Eadie's near death experience) is a contemporary expression of religious intent if not doctrine; in Orsi's words, "Religion is the practice of making the invisible visible, of concretizing the order of the universe, the nature of human life and its destiny, and the various dimensions and possibilities of human interiority itself . . . [made] tangible, present to the senses in the circumstances of everyday life" (2005: 73–74). There is sacredness without creed in that, a salvational quality powerful to those who experience images of presence, however odd they might seem to others. Whatever the peculiarities and variations, it is Sahlins's salvational ethos breaking through in a postmodern world.

I mentioned at an earlier point in the book an idea proposed by Michel de Certeau. Belief as creedal affirmation, traditionally referred to as "faith" in theologically traditional communities, is not really what belief is about. It is instead a manner of contracting with a cosmic partner, an Other on the opposite side of the table. As with any contract, promises are made and returns expected, gifts and debts circulating in a moral economy of exchange. Agreements are renegotiated from time to time, and their terms extended further into the future. ("Just one more year with this cancer, God, and I will faithfully do X, Y, and Z.") As with any contract, something better seems attainable, and we the living accept some debt service now in order to attain that goal later on. And as with many contracts, the partners are unequal, in this case radically so. What makes that particularly vivid to the parties, and to the living as believers, is what Orsi calls "the corporalization of the sacred" (2005: 74). The body will die and "our bodies, ourselves," as it was once described in another context, are the guarantors of the truth of the contract and all its entailments. What de Certeau calls "expectational practices" are the actions the living take to fulfill their side of the pledge. Then they hope for the best.[2]

Where does the prolific, even offbeat imagery people bring to their negotiations of a cosmic contract come from? Likely suspects are rebellion in the lower ranks against the commercialization and standardization of death, decline in the authority of hallowed religious institutions, and consumer diversion in a culture with little historical memory. But I suspect religious expression of an older, familiar American kind as well.

Historian Amanda Porterfield (2001) describes how the products of theological vineyards as old as 1620 have become the loose, individualistic spirituality of a late twentieth-century "post-Protestant" American culture. From the day the Mayflower arrived, she notes, "the emphasis on personal religious experience was a distinguishing aspect of Puritan thought" and "as a cultural group, it is the Puritans who introduced belief in the primacy of conscience and subjective experience into American religious life" (15). Their passion was inspired by the transformative possibilities of communion with "the Holy Spirit," achievable through devotional practices unmediated by clerics or creeds. The authority of personal experience was both the arbiter of religious knowledge and its only reliable source, whether one was theologically conservative or radical. An engrossing sense of self-assessment, personal surveillance, and hardy diligence in the labors of spiritual improvement were explicit in the old Puritan vision. That meant, of course, that there could be as many inspired visions of God's truth as there were visionaries. For these devotees of an inward looking piety, an enormous amount of energy went into self-doubt and contemplation of one's fate, for as Jonathan Edwards reminded them, they were all sinners in the hands of an angry God. Almost two centuries later, the New England Transcendentalists renewed and perpetuated that Puritan ideal, but with an important addition. Thoreau, who said he liked to walk at least four hours each day, is exemplary: "When I would recreate myself, I seek the darkest wood, the thickest and most interminable and, to the citizen, most dismal swamp. I enter a swamp as a sacred place—a *sanctum sanctorum*. There is strength, the marrow of nature." And just to be sure the readers of his 1862 *Atlantic Monthly* essay on walking did not miss the point, he added, "A town is saved, not more by the righteous men in it than by the woods and swamps that surround it" (1937: 616, 617). In a striking update of Pilgrim theologies, Nature and the natural world were consecrated as spiritual and sacred, the premier setting for cultivating self-knowledge and personal prophetic authority.[3]

A bundle of eighteenth- and nineteenth-century cultural enactments, then, are the sources of much in contemporary American spirituality, beginning with a piety of self-assessment and self-repair, a primacy of personal experience in matters of spirit, and a pragmatic embrace of nature as a repository of sacred truths. Porterfield adds, however, that "It was not primarily the moralism of the Puritan tradition that was revived in the late twentieth century . . . but rather its esthetic responsiveness to life. The identification of spiritual life with recognition of the beauty of being, expressed in the work of the eighteenth-century Puritan theologian Jonathan Edwards, would be endorsed by many recent proponents of spirituality" (2001: 231).

This personalized, utilitarian piety could not become a template for contemporary spirituality without one additional element. Up to the mid-twentieth century, these Puritan ideals were the cultural capital of denominational interests. To be a pious person, one had to be "in the tent" with the rest of the Methodists, Baptists, Catholics, or Lutherans. They were the sponsors and upholders of religious identification. But their authority in public life began to erode and has, with some exceptions, continued to do so for the last fifty years (Stark and Finke 2000). Gradually unhooked from familiar, church-based moorings, Porterfield argues, religious discourses of personalized piety have seeped into other sectors of American life, producing an exuberance of nondenominational pietistic activity. Just a short list of the sites for this activity would include self-help and multiple step recovery programs; the human potential movement with its technologies of transformation from Scientology to yoga; nature spirituality and ecological awareness; neopaganism from Wiccans to revived Native American traditions; decontextualized borrowings from Hinduism and Buddhism; affirmations of ethnic identity and the search for genealogical and religious roots; prophetic movements that are occasionally lethal; the politicized religious Right with its family values and antihomosexuality campaigns; feminist reinterpretations of biblical history; male sensitivity movements from Iron Man John to the Promise Keepers; Christian athletes; antiscientism as varied as alien abductions, faux shamanism and the so-called creation science; and religious tourism, including the revival of ancient pilgrimage routes and New Age gatherings. This list could be extended, but the point is obvious: in Porterfield's notion of a post-Protestant world, the historical imagery and ideology of some very old Protestant traditions have moved well beyond their originating institutions and are not always as recognizable as they once were. But their Puritan and Transcendentalist genealogy is unmistakable; their current manifestations are extensions of some very American, homegrown religious preoccupations.[4]

THE LAST ENEMY

Despite the enthusiasm for private spirituality and, through it, achievement of a good death, or at least a comfortable and meaningful one, death is for most people messy, painful, full of contradictions, and fearful. At the heart of it is ambiguity that will not go away. "The last enemy to be destroyed is death" says Paul in his (and the Bible's) most extended meditation on the subject. But that destruction has not yet occurred, and, all hopes for good deaths notwithstanding, it seems no closer now than it was then. Only the battle tactics are different, and whether or not they are an improvement is not yet settled either. I want to mention three current tactics, not to explore them exhaustively (others have done that), but to suggest the nature of the terrain where death as the last enemy is currently engaged.[5]

The commonly expressed desire for "quality of life" at the end, "to live until you die" and then exit with "dignity," is sometimes fulfilled, but often it is not. In a study of English hospice patients under palliative care, Lawton (2000) observed that we think of ourselves as "a bounded, physically sealed, enclosed body . . . [with] the bodily ability to act as the agent of one's embodied actions and intentions" (7). But at the end of life, the "corporeal capacity for 'self-containment'" collapses with a profound loss of agency and moral personhood. The body-as-subject becomes a body-as-object, a failing container that the dying and their medical partners attempt to control. The "hospice body" is an *un*bounded body, managed and addressed largely in reference to its failing functions and parts. It can enter into what Lawton calls "dirty dying"— unappetizing in the extreme. "Amongst the most common [ailments demanding symptom control are] incontinence of urine and faeces; uncontrolled vomiting . . . fungating tumours . . . and weeping limbs which resulted from the development of gross oedema in a patient's legs and/or arms" (2000: 129). Hospice bodies can, in a sense, be "rebound" with medications and wrappings, but those are temporary fixes. Dying people, she concludes, are sequestered in wards, home bedrooms, and hospices, not because their death is being covered up but because they are out-of-control bodies fast becoming unbounded ones. They have lost personal agency in the most evident and disagreeable ways.

Of course, the management of such disasters is what palliative medicine and care are about, and the benefits of good care are every bit worth it. Physician Ira Byock is one of the leaders of the palliative care movement and may be its best known public exemplar. *Dying Well* (1997), the title of one of his books, makes the case that there really is no good death to be had but that one can die well with a bit of luck, courage, and planning. He recounts the case of patient Anne-Marie Wilson, a middle-aged woman diagnosed with colon cancer that had spread to her liver. When she explained her condition to her sister, the latter insisted on taking over the physical demands of care in her own home. A visiting hospice nurse and social worker were part of the care team. Early in her stay there, a number of issues common to home hospice care had to be addressed—suicidal tendencies (there were none); the added workload of cleaning and feeding; and the patient's fear of making the house unpleasant for others. But there were benefits to her being in a home. Byock says that "In contrast to an abrupt, easy death, dying of a progressive illness offers precious opportunities to complete the most important of life's relationships" (53). Anne-Marie had a reconciliation with a sister, and she lived just long enough to know that a new grandchild had joined the family. She died as the people who loved her gathered at the bedside to tell her so. "The concept of dying well can provide a vision of a realistic and affirmative goal for life's end" so that "in the midst of profound suffering, not only comfort, but also triumph and exhilaration, are possible" (246, 245). Dying well, Byock argues, is the best that can be had. Maybe not a victory, but the next best thing.[6]

Physicians like Byock know there are limitations to what they and scientific medicine can do. They, too, share in the hope and pain of their patients, and it is interesting how sometimes their accounts are clothed in a vocabulary of near-religious inflection. In her aptly titled *Final Exam* (2007), surgeon Pauline Chen writes of "M and M" conferences: doctors' self-assessment of the treatment of morbidity and mortality among patients in their care.

> M and M, our professional ritual centered on death, attempts to heal the rents in our professional fabric caused by patient deaths. There are few other opportunities for surgeons to discuss death. We may mention it in passing, but we steadfastly reserve discussion for the conference, which will give us, as a group, ritual absolution (118).

An appearance before one's colleagues is a ritual and a confessional moment. Chen had her own when one of her patients died in the ICU. Before a group of attending surgeons, residents, and medical students, she presented the details of her failed attempt at resuscitation, speaking in the third-person monotone that is customary on these occasions. Then came questions from the audience, questions that probed every aspect of the case and the details of her care. After every successful answer, she says, the questions became more pointed and specific. Finally, after much scrutiny and interrogation, the last question arrived. "'So Doctor,' asked the department chief, 'How do you account for this death?'" Before she could respond, the questioner volunteered that the unfortunate placement of the patient in a back corner of the ICU, a temporary space that was hard to monitor, contributed significantly to his death. The impassive audience of professionals murmured their agreement. Chen was excused and went back to her seat. "I had been officially absolved of guilt"; and later, "The department chief put his hand on my shoulder. 'Good job with that code,' he said. 'These things happen'" (116).

Chen is critical of the philosophy that at one time ruled in M and M conferences. "Death is rendered optional, and mortality becomes a quantifiable and correctable error. By defining death only as the result of errors, we erase the face of our patients and insert our own fiercely optimistic version of immortality" (119). That, she notes, is now changing. M and M conferences are incorporating end-of-life education and care into the confessional moment. What was once a ritual expiation for failure is becoming an opportunity to rethink medical death in larger, more humanistic terms.[7]

DYING WELL FOR EVERYONE

Everyone dies, including those who are not part of the white, middle-class majority. Much less is known about these other groups, although that is changing. Beginning in the 1970s, the terms "cultural awareness" and "cultural competence" began appearing in the literature of social services and health care. They were inspired, in part, by the work of Arthur Kleinman, an anthropologist and physician who wrote of cross-cultural health care (his focus then was on China) and cultural variations in what he called "health seeking behavior" (1978, 1988). The issue was the ability (and inability) of health care institutions to provide effective services to people who were not white, educated, familiar with the workings of large bureaucracies, and financially able to access them. He saw that differing cultural practices and expectations were often obstacles to good care; providers tend to be highly educated whites comfortable in the specialized subcultures of hospitals and clinics, while those seeking help are often members of ethnic and immigrant communities with distinctive medical beliefs and health practices of their own. Early attempts to train professionals in these newly discovered realities, however well intended, were less than successful. "Cultural sensitization" workshops to which token representatives of diverse communities were invited to speak were not usually well attended nor much appreciated by overworked staff committed to service practices they felt were adequate for everyone. This, however, is something else that is changing.[8]

Psychologist Ronald K. Barrett is one of the authoritative voices on death and end-of-life care among African Americans, who, he notes, are less trusting of hospitals and medical professionals than many whites. There are good historical reasons for their concerns, including the long history of segregation and a pattern of underfunded health care in black communities.[9] There are also cultural issues that make relations between black patients and hospital staff challenging for both sides.

African Americans in hospital settings often give exceptional value to the sanctity of life. They want it preserved at all costs, and discontinuing treatment is not usually an option. DNR (do-not-resuscitate) orders are not likely wanted, assisted suicide is out of the question, and death as the "secondary effect" of pain control medication is highly problematic. Pain, too, is an issue, and not just a biological one. Nobody wants anyone to suffer, but, Barrett writes, "For many Blacks, there's almost an acceptance, if not the glorification, of suffering as a good thing. If Christian, they identify with Christ's suffering on the cross as being the most noble of experiences" (2001: 1). This obviously influences how patients report pain and how accepting of it they may be at the end of life. Barrett adds that occasionally he hears discussions at funerals of the admirable way someone died, enduring pain and choosing to take the harder way out. That is a value likely to be present in any clinical discussion of pain control and recommended medications.

Death is also a family event, which in the black community means family in a broad sense. There is a pattern of "creating fictive kin by esteeming good friends into relatives and by adopting foster children, those defined as 'like a child to me.' These networks for many African American elderly who reside alone are strengthened with fellow church members or neighbors, who often become surrogate family" (2005: 254). All of that bears on family decision making. Quick medical choices are not easy because people expect to consult others, sometimes many others, and to be consulted in turn. Rushing a decision is disrespectful. Where family factions exist, much discussion and negotiation may be necessary. That can be uncomfortable for hospital staff, including those who want to "do the right thing" but operate under hospital rules with a different set of timelines and expectations. It is additionally complicated because many African Americans do not have advanced directives and their explicit wishes may not be known.

Finally, Barrett adds that "attention to spiritual needs should be a *necessary and essential* part of the continuum of care that is provided at the end of life. It is almost unthinkable that you can have an honest, intelligent discussion about death and dying unless you deal with the centrality of spirituality in the black experience" (2001: 1). Wakes or "sit ups" are common and part of the "going home service." Belief in an afterlife is common, and whereas many (but not all) whites think of life in linear terms, with death as its end point, many blacks think of it as a continuation in a life beyond this one. Not only a continuation, but a place not far away. The dead can be physically gone but they are present nevertheless.

SPIRITUALITY IN A POSTMODERN MODE

Attention to matters of the spirit is not just an African American concern. In much of contemporary medicine, and in end-of-life care specifically, spirituality in some sense keeps creeping back in. "Quality of life," as that phrase is used, includes professional attention to physical, psychological, social, and also spiritual well-being. Of the four, the spiritual is said to be the least developed professional skill, although it is widely held to be important (Jocham, Dassen, Widdershoven, and Halfens 2006). But what qualifies as "spiritual" and how should health care professionals respond to it? In a large survey of the medical literature, Williams (2006) describes a continuum of patient experience running from spiritual despair to spiritual work to spiritual well-being. Despair has to do with alienation, loss of self, and dissonance. It includes feelings of abandonment, uselessness, pain; criticism of God; relational problems; and "vague, child-like perception of afterlife." Spiritual work is manifest in forgiveness; self-exploration; a "search for balance"; reconciliation; the reframing of suffering; letting go; and requests to God. Spiritual well-being is described as connection, self-actualization, and consonance: appreciation for life, connection with loved ones, transcendence, self-love, satisfaction with a life's work, inner peace, and wholeness. Obviously, not all these features are present in any given patient's experience, nor are all expected to be.

So what do medical professionals try to do in this diffuse area of practice? Spirituality is a lively topic in some of the medical literature, having first appeared well over a decade ago in the nursing journals. That makes sense, given that nurses (along with chaplains) have the most contact with patients once diagnoses are made and treatment prescribed. Stern and James (2006) write of education on spirituality as "enabling" good professional skill. By that, they mean the capacity to recognize the implicit spirituality of human relationships; those with self, others, groups, communities "and the world, or the whole" (901). Within these relationships, practitioners are advised to focus on awareness-sensing, mystery-sensing, and value-sensing. Awareness means awareness of one's own death; mystery refers to unconditional trust and love; and value here means the values people bring to their dying, which, of course, will be different for different people. When they envision spiritual training for staff, Stern and James propose that these three "boxes" (their term) be filled in by examples from the staff's own, as well as the patient's, experiences. "The presence of examples in clinical practice suggests evidence of the expressions of spiritual needs, allowing nurses to help meet those needs" (903).[10]

If this all seems a bit vague, it is. Mitchell, Bennett, and Manfrin-Ledet (2006) advocate something more specific that they call "care mapping." A care map is a chart with the named patient in a central box that is connected to surrounding boxes. In the boxes, the nurse fills in information on patient nutrition, oxygenation, nutrition, elimination, comfort and hygiene, psychosocial situation, and "spirituality and culture." In the example given, a Ms. Arcenaux, age eighty-eight, is described. She has colon cancer, speaks Cajun French, and her family does not want her put on life support. Her spiritual assessment is based on her answers to three questions: What is a strength for you? (Prayer). Where can you get it? (From saying the Rosary.) Where can you get more? (Pray with me.) A middle-aged man dying of AIDS, also Catholic, said strength for him was prayer also; by prayer he meant music, and he could get more if someone with a guitar would play and sing hymns. In this instance, his student nurse was able to do just that. The patient then "summoned the faculty to his room at the end of the clinical day to express his appreciation for the time and caring the student exhibited. The patient spent quality time with his family and friends until his death" (369–70).

A more systematic approach to spirituality in health care is the transcultural ACCESS model developed by Aru Narayanasamy (2002) of the medical school at the University of Nottingham. "Transcultural nursing can be conceptualized as a strategy of caring which takes into account, with sensitivity and consideration, the individual's culture, specific values, belief and practices" (643). More than just cross-cultural sensitivity, it "attempts to bring out the moral and ethical imperatives inherent in caring professionals" (650). ACCESS is an acronym for assessment, communication, cultural negotiation and compromise, establishing rapport, sensitivity, and safety, specifically "cultural safety" in the provider-patient relationship. Narayanasamy explicitly links culture and spirituality, making the model "wholistic" in the grand sense. How one would work with dying people is no different than how one would treat other patients, including those of varying cultural backgrounds. "The interventions intended to meet patients' spiritual needs included respect for privacy, helping patients to connect, helping to complete unfinished business, listening to patients' concerns, comforting and reassurance, using personal religious beliefs to assist patients and observation of religious beliefs and practices" (846).

These are all useful recommendations, but how they can be implemented, or evaluated, is a major challenge. An earlier study by Narayanasamy and Owens (2001) found four distinctive professional styles among the nurses sampled. Some used what the authors called "personal approaches," and not surprisingly, these nurses were the least likely to use conventionally religious language with their patients. Instead, they explored questions of meaning and feelings, and they gave more time to each patient than did other nurses. Those who used a "procedural" approach were more impersonal. They were less likely to recognize spiritual anxieties unless specifically voiced, and then they made referrals to chaplains rather than attempting to advise patients themselves. Those who took a cultural approach acted on perceptions of minority or immigrant status. They took practical measures such as working with the family, seeking outside information on religious beliefs that were unfamiliar, and arranging for private prayer spaces and special foods. They were inhibited, however, by lack of support from peers and management, and felt they lacked the skills and resources to do much more. Finally, a small number were explicitly evangelical, especially if they thought they shared a religious point of view with a patient. "Likewise, in the case of very ill babies and infants some nurses in this study went out of their way to baptize them in order to fulfill their own religious beliefs" and while "they avoided direct coercion, they were apparently very persuasive in encouraging parents to consider baptism" even in families where baptism was not the practice (452–53). Needless to say, that raised ethical questions about how spiritual issues can be appropriately addressed. Given these difficulties and the variety of nursing practices, the authors concluded that "there is confusion over the notion of spirituality and the nurses' role related to spiritual care" (446).

That there is confusion should not come as a surprise, and I suspect the reason for it has less to do with training methods and bedside manners than the concept of "spirituality" itself. That it is vague and open ended is both a strength and weakness. The interesting history of this concept has a lot to do with its current imprecision (Bregman 2003, 2006). In 1799 the liberal Protestant theologian Friedrich Schleiermacher invoked it as a challenge to the confessional styles of church orthodoxy in his day. Spirituality, he argued, has little to do with the recitation of creeds; it is rather a cultivated sense of interiority combined with a taste for the mysterious and wondrous. Spirituality is about how one feels, not what is professed, and he thought it should be incorporated into all formal worship. Schleiermacher envisioned spirituality as a feature of traditional, denominational practice, an improvement on it rather than a thing apart. But the modern usage, an invention as recent as the 1980s, makes of spirituality something diffuse and divorced from institutional expression and formalized theology. Bregman sites one study of ninety-two current definitions grouped into categories as varied as relationship to God, transcendence unconnected with identifiable agencies, meaning and purpose in life, the individual life force, and a strange "not of the self" (8–11). One of the signal characteristics of most of these definitions is their ahistorical character; they are used without reference to cultural context and lack mooring to named traditions or historically familiar spiritual agencies. "'Spirituality' refers principally to some human realm or capacity and this realm or capacity or level of experience has been neglected and devalued in contemporary Western societies, say advocates on its behalf" (11).[11]

Any allegation of neglect and devaluation seems, however, an overstatement. Free-floating spirituality is abundant in the endless run of self-help books; in most twelve- or seven- or five-step self-improvement programs; in much daytime television programming; among enthusiasts of co-opted shards of Eastern and shamanistic practices; and on the wards among many of the nurses surveyed by Narayanasamy and Owens. The looseness of the term creates special difficulties for those who want to train medical staff in spiritual sensitivity. What specifically does one train for, what counts as "spiritual care," and how would one ever evaluate it? Walter (2002) writes that spirituality as an undifferentiated category creates opportunities, but it also burdens. Said one frustrated nurse in Narayanasamy and Owens's study: "Some family members needed more support than others, although with a young family I felt it was hard coping with them, [my] work, and my own emotions to try to meet their spiritual needs" (452). In a pluralistic culture such as that found in North America and, increasingly, in parts of Europe, not everyone is "spiritual," even in the postmodern sense. Some are committed to established religious institutions and their creeds. Those from immigrant communities have traditions of their own, with variable degrees of attachment, and with needs that native staff may not recognize or understand. And some people are not spiritual at all, either by creed or inclination. Diversity is what the modern world offers, even at the end of life. There may be as many "spiritual solutions" to the problem of dying as there are ways to make one's exit.[12]

IS DEATH THE END?

Some years ago I interviewed a number of people who told me they had died, traveled to the afterlife, and were allowed to return so they could complete their assigned tasks in this life. They were willing, even eager, to explain what awaits in the world to come. I described that vision and my interpretation of it at a meeting of the Society for the Anthropology of Religion, and during the question and answer period, an older woman in the back stood up. The room was immediately silent. Having never met her, I did not know she was a senior anthropologist whose work I had used in my teaching. "Young man," she intoned critically and pointed in my direction, "have you ever had a near-death experience?" I had not, I said, and added, unnecessarily, "I'm probably not the kind of person who would." The silence was thick. Finally Edith Turner waved in a gesture of futility and sternly pronounced judgment: "I didn't think so. You have never died."

She won the point. I was only a bystander in the world of the people I interviewed. I have not experienced their exposure, their terror that death is going to happen, right now. Nor have I ever sensed my body so damaged I can not live in it anymore; or, wondrously, that I can willfully abandon it for something or somewhere else. My interviewees described experiences that jolted them out of all normality and safety, and their need to make some sense of it was overwhelming. Thus they recalled a realm where the dead continue on, much as we do, only better; and the dramatic, fearsome journey that got them there. The issue Turner demanded I take seriously, given my never having experienced the immediacy of my own death, was why imagining a place like that should in any way be peculiar. I have to agree with her. Alister McGrath, a historical theologian, has commented that human reason persuades us that something is true, but human imagination persuades that it is real (2004: 185).

Do people really travel to an afterworld where deceased family, friends, and godly beings welcome them? Posing the question that way, as an either-or, yes-or-no proposition, does not seem to me helpful. Something more interesting is at work. In thinking about the near-death experience, the issue is less the dramatic imagery than why it seems appropriate and reasonable to those who have had the experience. Interesting in the details, even fascinating, these accounts are also familiar, within context even quite conventional. They draw on expressive imagery that is culturally familiar, yet intensely personal and creatively presented. These events are also existentially real, dramatically so; a more impressive encounter with "presence" in Orsi's sense is hard to imagine.

Émile Durkheim made a useful point about how things can be both real and true in the manner McGrath suggests. "A society," he said, "can neither create itself nor recreate itself without at the same time creating an ideal . . . it is the act by which it is periodically made and remade. . . . It is society which, by leading [the individual] within its sphere of action, has made him acquire the need for raising himself above the world of experience and has at the same time furnished him with the means of conceiving another" (1965 [1915]: 470, 471). Daily life in any particular time and place generates its Other, sometimes many Others, idealized conditions that exceed the mundane yet are recognizable because they incorporate it. Dying, I suggest, is an occasion for expressing hopes about that imaginary *habitus*, the one future everyone has in common.

This way of thinking about death, as culturally inspired mythmaking, has nothing to do with escapist fantasy or "denial," skeptics and the village atheist notwithstanding. (They have certitudes of their own.) I will make a guess at how mythmaking, Durkheim's refraction of the everyday in supramundane realities, is done. Recall Lambek's discussion of memory as a moral practice, particularly his reference to Aristotle's *poiesis* as poetic creativity. He contrasts this with Plato's more abstract notion of the good, a cosmic ideal toward which humans imperfectly grope. While "the good" in some grand sense is attractive, especially to academic theologians, anthropologists are more interested in "the practical judgments people make about how to live their lives wisely and well and, in the course of making them, do live their lives, albeit in the face of numerous constraints . . . [including] culturally dense under-standings of the complexities of judgment, the social context of commit-ments, and the fine line between happy and unhappy actions" (Lambek 2000: 315). Mythmaking is poetic creativity occurring in a practical context, and memory is one of myth's cogwheels—engaged in imaginative recalculation of the meaning of the past from the point of view of the present and, in light of that, a reestimation of future prospects. It is what the near-death experiencers do and what the rest us do, including the mythmakers of formal theology and of hierarchical religious bodies.

The loose agglomeration of features that typify the American way of death exemplifies that. I have argued that a very long historical trajectory underlies the diverse ways contemporary North Americans think about and respond to death. Sahlins's notion of a salvational ethos identifies that continuity. Within it, there is a continuous and active process of mythmaking and myth enact-ing, opportunities for poiesis, although no one thinks of it that way while at the bedside or when discussing "final arrangements" at the funeral company. The entire sequence of dying and being laid to rest ("rest" being another imaginative trope) is both artful and artifactual, arising not from nature or demands made by the supernatural but from our experience as social beings. The eclecticism of a pluralistic, individualistic democracy runs through it, from romantic depictions of the redeeming potential of nature to images sur-viving from older, scripturally inspired visions. The eternal future is not the opposite of the present or the remembered past; it is more of it, perfected and fulfilled. When death is at hand, there is little else the future can be.

Some among the traditionally minded might find that kind of future uninspiring, stripped as it is of angelic choirs, postmortem encounters, and final judgments and redemptions. They could complain that it is less than majestic, an imagined state of Otherness built of metaphors and images we already know. But I see a certain strength in that. If, as the ancient story goes, we were once innocent life-forms nakedly wandering in a primeval garden of abundance, blind to the world-making potential of our thoughts, we are such no more. We have become practitioners of poiesis. The mystery is not that we live and die—bugs and trees do that too. It is that we know the difference and do not have to take it, as it were, lying down. Eschatological imagining is a last defense against what nature is going to inflict on us. Given the odds, it seems a reasonable thing to do.

NOTES

CHAPTER 1. GETTING DEAD

1. How far that idea has reached and how much more complex it has become can be seen by comparing popular books on the topic (often shelved in the self-help sections of bookstores) with something substantial like Ira Byock's clinically based "dying well" (1997). Dying is not easy, nor is it a last "great" adventure in fulfillment, even in a hospice (Lawton 2000; Henig 2005).

2. Despite cautions against using the five-stage model as a prescriptive guide for managing individual dying, Kübler-Ross opens her discussion of acceptance by saying that if the dying person "has been given some help in working through the previously described stages" (1969: 123), he or she will have expressed feelings about anger and depression, mourned the losses to come, and entered a more satisfactory state of "quiet expectation" (124). Success, according to the model, occurs when the futile idea of struggle is abandoned and, almost Zen-like, the patient experiences less anxiety as the circle of interest narrows to a loved one or two who will be present to the end. She adds that some "patients who fight to the end, who struggle and keep a hope that makes it almost impossible to reach this stage of acceptance" (125) will never know that final peace. Their resistance is often abetted by family and medical staff who encourage them to be brave, strong, and unyielding. But raging against the failing light does them no good because "the harder they struggle to avoid the inevitable death, the more they try to deny it, the more difficult it will be for them to reach this final stage of acceptance with peace and dignity" (125). She does not explore whether "peace and dignity" might be attained by other means, through participation in a deeply felt liturgical performance, for example, or limited engagement with lifelong projects. Her interest is in promoting a highly privatized inner state, one uncoupled at the last from a lifetime of social and cultural moorings.

3. There are all kinds of contemporary ars moriendi, from bereavement cards to Web sites, but none more wickedly fun than Edward Gorey's book illustrating 26 ways to die, from A ("is for Amy who fell down the stairs") to Z ("is for Zillah who drank too much gin"). See and enjoy *The Gashlycrumb Tinies* (1997).

4. There is precedent for viewing control as an important aspect of American culture. Impulse control and self-mastery are long-standing religious and cultural themes, famously described by Max Weber in his study of the Protestant work ethic and ridiculed by literary figures as diverse as D. H. Lawrence and Allen Ginsberg. Control is a necessary component of individualism in both its utilitarian and expressive varieties (Bellah et al. 1985), as a feature of everyday speech (Lutz 1990), and in religiously inspired conceptions of the self (Csordas 1994).

5. Bernadin would most likely refer us to his own mythic preference, Paul's first letter to the Corinthians, chapter 15, which includes the well-known line, "Death, where is your victory? Death, where is your sting?" (verse 55). Biblical scholar Victor Furnish (1999) summarizes Paul's views, noting that he had a vision of the

whole person that included the body as well as an imperishable spirituality that is "known" by God and which at death "puts on" immortality much like someone putting on a new set of clothes (1999). Paul himself was working the mythic categories of his Mediterranean tradition to do just as Bernadin did, instruct his audience. The complexity of his teaching task is discussed by Dale Martin (1995). To paraphrase the latter (much too briefly), many working-class converts living in the port city of Corinth would have accepted uncritically the view that the body as a fleshly entity will be revived, reconstituted, and taken whole into heaven at the end of time. They were busy baptizing each other and their dead to make sure that happened. By contrast, educated converts would have dismissed rejuvenation of the flesh as superstition, insisting on familiar Greek philosophical arguments that at death the soul, a form of rarified matter, separates forever from flesh and rises alone into the heavens. Paul sought a middle way that became the mythopoetic centerpiece to his argument and gospel truth to believers for two millennia.

6. Viewed as a cultural ethos rather than religious doctrine, salvational beliefs and practices transcend denominationalism and formal affiliation. One need not "be religious" to draw on an ethos for guidance in private decision making. Writing of salvation as a formally religious theme, historian Paul Conkin describes in denominational terms what Sahlins would understand as an ethos. "Salvation doctrines are most critical for an understanding of the present varieties of Christianity in America. These are very complex. All orthodox Christians affirm the following doctrines: Humans in their natural capacity are so alienated from their personal and masculine god, so full of pride and ego, that they are incapable of giving their full consent or love to him. They are sinful. This does not mean that they are mean or immoral from the perspective of some system of moral philosophy or law, but that they cannot so act as to further the will and purpose of God. They are therefore doomed to a life apart from God, to some type of hell, unless God is merciful to them. Only he can save humans. . . . God has provided, at least for some people, a pathway back to reconciliation, even though no one deserves such salvation. Thus, salvation is an unearned gift" (1997: xi). Substitute here "citizen" for Christian, "community" for God, and lack of public spiritedness for sin, and the statement reiterates themes familiar to the written constitutions of Western liberal democracies. Or, dress the statement up with the jargon of pop psychology and it is still that old-time religion, proclaimed by Oprah and Dr. Phil rather than Billy Graham or Norman Vincent Peale.

7. This phrase, "canonic memory," comes from a theologian, but it does not seem out of place here. Michael Welker's view, similar in some ways to that of Sahlins, is that there exists in any culture a basic stock of texts that are worked and reworked as historical changes occur. "A canon and a canonic memory cannot be planned, launched, or constructed. They arise out of complex historical and cultural lives and patterns" (2000: 286). Canonic memory is tradition in an active sense, as a source of ideas for inventing responses to new perspectives and new problems. For example, Welker argues that the resurrection of Jesus is, for many in the Western world, Christian or not, a key feature of canonic memory. One does not have to believe in a literal resurrection, or even be Christian, to appreciate that the idea of "the Resurrection" shapes contemporary talk and imagery about what happens to us after we die. In that sense, a historically remote event can be a continuing influence

through very long chains of presentation and re-presentation, appearing in the present in forms as varied as near death experiences and expectations of being reunited with dead pets.

8. By "vernacular" I have in mind practices and expressions originating outside or at the margins of institutions historically associated with the "ownership" of death, namely denominational and, increasingly, medical ones. "The vernacular" implies its opposite, a dominant superstructure where claims to authority, precedent, and authenticity are made. Vernacular is what Geertz calls "local knowledge" (1983). It lives at the fringes of someone else's respectability. It is about diversity, proliferation, imagery, and talk that exceeds and overlaps official boundaries and expectations. In that sense, vernacular or "popular culture [is] a site where the struggle for hegemony unfolds" and "creative appropriations of cultural commodities by consumers" is the norm (Traube 1996: 132–33, 135). Popular death imagery in American culture is an instance of that, a rampant, weedy growth well documented by sociologist Michael C. Kearl (2001), who lists death themes and imagery in best-selling books, cinema, advertising, music, cyberspace, halls of fame, and postage stamps. Of the latter, he mentions a series of first-class stamps with the likenesses of Dracula, the Wolf Man, the Mummy, Frankenstein, and the Phantom of the Opera. All such imagery operates in what he tellingly calls a "transcendence market" populated by deceased "postselves" and eager consumers. His fascinating discussion may be found at http://www.trinity.edu/mkearl/death-3.html

9. Several years ago I was visiting the cemeteries of Colma, California, a few miles south of San Francisco, that town being a genuine necropolis unlike any other in America. My intent was to photograph a display of life-size Disney figures in the children's cemetery. Sadly, they had been vandalized and so removed. But an attendant suggested I look at a large tree nearby, one that had drawn crowds just the month before. As part of spring pruning, a sizeable limb had been sawed off, leaving a flat, oval cut. Within a day, sap formed on its surface in the shape, some said, of Mary's face, and for a time the tree was more popular than the headstones. Candles, flowers, personal objects, and prayers both oral and written were left by admirers until the sap merged and hardened, leaving no further suggestion of a human face. That was not a singular event. Within the last year or so of this writing, there have been sightings of sacred images, faces, and whole bodies on the wall of a freeway underpass in Chicago, in the shadows of a California church where new lighting fixtures had been installed, and on the surface of a bagel and also a pizza in several East Coast cities. These events, of course, are picked up by the tabloids and occasionally by the legitimate news organizations. Many scoff and joke, but apparently others find reassurance. In either case, these events enter into the lore of esoteric appearances and are, for those so inclined, legitimate moments of presence, occasions of wonder and possibility. A fascinating study of this phenomenon, and of the Internet as a means of promoting it, is that of Paolo Apolito (2005). He lists multiple locales of reported Marian sightings, including "furniture, plates, glasses, bathrooms, parlors, bedrooms, hospitals, shops, garages, soccer fields, streetlights, car dashboards, puddles . . . plates of spaghetti, tortillas, buns, cakes, pastries, pieces of fruit," and more (50). His point is that through the agency of the Internet, opportunities for presence are everywhere, virtual and otherwise.

10. The materiality of images of presence cannot be overstressed. Orsi discovered, for example, that in the post-World War II years, when all Catholic children were said to have a guardian angel, angelic representations were always near in coloring books, on the covers of communion missals, and on posters and postcards. In stories and visual imagery, they warned children of danger, "So angels were etched into children's imaginations by an implicit but deeply imbedded threat of physical harm and death . . . . [they] brought a particularly intense moral self-reflexivity into children's experience" (105, 106). So intense, in fact, that some children sat on only half their desk chair to better accommodate a seated angel. So personal that many believed their angel cried when they did, laughed when they did, and when they misbehaved, especially out of sight of others, their angel saw, knew, and turned aside in shame. Angels bore in angel bodies the hurt a child might feel but also felt the satisfaction of a task well done. It was rumored that some children, those who were very, very good, actually saw their guardian angel. All that, Orsi notes, must have been a significant compromise in personal autonomy, one's body and one's self intertwined with and given over to a heavenly Other. Not only a compromise, but sometimes a powerful visceral experience.

CHAPTER TWO: EXIT STRATEGIES

1. In his book, Heilman adopts a voice comparable to that of some other ethnographers who write of death: really two voices, complementing one another. Energetically committed to his faith, he nevertheless states that "I have tried to provide an answer [to questions about the religious meaning of death] that is different from one offered by those who speak purely in the language of faith and consolation." For those who would engage a religious tradition, yet want to retain critical sensibilities, the language of conventional pieties can be off-putting. It is his hope that the comparative, analytical language and procedures of good ethnography will appeal to them. "Thus, while my book aims to sociologically and anthropologically analyze Jewish custom and tradition following death, it also, in some small way, may cross over into the domains of religion if it simultaneously makes custom and tradition more transparent and attractive for contemporary Jews" (2001: 5).

2. Heilman is critical of the preference of some in the Jewish community for commercial body handling. Despite the expectations of their faith, "most Jews today rely on the services of a 'Jewish' funeral parlor, assuming the undertakers will do the job right. The 'Jewish' character of these parlors often is little more than their Jewish-sounding name, ownership, or willingness to supply some Jewish amenities. . . . they do not carry out *tahara*—indeed, frequently their employees, the ones who actually work on the body or handle the details, are not Jews" (2001: 33). But commercial services are easily available, and it can be hard to find volunteers for *chevra kaddisha* duty even where there is a large Jewish population. In the suburbs of east coast cities, he says, no one is "knocking down the doors" to wash and wrap bodies.

3. InnerNet Magazine, http://www.heritage.org.il/innernet/archives/chevra.htm (accessed April 22, 2005). Women's participation in the *chevra kaddisha* is discussed at the Jewish Orthodox Feminist Alliance Web site at http://www.jofa.org/social.php/life/illnessandde/chevrakadish.

4. How Gillman frames his understanding of the body, dead and alive, is as interesting as the theology on which he depends. He recognizes that there is a sense in

which all talk of souls as well as bodies is mythic but that this is not to say it is false. Myths are not the opposite of facts. They are narrative devices that string apparent facts together, suggesting the larger sense the individual facts only imply. Noah's ark, psychoanalysis, and the Big Bang are all myths not because they are untrue (although they might be) but because they explain more or less efficiently something otherwise inexplicable. It is in that sense that myths "work." Gillman puts it neatly: "Myths are the connective tissue that knit together the data of experience, thereby enabling these data to form a cohesive pattern and acquire meaning . . . the lines that connect the dots on the page so that we can see the bunny rabbit." The two-dimensional bunny is a line-myth, never a rabbit itself. So too with souls and resurrected bodies. Any debate about them cannot be about their existence since, unlike rabbits, their reality is terribly hard to prove. We can only know that as narratives they connect a few observable dots, and that helps some people get through hard times. Myths can be true when they enable meaning, untrue when they do not do that anymore; their truth is always social and contingent. Human hope is what makes them cosmic, and it is our only real weapon against death. Gillman's interesting discussion of this, from which I have quoted, is available at http://www.shma.com/jan02/neil.htm.

5. Justice's point is especially poignant post-Terry Schiavo. The decision to end artificial feeding and hydration for her was characterized either as an act of kindness on the part of her husband and doctors ("she wouldn't want to be like this") or a medical murder, as alleged by her parents, their priest, and an eager throng of political opportunists ("Terry wants to live"). Justice, of course, wrote about Hindu voluntary starvation well before Schiavo, but his insight from the Ganges gives context to that sad event. The American desire to supply food and water to the dying to the very end, a kindness that is touching, is as culturally generated and arbitrary as the Hindu preference for self-starvation is a noble and sacred one.

6. Dying out of sequence, as that is conventionally understood, creates one set of problems, as the death of this woman illustrates. But dying out of place creates problems as well. Stephen White (1997) describes the difficulties experienced by Hindu residents of the UK who wish to cremate family members in an open air, riverside pyre. There have been such cremations but they are rare. The possibility of scattering ashes in the Thames after removal from a licensed crematorium was considered by authorities in 1971 but denied. Permission was given instead for scattering "in certain tidal and estuary waters with a license from the Ministry of Agriculture, Fisheries and Food" (145). Edinburgh was the first British city to authorize riverside scattering.

7. My thanks to colleague Jeanelle Taylor, who brought the society to my attention. Hecht's fascinating study examines a number of issues associated with the intellectual life of nineteenth-century France, many of which generated controversy then and still do: the reality of souls; the challenges of science to religion and religion to science; the proper role of religious institutions in a democratic polity; the humanist, often politically leftist stance of many early anthropologists; and the uses and misuses of science, including anthropology in public policy and discourse.

8. Beyond personal desire and political partisanship, these nineteenth-century intellectuals and their followers were inspired by an influential group of thinkers known as *physiocrats*. About the time of the French Revolution, the latter called for

development of a "moral science," essentially a variety of laissez faire economics, to replace older feudal ways of production. But their economic theories, deduced from dense metaphysical cogitations about the nature of human nature, suggested more than just economic reform. The moral sciences would be something new, a rational basis for taking control of human affairs through naturalistic observation, rational calculation, and enlightened public policy. They would include fields of inquiry such as economics, psychology, business management, and statistics, all data based. The payoff would be a true "science of man" that would generate greater happiness and a harmonious social order. Such goals were now within grasp.

9. For readers who want more, consult Mim's clinical account. Like all animals, we are a bag of water, proteins, fats, and minerals, and what remains of us is food for other living things. If a body is left minimally protected above the ground, there is a feeding sequence of insects and molds determined by local flora and fauna. Knowing about that is useful to forensic investigators trying to determine an approximate time of death. Ants typically arrive first, followed by various species of flies and beetles. They all have their preferred conditions of decay, and that determines where they settle down at table. Predators such as rats, dogs, and birds arrive early too, cleaning off bones and scattering parts where insects and mold spores will eventually find them. If in a casket underground, microbial action on the body generates gas, mostly hydrogen sulfide and methane, and gas pressure swells the torso, forcing the tongue and eyes to protrude. Decay proceeds more slowly in a coffin, usually lasting several months. "Bones and teeth are even more resistant, and within a year or so all that is left is a skeleton. The bones are still a bit greasy and contain organic material . . . [and it] takes forty to fifty years for them to become dry and brittle in a coffin or in fairly dry soil" (Mims 1999: 123). Ironic it is that our teeth, so subject to decay and loss during life, outlast the rest of us. Can embalming prevent this unappealing spectacle? "Yes, no and maybe," says Kenneth Iserson (2001) in his encyclopedic study of forensics. The critters that feed on our remains do not like the taste of embalmer's chemicals. They are applied mostly to the body parts put on view, the face, head, neck, and hands. The rest is subject to the usual predation. For more detail on all of this, try Mary Roach's aptly titled *Stiff: The Curious Lives of Human Cadavers* (2003).

10. Two Poe stories that come to mind—there are probably others—are "The Fall of the House of Usher" and "The Cask of Amontillado." Poe also wrote an essay on the topic, "The Premature Burial." In the Usher story, a woman buried alive returns to destroy her obsessed brother and their family castle, her revenge for wrongful consignment to a cellar tomb. In the premature burial piece, Poe was prescient of what was to come in cases of coma and persistent vegetative state: "The boundaries which divide Life from Death are at best shadowy and vague. Who shall say where the one ends, and where the other begins? We know that there are diseases in which occur total cessations of all the apparent functions of vitality, and yet in which these cessations are merely suspensions, properly so called. They are only temporary pauses in the incomprehensible mechanism. A certain period elapses, and some unseen mysterious principle again sets in motion the magic pinions and the wizard wheels. The silver cord was not for ever loosed, nor the golden bowl irreparably broken. But where, meantime, was the soul?" Out of such fears, a Society for the Prevention of Premature Burial was organized in the 1820s (Powner et al. 1996).

Nor was fear of live burial unique to the Victorians. Bruce Gordon (2000) cites examples of the terror it inspired in medieval Europeans.

11. Schiavo commentary is now a cottage industry, as anyone using her name in a Google search knows. I use Hook and Mueller (2005) as my map through this saga. A special issue of the journal *Death Studies* (vol. 30, 2006) focuses on Schiavo with articles on family care giving, disability rights, surrogate decision making, and medical ethics. A timeline of the case with links to many legal and medical documents is at www.miami.edu/ethics/schiavo/timeline (verified February 2, 2006).

12. A persistent vegetative state (PVS) is not a coma. According to the National Institute of Neurological Disorders and Stroke of the National Institutes of Health: "A *coma* is a profound or deep state of unconsciousness. An individual in a state of coma is alive but unable to move or respond to his or her environment. Coma may occur as a complication of an underlying illness, or as a result of injuries, such as head trauma. A *persistent vegetative state* (commonly, but incorrectly, referred to as 'brain-death') sometimes follows a coma. Individuals in such a state have lost their thinking abilities and awareness of their surroundings, but retain non-cognitive function and normal sleep patterns. Even though those in a persistent vegetative state lose their higher brain functions, other key functions such as breathing and circulation remain relatively intact. Spontaneous movements may occur, and the eyes may open in response to external stimuli. They may even occasionally grimace, cry, or laugh. Although individuals in a persistent vegetative state may appear somewhat normal, they do not speak and they are unable to respond to commands." Accessed February 3, 2006 at http://www.ninds.nih.gov/disorders/coma/coma.htm.

13. The concept is paralleled by that of "social birth," and for about the same reasons. "The notion of social birth is useful because it highlights the gradual, malleable, and contested processes through which personhood is often ascribed. . . . The willingness to anthropomorphize or grant social personhood may be contingent on factors—such as kin relations, physical health and vitality, parenting expectations, spiritual considerations, economic wellbeing—that have little to do with the ontological status of fetuses or infants. Delaying or denying personhood may justify abortion, infanticide, or infant neglect" (Kaufman and Morgan 2005: 321).

14. Video clips showing Schiavo are available at several sites. Those quoted here are http://www.blogsforterri.com/video.php and http://www.sacramentolifechain.org/ schiavo.html respectively (accessed February 18, 2006). See Arthur L. Caplan, *The Case of Terri Schiavo: Ethics at the End of Life* (2006) for a comprehensive overview.

15. My source for all the BlogsforTerri quotes in this paragraph is Diane Waldman (2006). Her online article, one of several perceptive discussions of the visual aspects of the Schiavo case, appears in *Jump Cut* 48 (Winter 2006), www.ejumpcut.org. I commend it and the other articles there to readers interested in the power of visual images.

16. Apolito puts it this way: "Every image captured is an actualization of an infinite chain of virtual depictions of the divine; but a divine that is immanent to the Web, produced by it and embedded in it. The divine offline, with its well-defined properties and boundaries, evaporates from the images on the Web, vanishes as an otherworldly point of reference, and is replaced by a self-referential universe of the virtual divine" (2005: 181–82). So too with the Schiavo clips, the conundrum of an artificially maintained body lacking apparent agency is presented electromechanically as

willful, as agency seeking release from bodily entrapment. Like the apparent magic of sonograms and CAT scans, the clips of a seemingly responsive Terri reveal obvious truths to those willing to see them, truths lost on skeptics who will not "read" the images for what they virtually are.

17. The examiner's report is at http://news.findlaw.com/hdocs/docs/schiavo/61305autopsyrpt.pdf (accessed August 23, 2005). The autopsy report is at www.miami.edu/ethics2/schiavo/061505-autopsy.pdf (verified February 2, 2006). There is no likelihood that Schiavo would have "awakened" from fifteen years in a PVS, something the Schindlers seemed to know. They talked of rehabilitation but also of taking her home for private comfort care. In 1994 a Multi-Society Task Force of the American Academy of Neurology determined that the chances of moderate to good recovery by patients in a PVS for 3 months is 1 percent; after 6 months, 0 percent. No patient has been known to recover spontaneously after one year. The Task Force statement is available in the *New England Journal of Medicine* 330 (1994): 1499–1508.

18. The Schindlers' press release was issued through terrisfight.org, June 16, 2005 (accessed August 23, 2005).

19. MSNBC news items of March 30, 2005, accessed at http://msnbc.msn.com/id/7335806/ on February 21, 2006.

20. Related expressions such as "death with dignity" and "natural death" are, like "quality of life," vague, even abstractly romantic. They come out of the "right to die" movement and are used by those hostile (sometimes for good reason) to the technological prolongation of dying. Their limitation is imagining that "death under such circumstances [can be] envisioned as a peaceful, painless, technologically unencumbered, more humane process. No guarantee exists, however, that this will be the case. In fact, many natural deaths can be quite painful and far from peaceful. They may be less prolonged, but they are not necessarily easier" (Kleespies 2004: 18–19). Physician and dying-guru Sherwin Nuland remarks simply that dying is an unpleasant business, with no dignity in it: "the quest to achieve true dignity fails when our body fails" (1993: xvii).

21. Address of John Paul II to the Participants in the International Congress on "Life Sustaining Treatments and Vegetative State: Scientific Advances and Ethical Dilemmas," http://www.vatican.va (accessed February 23, 2006).

22. The Schiavo case broke no new legal ground, but as a media event it became an attack on the "right to die" precedent. Commenting on the legal implications for medicine, lawyer George Annas wrote in the *New England Journal of Medicine* that it would not be wise to legislate on the patient's right of refusal as it pertains to specific diseases. "'Erring on the side of life' in this context often results in violating a person's body and human dignity in a way few would want for themselves. In such situations, erring on the side of liberty—specifically, the patient's right to decide on treatment—is more consistent with American values and our constitutional traditions" (2005: 1754).

CHAPTER 3. THE BODY AS RELIC

1. An additional attempt at clarification was made in 1981 by a presidential commission that proposed the following: "An individual who has sustained either

(1) irreversible cessation of circulatory and respiratory functions, or (2) irreversible cessation of all functions of the entire brain, including the brain stem, is dead. A determination of death must be made in accordance with accepted medical standards" (Jonsen 1998: 243). That commission stayed close to what it saw as standard clinical practice rather than attempting a definition of what death is in principle. The literature on this topic is large, wide ranging, daunting, and full of contentious discussion but an excellent overview is Margaret Lock, *Twice Dead* (2002). See also *The Definition of Death: Contemporary Controversies* (1999), edited by Stuart Youngner et al. Of related interest is a recent review of arguments for brain death as a sufficient definition of death generally. Chiong (2005) suggests that any such idea is inadequate; no definition will ever be possible as long as medical researchers and ethicists keep looking for a single, specific, namable criterion that can be used as a bedside test. Life, he says, is really a cluster of characteristics including but not limited to consciousness; spontaneously maintained vital functions; behavior that is responsive to the environment; internal organization; resistance to decay; and the ability to grow, persist, and reproduce. Any of these can be lost or seriously compromised, yet life can continue, at least for a time. It is plausible, then, that "in the course of dying, many people pass through a borderline state in between being determinatively alive and determinatively dead. . . . We may then look upon competing criteria for death not as attempts to state necessary and sufficient conditions for death, but instead as proposals for sharpening the distinction between life and death. Presumably there is no uniquely admissible cutoff" (26–27).

2. An instance from popular culture well illustrates the point. When issued in 1989, the French-Canadian film *Jésus de Montréal* became something of a hit and has been a cult favorite since. The story is of a group of unemployed actors asked by the priest of a cash-strapped church to stage nightly reenactments of the Easter story for tourists. The performances go well and the parish is restored to solvency. But the actors are changed. Imperceptibly they become the characters they were hired to play. Everyday life becomes a reenactment of episodes from the gospels amid the noise, corruption, and secular sophistication of modern Montreal. Midway through, it becomes apparent that there is going be a resurrection scene; the only surprise is how it will be portrayed. Like the original, the Jesus figure dies, victim of a crowd rush. He later expires in the ER where the physician has a request. He wants to take body parts and rush them off to other hospitals where they will bring restored life and healed vision to those who get them. That is Québec filmmaker Denys Arcand's solution, one modern imagining of resurrection and salvation—sacrificial transfer of body parts to needy strangers. Death is cheated when the "gift of life" is shared.

3. Available at http://www.donormemorial.org. Statistics cited in this paragraph may be found at http://organdonor.gov and http://unos.org, accessed August 24, 2005.

4. According to the Funeral Consumers Alliance, "1. Embalming is rarely required by law. The Federal Trade Commission and many state regulators require that funeral directors inform consumers that embalming is not required except in certain special cases. Embalming is required when crossing state lines from Alabama, Alaska, and New Jersey. Three other states—Idaho, Kansas, and Minnesota—require embalming when a body is shipped by common carrier.

2. Embalming provides no public health benefit, according to the U.S. Centers for Disease Control and Canadian health authorities. Hawaii and Ontario forbid embalming if the person died of certain contagious diseases. Many morticians have been taught, however, that embalming protects the public health, and they continue to perpetrate this myth," http://www.funerals.org/faq/embalm.htm, accessed March 6, 2006. Professional embalmers wear rubber gloves and protective clothing (required by OSHA), and I have seen autopsies performed by technicians wearing moon suits. Handling a corpse is usually safe, but questions can be raised about the fluids pumped into and out of one. Blood drained from a corpse commonly goes into the local sewer system. With each burial several gallons of highly toxic embalming fluid, mostly formaldehyde and methyl alcohol, go below ground. The deceased is in a sealed casket, which is often in a vault, but no container is forever. Vaults have weep holes in the bottom for drainage, so eventually something may get into groundwater. Whether that is dangerous or not depends on local hydrological conditions and the chemicals themselves. Arsenic was used in all embalming during and after the Civil War but was banned about 1900. Many historic cemeteries have high concentrations of arsenic, which does not degrade and remains as a health and environmental threat. Cremation is cleaner and crematorium smokestacks have scrubbers to control air pollution.

5. http://www.dartefuneralhome.com/Embalming_-16913.html, accessed August 27, 2005. A lively popular account of this, and "lively" is the correct word, is Mary Roach, *Stiff* (2003), especially chapter three, "Life After Death, On Human Decay and What Can Be Done About It." As she puts it, embalming "will make a good-looking corpse of you for your funeral, but it will not keep you from one day dissolving and reeking, from becoming a Halloween ghoul. It is a temporary preservative, like the nitrites in your sausages. Eventually any meat, regardless of what you do to it, will wither and go off" (82). In addition to the work of Laderman (1996, 2003), an interesting review of the history of the American funeral industry is Troyer (2007). He describes an unlikely intersection of interests in the mid- to late nineteenth century—the popularization of photography, rise of the railroad industry, and improved embalming practices—which led to the creation of the durable corpse as a consumer product. They generated an "embalmed vision" (photography) which could "circulate" or travel distances (via railroads, now airlines) when, prior to that, bodies were usually buried within a day or two of death depending on the climate and the season of the year.

6. My source for much of this material is a series of articles by Jack Adams, "Restoring Emaciated Remains: Parts 1–7," appearing in *Dodge Magazine* from March 1998 to June 1999. The Dodge Company of Cambridge, Massachusetts, is a major supplier of chemicals and equipment to the funeral industry, and their magazine, intended for in-house professionals, dates to 1921. The company founder established a school for embalmers in 1907 and pioneered continuing professional education. Adams's comment is in Part 5, January 1999, 21. My thanks to Chris Robinson of the company for making the articles available.

7. Holloway (2002: 131). Examples of Van Der Zee's work are online at http://www.lightfactory.org/jameszee.htm, accessed March 9, 2006. A more complete collection is in Van Der Zee, Dodson, and Billops (1978). He was "discovered" in 1969 after which the Metropolitan Museum of Art arranged an exhibit. For a history

of African American cemeteries, see Roberta Hughes Wright and Wilber B. Hughes III, *Lay Down Body* (1996).

8. Photography is becoming a standard feature of the funeral as well. The reception is an opportunity for displaying a montage of life events alongside personal items, from military uniforms to handicrafts to published books. In addition, some video and funeral companies advertise digital recording of funeral services, including online streaming, if that is wanted. One promotes its "customized memorial web page with photo album, same day setup and availability online for a duration desired by family members. Private or Public broadcast of the services. The recording of the Funeral ceremony on CD-ROM or VHS" (http://www.online-funeral.com/). Another offers "Video montages (still photographs transferred to VHS videotape) [which] can be produced, showing a collection of photo or video images of the deceased from his/her life. Set to soothing music, these productions are perfect for showing at wakes and viewings and are great mementos for the family, because they allow rare or unique family heirloom photos to be shared with other relatives and friends" (http://www.allvid.com/funerals.html). One industry rationale for these services is that they make the memorial event available to those unable to attend (sites accessed March 9, 2006).

9. One other medical use of body imagery, unusual in its own way, can be accessed at http://www.nlm.nih.gov, the homepage of the National Library of Medicine. Once there, look for the Visible Human Project. The project is described as "the creation of complete, anatomically detailed, three-dimensional representations of the normal male and female human bodies. Acquisition of transverse CT, MR, and cryosection images of representative male and female cadavers has been completed." Behind that abstract language is a peculiar story, well told in the German documentary film *Blue End*, directed by Kaspar Kasics. Joseph Paul Jernigan, a convicted murderer, was executed by lethal injection in a Texas prison in 1993. He volunteered his body "to science" without being told what was planned. His corpse was quartered horizontally, each section frozen in a block of blue gel, and shipped to a research laboratory in Colorado, where he was sliced and photographed one millimeter at a time from head to toe. The National Library of Medicine site has no mention of him other than an acknowledgment that the body parts on display, digitally enhanced, once belonged to a prisoner. Jernigan is their man, nameless and without history, mentioned only in euphemisms as the world's first fully digitized human being. He is immortalized, in a sense, in cyberspace. A review of the film is in the British journal *Mortality* 8 (February 2003): 97–99.

10. There are, of course, many variations. The Catholic Church, for example, specifies three elements for a complete funeral rite. A Vigil for the Deceased is what many would consider "the funeral"; it includes hymns, scripture readings, a homily, prayers, and a blessing. It can be held at a funeral company or church. A Funeral Mass adds the Eucharist and requires removal of secular symbols such as those associated with nationality or fraternal organizations. The Rite of Committal is performed at the grave site with the casket present. A reception usually follows.

11. A concise summary of federal action on consumer issues is available in Laderman (2003: 119–69). Mitford complained that funerals cost too much, and subsequent government regulation has not changed that. Funerals can be expensive, and the add-ons, as with buying a new car, run the price up dramatically. Further,

consumers are making a major purchase exactly when they are most vulnerable to sales pressure. And needless to say, comparison shopping is a rarity. Laderman notes, however, that "consumer-driven modifications in the specifics of disposal have led to increasing customization of ceremonies to suit the individual traits of the deceased and the tastes of the family" (2003: 139).

12. http://www.funerals.org/, accessed April 1, 2006.

13. In fact, there are "transgressions" at Carlisle and probably at other ecocemeteries as well. Families occasionally "tidy up" their green burial by pulling weeds, trimming grass, leaving mementos, and inadvertently trampling adjacent graves. June Carswell, the cemetery director, discussed with me the care and tact she uses to convince customers that green means green, and that is what they signed up for. That is not a problem at the old Holywell Cemetery in Oxford, however, which was filled to capacity many years ago. Its paths divide the cemetery into quarters, and they are treated as if in field rotation, one quarter cleaned off each year. The rest grow wild, providing homes for pheasants, rabbits, hedgehogs, butterflies, foxes, and even the occasional deer. The idea, as with Carlisle, is to create, in urban settings, habitats friendly to wildlife.

14. *San Francisco Chronicle*, August 22, 2004. The Memorial Ecosystems Web site is at http://www.ramseycreekpreserve.com/index.html, accessed April 6, 2006. Green promoters are fond of quoting statistics on the wastefulness of traditional burial, and they all use the same numbers from an unnamed source. Based on yearly consumption, the numbers are 827,060 gallons of embalming fluid sent underground along with 90,272 tons of steel and 2700 tons of copper and bronze in caskets; 1,636,000 tons of reinforced concrete and 14,000 tons of steel in vaults; and 30 million board feet of hardwood (much of it from tropical forests) in caskets.

15. Three Ladies in White including the founder, Frances Coover, are shown purposively hiking into Montana's Rattlesnake Wilderness in the *New York Times*, March 30, 2007. There is a Green Burial Council that promotes environmentally responsible burial and scattering practices and they are developing a certification program for green burial organizations and promoters. But not all burials have to be land-based. For those with a more aquatic orientation, www.eternalreefs.com offers another choice. They will mix your ashes into cement (or let someone who cares about you do the mixing) and pour it into a mold to harden as an "eternal reef." Reefs are of various sizes, two to over four feet high and shaped like half a hollow ball, with sizable holes for fish circulation. A charter boat takes reefs and families into the waters of the Atlantic and Gulf coasts for a "placement." Prices range from $1,000 to $5,000 and for that survivors get the trip, a GPS location, and a memorial certificate. The reef itself bears a small bronze plaque with a name. The service is advertised for those who want "to give something back to the earth. Helping to repair and restore the ocean environment is a permanent mark and legacy to honor their time and existence."

16. "A Family Undertaking" is available at Fanlight Productions, http://www.fanlight.com. Lisa Carlson wrote *Caring for the Dead: Your Final Act of Love* (1998), the bible of the DYI movement. Thomas Lynch's remark was made in a 1997 National Public Radio interview and is posted at http://www.npr.org/programs/death/971208.death.html

CHAPTER 4. SOULSCAPES

1. The percentage of those who subscribe to some version of the afterlife has been going up over the last several decades. Greeley and Hout note that "In 1998, 82 percent of American adults reported to the GSS [General Social Survey] that they believe in life after death" (1999: 815). By affiliation, that included 86 percent of Protestants, 83 percent of Catholics, 56 percent of Jews, 68 percent of other affiliations, and 63 percent with no organizational preference. Figures for the early 1970s were about ten percentage points lower.

2. Dialogues with the dead are literally an everyday event. Vitebsky notes that in a village of 500 people, they can occur as often as five times aweek, even ten times in one day. They can happen anywhere—along a path, in a house, or at the cremation ground. "According to the mood of the dialogue and the degree of their involvement, [participants] may squat on their haunches and huddle intently around her [the shaman] arguing vehemently with the dead, weep and embrace her, or else come and go to the edge of the proceedings and interpose a careless remark. A sequence of dialogues can last up to several hours and range from casual gossip to extremes of emotion which I could never learn to observe while remaining unmoved. But dialogues with the dead are not all tears: they often include moments of good humour and of obscene joking amidst uproarious laughter" (1993: 5–6).

3. The Sora are not fools. They can distinguish a convincing shamanistic performance from an inept one and know that shamans can be, on occasion, charlatans. One, says Vitebsky, "was known for the rest of his life as 'Oops!' [Gege] because a crab he was hiding for a conjuring trick popped out his pocket before its cue" (1993: 21). Sora are of course interested in who their shamans are, but more important, they respect solid "shamanship" just as anyone might respect good musicianship. The talent, like any other, is distributed throughout the population but some people are better at it than others.

4. For an alternative interpretation, see Elaine Pagels, *Beyond Belief: The Secret Gospel of Thomas* (2003). In this surprise best seller, she argues that the hostile depiction of a doubting Thomas in the Gospel of John is but one side of an acrimonious debate among early Christians, the other side advanced by Gnostic thinkers who circulated a competing Gospel of Thomas. Their agenda, too, was cultivation of an interior state of religious awareness, but one not bound by the emerging orthodoxy that John so revered. Clearly, John won the argument, but of late the gnostics are getting another hearing.

5. I appreciate that I am hopping over huge chunks of historical and interpretive territory in just a few paragraphs, but I think this claim is generally true: in the modern (as well as traditional) Christian understanding, "belief" is held to be a type of knowledge that is (1) superior to empirical, rational, evidentiary "truths" and (2) a property of the individual's psyche. Williams James spotted it a century ago in his classic *Varieties of Religious Experience* (1936) when he wrote that in the instance of religion it is mood and instinct that lead us, while intelligence is their follower. Nearly a century later, David Lyon, in his lively and challenging *Jesus in Disneyland*, describes the contemporary face of James's "impulsive belief": "The idea of making up your personal bricolage of beliefs, choosing what fits and what does not, appears to be a popular mode of religiosity or spirituality today, especially in North America. And what goes on in such mixed religious realms, or in the religious regions that lie

well beyond the conventional, relates increasingly to religious identity. A careful sociological listening to contemporary voices reveals a trend towards the more general sacralization of the self" (2000: 18). Contemporary belief, faith, and spirituality are approaching something more akin to emotional solipsism, well labeled by Robert Bellah (1985) as "expressive individualism."

6. Native American religions, according to Vine Deloria (1973), challenge the claimed universalism of Western Christianity, but on grounds different from those I am discussing here. As he sees it, belief as understood within Christianity is peculiar in that it is event-dependent, representing cosmic history as a linear progression from an originating moment of creation to the realization of the Christian deity's purposes at the end of time, a process paralleled in miniature in the personal lives of many followers and especially converts. Key events throughout that cosmic unfolding are taken as proof by believers of the doctrines they affirm. On this, Deloria may be right. What kinds of beliefs would Christians affirm without the Resurrection, Jews without the Exodus, Muslims without The Prophet's (p.b.u.h.) hijra to Medinah? By contrast, he says, belief among many traditional Native American peoples never depended on the veracity of past events. They emphasize instead the order and integrity of the natural world, irrespective of how it may have begun or may end. "In the Indian tribal religions, man and the rest of creation are cooperative and respectful of the task set for them by the Great Spirit. In the Christian religion both are doomed from shortly after [the Fall] until the end of the world" (1973: 96). Whether or not Deloria is overstating the case in assuming as much commonality among traditional tribal religions as he does, his point is still worth taking. Not all cultures conceptualize belief as do adherents of the three major religions that came out of the Middle East. Mental endorsement of ancient propositions inherited from arcane debates centuries old, or affirmation of ancient events not easily verified except by scriptural sources, is not the only way to think about belief, including belief in the reality of the afterlife.

7. What Vitebsky may have found among the Sora is a culturally specific way of experiencing grief, one quite unlike anything in Western practice. American cultural orthodoxy of so-called "normal grief" calls on the mourner to disassociate himself or herself from the deceased relatively quickly. The "reality testing" that many authorities on grief say is necessary includes things like viewing a cosmetically prepared corpse and giving away the deceased's clothes or toys, said to be psychologically healthy ways of convincing ourselves that the dead really are irretrievably gone. It can be pathological, in Freud's model of unresolved mourning gravitating toward melancholy, if we cannot find our way through death's thicket of suffering and discover a new set of interests that restore us to our normal selves. However that is accomplished, by five-step programs or by prayer, survivors are expected to do some serious "grief work" and then, as we say, "move on." This seems to work because it is an enactment of *our* cultural assumptions, which view the dead as truly extinguished and beyond our reach forever, something the Sora know is manifestly untrue. Death, in their experience, is not the end of everything at all but an exceptionally difficult point in the individual's trajectory of being. What is different among them is that things said and unsaid prior to a death can be voiced, and the deceased can be counted on to carry their end of the conversation. As they are still around us, how could it be otherwise?

8. My use of the term soulscape is an extension of Appadurai's well-known formulation of ethno-, techno-, media- and ideoscapes in contemporary globalization theory. "The suffix -*scape* allows us to point to the fluid, irregular shapes of these landscapes" that "are not objectively given. . . . rather, that they are deeply perspectival constructs, inflected by the historical, linguistic, and political situatedness of different sorts of actors: nation-states, multinationals, diasporic communities, as well as subnational groupings and movements (whether religious, political, or economic), and even intimate face-to-face groups. . . . [Actors engage these -scapes] in part from their own sense of what these landscapes offer" (2002: 49–50). Modern landscapes of eternal repose are more than psychological fantasies or sociological collective representations. They are meaningful places, advanced as alternatives to older, historical (usually medieval) models. Their diversity of form, as well as their general failure to inspire widespread consent, is what one would expect in a postmodern world of "fundamental disjunctures," as Appadurai calls it.

9. "The doctrine that the human soul is immortal and will continue to exist after man's death and the dissolution of his body is one of the cornerstones of Christian philosophy and theology" says the *New Catholic Encyclopedia* (1967, 13: 464). The more recent *New Dictionary of Catholic Spirituality* (1993), issued by the Order of St. Benedict, acknowledges the traditional Platonic view but then moves to more recent doctrinal statements coming out of Vatican II, noting that "Whatever the term, what is agreed is that human beings are spirit as well as flesh. Yet we have no experience at all of this spiritual aspect of ourselves except as rooted in our physicality, in our bodies" (1993: 908). They conclude, somewhat startlingly, that despite the overwhelming presence of pagan Platonism in two millennia of Christian theorizing, "modern anthropology [with its focus on the body] is nearer to biblical thought than the intervening nineteen centuries of Christian tradition" (910). "Biblical thought," as they put it, apparently did not favor the church's mind/body dualism. One has to wonder why, on a subject as important to believers as the soul, the views of the pagan Plato managed to trump the Holy Bible for two millennia. Perhaps there is a lesson there for theological purists of all kinds.

10. The complex mixture of belief about souls in various pagan sources; in ancient Jewish thinking; among Diaspora Jews throughout the Ancient world; in the multiple forms of early Christianity; and as interpreted by Paul, Augustine, and early church theologians is an incredibly complicated story. There was never a "party line" on this topic either among the first generations of Christians (who were mostly Jews simply calling themselves followers of "the way") or in subsequent generations of believers. A very readable overview is Osmond, *Imagining the Soul, A History* (2003). The diversity of opinion among people who had direct contact with Paul is well covered in Martin, *The Corinthian Body* (1995). For a fascinating interpretation of Paul's views on the soul, body, and death, an interpretation that shows him to be a challenging first-century intellectual as well as an apostle, see Crossan and Reed (2004: 341–45). A related idea is resurrection, which is for most Christians the central tenant of their religion. Resurrection theories were common in the ancient world, they were not a uniquely Christian invention, and generally they held that resurrection is reserved for a lucky few such as heroes or leaders. Death for everyone else is less glorious. In early Jewish sources (Genesis, Psalms, Isaiah), all who die descend to a shadowy realm under the earth called Sheol to

remain as woeful spirits trapped in gloomy inactivity forever. In the postexile period, Diaspora Jews familiar with Greek philosophical debates began to imagine a general resurrection, a Last Judgment at the end of time when all would be called forth to answer for how they lived (Bremmer 2002). The founding figure of Christianity apparently shared that common Jewish view, having said very little about death or an afterlife during his preaching career (Meier 2000). He focused instead on a soon-to-arrive "kingdom of God," something imminent and transformative of this life now. Yet within a generation, his followers began promoting their view of personal resurrection, a theme developed in their liturgies and their accounts of Easter. Paul is the most prominent of these advocates, and his doctrines, as enunciated in 1 Corinthians 15, have had great durability. Three centuries later, when Christianity emerged as the state religion of Rome and empire, notions of individual resurrection as well as reconstitution of the whole body in paradise came into vogue. By that time, the movement was far removed from its Palestinian origins and inflected with Roman theologizing and the institutional church's needs for foundational dogmas. Souls are still represented as substantive "things," stuff or properties inside us just as Plato and Aristotle said, and they are closely associated with the resurrected body as early Roman and medieval theologians claimed (Bynum 1992, 1995). They are the essence of the self and the only part of us that will outlast our limited time on earth.

11. Lachman (2004) argues that Swedenborg's heaven is not really a "place" (although *Heaven and Hell* often reads that way) but a state of being. Swedenborg worked with a "doctrine of correspondence," the present and the afterlife being isomorphic and within us. "We are as we are because the Divine is human, and the worlds, spiritual and physical, represent this fact. Just as we can perceive aspects of our own being in contemplating natural phenomena, we find evidence of the Divine by looking into ourselves" (in Lachman 2004: 231). If at death we move into a higher or lower place in the hierarchy of heaven and hell, that is due to the kind of life we have already lived. Thus hell will be a place that some among us will recognize: "In some hells, one can see something like the rubble of homes or cities after a great fire. . . . Within our houses are hellish spirits, constant brawls, hostilities, beatings. . . . In some hells there are nothing but brothels that look disgusting and are full of all kinds of filth and excrement" (Swedenborg, quoted in Lachman 2004: 230). This graphic imagery is appropriate to the idea of correspondences: the world to come is simply more of what we create for ourselves now. Perceptions of heaven and hell are our inner experiences of this life and a foretaste of what we store up as our future. Swedenborg's own inner life was certainly intensive and active: "To prevent [the contrary views of clergy] from infecting and corrupting people of simple heart and simple faith, it has been made possible for me to be right with angels and to talk with them person to person. I have also been allowed to see what heaven is like and what hell is like; this has been going on for thirteen years" (in Lachman 2004: 227).

12. Current academic theological speculations about the afterlife are not outside the range of this discussion and are a fascinating topic in their own right; only space limits their inclusion. But it seems unfortunate, at least to me, that so little of it rarely makes the transition from seminaries to the pews. In their chapter "Heaven in Contemporary Christianity," McDannell and Lang (1988) describe the insipid theo-

rizing of the afterlife of some of the twentieth century's leading theologians who offer a sketchy "theocentric minimalism" at best. Meanwhile, some on the fundamentalist Right indulge extravagant visions of an apocalypse, and New Agers wander off into their own Disneylands of the mind. Hometown congregations are often decades (perhaps centuries) behind what at least some seminarians are up to. But that may be changing. Corcoran's *Soul, Body, and Survival* (2001) takes up where Cartesian mind/body dualism left off and recasts what we understand to be a self, a body, and whatever the word "resurrection" might mean for people today. Equally adventurous is Brown, Murphy, and Malony's *Whatever Happened to the Soul?* (1998). The contributors, many connected with Fuller Theological Seminary, seek to reconcile theological and scientific views of human nature. Their speculations are not calls for gentlemanly compromise in the tiresome wars between science and religion but newly creative ways of imagining what we mean by human nature and human spirituality in both scientific and theological contexts.

13. I owe special thanks to Thomas Murphy, former graduate student and fast-rising star in the world of Mormon scholarship. He critiqued this section of the chapter with special care, bringing to it an insider's understanding of the tradition plus the comparative perspective of anthropology. The statements and interpretations are, of course, my own.

14. I am indebted to Erich Robert Paul (1992) for his discussion of LDS thinking on theology and science. One practical consequence of Mormon views on the nature of science is that the hostility toward Darwinism and evolution that bedevils some conservative Protestants and Catholics, regularly erupting in attempts to modify biology texts and dictate teaching practices in public schools, has been less of an issue for them. But there have been, on occasion, reactive assaults on evolution, notably Joseph Fielding Smith, *Man: His Origin and Destiny* (1965) and Bruce R. McConkie, *Mormon Doctrine* (1958). To my knowledge, their positions are not those of the LDS church in a formal sense.

15. The role of Jesus in this arrangement is quite different from that proposed in other Christian denominations. Conventionally, through his "atonement," Jesus "reconciled" God and humankind, bridging the gulf of sin separating mortals from the godhead and defeating death for all time. That has always been the theological import of Easter. But the Saints' see this differently. In God's larger plan, populating heaven required that two tasks be completed. First, premortals had to be introduced to mortality and, subsequently, undergo their death and resurrection. Those were the preconditions for admission to paradise and Adam was chosen by God to take care of the first task, Jesus the second. Adam gets credit not for an unfortunate "Fall" but for unlocking the first gate on the pathway to salvation. Jesus advanced the plan through its next stage. Nor is heaven only for the elect or the devout. Everyone gets there one way or another and additionally, everyone arrives in a corporeal albeit refined state. The *Book of Mormon* advises, "This restoration shall come to all, both old and young, both bond and free, both male and female, both the wicked and the righteous" (Alma 11:14). This apparently includes even the unfortunates who inhabit a lesser known fourth realm of the afterlife, that of "Outer Darkness" reserved for "only a handful of people who once accepted and later knowingly rejected the Holy Spirit." (Murphy, personal communication). Presumably, those are Mormons who left the faith.

16. Historian Klaus Hansen (1981) points out that however much anti-Mormon critics may have thought polygyny was a ploy to increase the number of Saints, in fact it did not work out that way. Women were scarce everywhere on the frontier, whatever their religion, and those in plural marriages often had fewer children than women in monogamous relationships. More important, he argues that in antebellum America the old Puritan sexual codes were breaking down, individualism and diversity in sexual practice were becoming more common, alarmed antisex reformers were active and vociferous, and a culture of upheaval, at least on issues of sexual morality, was apparent. Given the trends, Smith was sensitive to his followers' desires for moral clarity, and his real interest was in establishing patriarchal authority (based on Biblical precedents) for church families, whether monogamous or polygynous. But one consequence of his doctrine on plural marriage was to create for the Saints an instantaneous and unambiguous ethnic identity in a chaotic, multiethnic, multiracial frontier society.

17. The LDS church offers an explanation of this on their "FamilySearch—FAQ Family History Library" Web site. "Through priesthood authority from God, marriages are performed in temples. These marriages can continue throughout this life and for all eternity. In addition, children are "sealed" to their parents, meaning that their relationship to their parents will continue even after death. In order to give these same blessings to their deceased ancestors, Church members seek information about them so they can perform marriages and sealings on their behalf. These ancestors may then choose to accept these sacred rites." The site is at http://www.familysearch.org/.

18. Owens's paper can be accessed at http://www.webcom.com/~gnosis/jskabb1.htm. For additional sections on alchemy and freemasonry substitute jskbb2 and sjkbb3 respectively, accessed January 24, 2007.

19. Smith's involvement with Masonry and what are generally known as hermetic traditions needs to be seen in context, for it is not as unusual as might first appear. His interest in esoteric knowledge began in the 1830s, the same time other countercultural movements were emerging in a pattern reminiscent of today's "cultural wars." They included groups now reduced to historical footnotes—Cochranites, Rappites, Millerites, Brook Farm, New Israelites—and others who are better known including Shakers, Christian Scientists, and Theosophists. Ralph Waldo Emerson and some among the Transcendentalists took up the same themes, giving them public visibility and intellectual respectability. But heated religious enthusiasm does not last unless, in the classic formulation of Max Weber, it is routinized, and for Mormons that was the priority once they arrived in Utah. Brigham Young and the leadership of the community deemphasized esoteric doctrines in favor of the hard work needed to survive in a desert. "The faithful were not to expect miracles or visions, rely upon their endowments, or search out the mysteries. Nor were they to neglect meeting, sell valuable grain to gentile wagon trains on the trail west while fellow Mormons suffered the effects of drought and grasshopper infestation, or themselves drift off to California" (Brooke 1994: 284). From the mid-nineteenth century on, Smith's church, begun as a separatist and reformist enterprise, walked a fine line, preserving its traditions while living within the national culture. That meant a doctrinal move away from hermeticism and toward something like the conservative Protestantism now common to large parts of the country including the

Mountain West. Both in its origins and current practice, the Saints' church was and is deeply and uniquely American.

20. An eclectic Christian spirituality runs throughout Eadie's work, but her contacts with the Mormons were obviously important to her. Parallels to LDS theology in *Embraced by the Light* include our premortal existence (1992: 35, 47), spirit as matter (47), levels of achieved spirituality in the afterlife (45), the importance of the written Word and lifelong and eternity-long learning (72–77), a "God who wants us to be as he is" by taking on his attributes (61), and a description of the peopling of the earth that invokes the imagery of westward-heading nineteenth-century Mormon wagon trains: "Then we watched as the earth was created. We watched as our spirit brothers and sisters entered physical bodies for their turns upon the earth. . . . I distinctly remember watching [from a heavenly vantage] the American pioneers crossing the continent and rejoicing as they endured their difficult tasks and completed their missions" (52). None of this should be surprising given Eadie's Sioux background and the signal importance of Native Americans in LDS theology. Not without good reason, in one of her promotional videos, a two-hour talking-head performance before an appreciative white audience, she wears a stylized Indian dress with what appear to be buckskin streamers hanging from the sleeves and hem. As she speaks she gestures with an eagle feather. Her video production company and quarterly newsletter are both called Onjinjinkta, her Native American name. Eadie's relationship to the LDS church, including variations in early manuscript versions of *Embraced by the Light* handled by a Mormon publisher before she went "national" with Bantam Books, is somewhat controversial. On the latter, see Introvigne (1996) in *Dialogue: A Journal of Mormon Thought*.

21. Greyson's list of publications is lengthy, but a sample of his work includes biological features of the NDE (1998), clinical aspects (1997), posttraumatic stress and NDEs (2001), and his interest in developing scales for measuring the intensity of the experience (1983). All this work appears in peer-reviewed medical journals.

22. Not everyone in the NDE community agrees with Morse's interpretation. A reviewer of *Where God Lives*, writing in the *Journal of Near-Death Studies*, the in-house publication of IANDS, lauds Morse's effort to present to a wider audience "the New Paradigm" of science, healing, and the spiritual. But he faults the author for not supporting his propositions more fully, especially the conjecture that the right temporal lobe is where God physically connects with human bodies. Nevertheless, the reviewer is appreciative of the book: "integrating vistas of plausibility from Mind/Body Medicine, the New Biology and the New Physics, Morse and co-author Paul Perry suggest that science is on the verge of coining a new version of reality, one that is decidedly more spiritual and belief-oriented." See *Journal of Near-Death Studies* (Fall 2002): 47.

23. My data come from several years of participant observation, casual talk, interviews, and reading accounts by people who say they have had a near-death experience. I have attended national and local meetings of their organization, IANDS, and once worked with several leading members on an (unsuccessful) grant proposal to explore the matter ethnographically. In addition, I have consulted the largest online data base of NDE accounts now available, developed by physician Jeffrey Long and his associate Jody Jovanovich and posted at www.nderf.org. Their collection is a remarkable and valuable resource. As an interested observer, my impression is that

experiencers are as varied in their social origins, education, and occupations as the population as a whole, although I see very few minorities among them. Many seem to be religious "seekers," and I have a hunch that more than a few have struggled to separate themselves from a religiously conservative or fundamentalist upbringing. I know one fellow anthropologist who had an NDE. Individuals I have talked with, a small and unscientific sample, have understandably emphasized the uniqueness of their NDEs and might find my anthropological way of generalizing about their stories an odd way of doing business. The spiritual realities they say they encountered are things I cannot verify. But I do not doubt the intensity and terrifying reality of their experience.

CHAPTER 5. PASSING IT ON

1. My thanks to Erik Seeman of the Department of History at SUNY, Buffalo, who gave helpful advice on this chapter. Thanks also to Gayle Richardson of the Seattle Public Library, who introduced me to the children's literature on this topic.

2. As noted in Chapter 1, Orsi works with a particular theory of religion that is particularly applicable to thinking about end-of-life issues and how they are presented to children. He thinks of religion as material practices wherein the sacred breaks through the ordinary and becomes visible to those willing to see and respond. The embalmed corpse, a headstone, a familiar photograph at the bedside can be media of presence, emotionally vivid to those who would engage them, devices signaling realities well beyond themselves.

What a book teaches and how its message is first conceived, delivered, and heard is, of course, variable. One well-known author of children's fiction is Katherine Paterson, who, writing in an academic theology journal, disavows any attempt to teach children specific "lessons." Her view is that readers will find in her prose what they want to see there; fiction is an independent, uncontrollable medium. "We don't trust fiction. It is too wild, too untamed. It might carry meanings we don't approve of beforehand. . . . [I am sometimes asked] 'What message do you want to convey to children in this book?' 'That is not my job,' I answer to the distress of the questioner. 'My job is to tell the best, the truest story that I can tell. It is the reader's privilege to choose what she or he will learn from reading the book'" (2000: 570). While I admire Paterson's authorial respect for the independence of her audience, I would observe that the "privilege to choose" the meaning of a text is never free but always constrained by a cultural context, more so when the topic is a charged one such as death and the readers are children.

3. Scheper-Hughes and Sargent remark that "Childhood illnesses are often metaphors of social disruption" (1998: 17), something that could be said of childhood experiences of death as well. They allude to what they call a cultural politics of "small wars" at the borders of the adult and child worlds; perhaps in some ways the ambiguities of death in contemporary children's stories express that. The well-documented sequestration and commercialization of death in American culture is due to a number of historical developments, including the dominance of the middle class and the nuclear family (in fact and in mythology), the control of health care and death care by medical bureaucracies, the commercialization of body handling and disposal, and a popular shift in religious allegiances from traditional denominations to contemporary laissez-faire spirituality. What adults struggle to tell children

about death is what they struggle to understand from their own experiences with these larger realities.

4. About forty children's books whose central theme is death were reviewed. This is a small, niche genre, and I believe I have read most of it. My choices were based on sales, easy availability from commercial sources, author reputation, and the recommendations of public librarians and educators whom I contacted. Three titles in the sample are published by the American Psychological Association with their endorsement. I also looked at numerous book reviews, including those used by librarians who purchase for their collections, and reviews written by customers and published online by Amazon.com. My selection was limited to books for younger children just learning to read, sometimes categorized in libraries and by educators as "picture" or "easy reading" books. I focused on these because, if their effect really is "vicarious socialization" as Moore and Mae say, then they are a child's earliest experience in learning the death practices of the adult world. There are many books for pre-teen and teenage readers, as well, where death is a feature of the story line (Disney's *Bambi*, for example), but those were not part of the sample.

5. The communities described in these books are highly circumscribed. With several exceptions, they are white, middle class, and urban, although sometimes the scene of a death is distant and the story's action occurs in a rural, pastoral setting. Only three books featured minority families: children's television notable Fred Rogers's *When a Pet Dies* (1988), African American poet Lucille Clifton's *Everett Anderson's Goodbye* (1983), and Brown and Brown's wonderfully anthropomorphic *When Dinosaurs Die* (1996), which includes cameo appearances by Chinese, Jewish, Christian, and South Asian funeral celebrants. Only three, Mary Kate Jordan's *Losing Uncle Tim* (1989), Lesléa Newman's *Too Far Away to Touch* (1995) and Jeannine Atkin's *A Name on the Quilt* (1999) mention AIDS. For the most part, the family units depicted and the communities of bereavement are small, sometimes almost claustrophobically so. Perhaps intending to emphasize a child's sense of isolation in a world where death is an adult affair, *Gran-Gran's Best Trick* (Holden 1989) has only two characters, a grandfather and his granddaughter. In the few scenes where adults are shown in this title, they are remote. At a viewing in a funeral establishment, they cluster in a small circle between the heroine, standing in a darkened corner, and Gran-Gran's open casket, displayed in dappled light at the other end of the room. During the funeral the adults sit distinctly apart from one another in a long, straight row of institutional-looking chairs, as isolated emotionally as they are physically. Other stories feature nuclear families and sometimes include a playmate or two. Friends and mothers are important in offering comfort, and fathers are sometimes helpful, although one who brings home a replacement puppy too early in the grieving process seems a bumbler (Keller, *Goodbye, Max* (1987). In a few books, large extended families with neighbors and friends gather for the occasion and there is intense interaction among cousins, aunts, uncles, and "friends of the family." In Jane Thomas's *Saying Good-bye to Grandma* (1988), while the adults are in the viewing and reception areas of the funeral company doing, at a remove, whatever adults do, the children use a shoe to play "capture the flag" among the caskets in a dim showroom. A tolerant mother who finds them deadpans, "I'm glad you found a quiet place to let off steam." Family gatherings are often part of a trip to a distant,

rural place where a death occurred, suggesting widely extended networks of loosely affiliated kin rather than localized, ongoing communities. Games, swimming, story telling, and adventures are part of these trips, a "normalizing" touch making a sad occasion more like a summer vacation.

6. Judith Viorst's widely read title *The Tenth Good Thing About Barney* (1971) avoids celestial rumination and offers practical and straightforward answers to a child's questions. Barney the cat has died and an unnamed boy wants to know where he has gone. Annie, a neighborhood friend, argues in favor of heaven, but the boy is doubtful, so they ask father for his advice. Heaven is a possibility, he says, but he is not sure. "We don't know too much about heaven, he told Annie. We can't be absolutely sure that it's there. But if it is there, said Annie in her absolutely sure voice, it is bound to have room for Barney and tuna and cream." At this point, father announces he has work to do in the garden and invites the boy to join him, while Annie has another cookie before going home. As the two work in the garden, the problem of Barney's fate is resolved. The boy had wanted to recite ten good things about his cat at the funeral. But he could only think of nine, and as the memory of Barney's presence begins to recede, he struggles to name a tenth. Fortunately the gardening has an inspirational effect. Some seeds (sweetpeas in the illustration) are pushed into the soil of the fresh grave, and that night the boy tells his mother he has at last discovered the tenth best thing. "Barney is in the ground and he's helping grow flowers. You know, I said, that's a pretty nice job for a cat." No heaven for Barney, whose fate pushing up sweetpeas is more ecological than ontological.

7. Colleague Paysha Stockton, who read this in draft form, had an interesting response to the nature imagery of some of these stories. "I'm having a 'Fantasy Island' flashback! Isn't it interesting [how] this view of heaven mirrors our idea of a tropical vacation? Now, not only is a sad occasion like a summer vacation, death itself is an eternal opportunity for suntan lotion and beach bumming. Heaven might not be clouds and Mediterranean palaces and harp music—it could be sand and palm trees and reggae." For those like myself not inclined to palm trees and tropics, especially not forever, there is another option, the moody, slanting-light mountain-scapes of more northerly latitudes in Robin Williams's 1998 film *What Dreams May Come*, also a nature-centric, feel-good take on the afterlife.

8. An interesting and creative example of a book used this way is *My Hospice Book: For Children with a Special Person in the Hospice* (Macpherson and Cooke 2003). This is an unpublished workbook in which children draw and write about their hospice visits, its usefulness having been tested in a pilot study at a Scottish institution. It is designed so children can express their feelings but also so parents and staff can access the children's anxieties and state of understanding. Children are encouraged to draw and discuss their artwork with others, and in the study, most welcomed the chance to do that. But one independent soul requested privacy: "My mum watched me doing it but I prefer to do it on my own . . . . I says to her to go through and watch the telly or that because I was fine doing it myself" (2003: 401). Generally, parents liked the idea, if only to give their children something to do while adults talked.

9. An ecumenical variant of the theme occurs in the curiously titled *Kaddish for Grandpa: In Jesus' Name, Amen* (2004) by James Howe and Catherine Stock. Curious, but reflecting some modern demographics. A child asks her mother about

the planning for grandpa's funeral. "She told me that even though we were Jewish, the funeral would be Christian because that's what Daddy's family is. Daddy chose to be Jewish when he was grown-up. Mommy was born Jewish, like me." The child then adds her own insight: "I don't understand that part. If a funeral was a time for singing songs and telling stories, why did it have to be Christian or Jewish?" As things turn out, it does not have to be.

10. Erik Seeman's inspired reading of an earlier draft led him to the term "me-odicy." It seems an apt characterization of some of the theodicies of American popular culture. My thanks to him. It is useful to add that there is a possible middle ground between pietistic renderings of Bible stories "retold" for children in sectarian titles and the current nature-and-memory genre I have described here. It is the well-known literature of fairy tales, particularly those of Hans Christian Andersen, and Jacob and Wilhelm Grimm. Sadly, most of us know these stories only through corruptions cooked up in the Disney studios. Two children's classics, however, are Andersen's "The Little Mermaid" and Margery Williams's *The Velveteen Rabbit*. Both are tales of love, fallibility, and immortality that carry in their imagery a significant theological presence. Certainly not preachy in the way explicitly religious titles usually are, they presume the reader's familiarity with an old and complex theological tradition that is inspirational in its own right. For an enlightening discussion of how these fanciful stories can inspire children's understanding, see Vigen Guroian's (1998) interesting *Tending the Heart of Virtue: How Classic Stories Awaken a Child's Moral Imagination*

CHAPTER 6. IN OUR HEARTS FOREVER

1. What is good for football is good for baseball too. Check out "Major League Baseball ™ Line of Urns and Caskets" at http://www.eternalimage.net/mlb_page.html, accessed April 9, 2007. The urn shown looks vaguely like old-fashioned food-storage pottery, but they are made of aluminum, bear a team logo, and are attached to a simulated home base. A "display dome" is mounted on the top and the manufacturer thoughtfully advises that "the urn comes with a baseball, which the purchaser or family can replace with a special ball from their own collection."

2. For readers who share Rasberry's can-do enthusiasm but lack her handicraft skills, check out Dale Power's *Do-It-Yourself Coffins for Pets and People*, subtitled a "book for woodworkers who want to be buried in their work" (1997). Power offers complete specifications for materials, designs, and needed tools. Richly photographed, his book takes the reader from initial sketches to beautifully crafted and finished coffins. At the end he poses impressively in a black suit and black top hat with one of his products.

3. As a shrine, the Vietnam memorial is distinctive among the other well-known monuments on the Mall. In addition to its appearance—below grade rather than ascending grandly to the sky—the hushed atmosphere, quiet and reflective conversations, slow movement of visitors, and objects left in remembrance all create a distinctive mood. Even the tawdry souvenir and T-shirt stands once propped up in the trees at one edge of the memorial are suggestive of the link between commerce and piety that is common to religious shrines and festivals throughout the world.

4. The number of suicides among all Vietnam veterans has been estimated to be between 20,000 and ten times that number. If 200,000 is even close to correct, it

means almost four times as many have died by their own hand following the war than died as combat casualties. A novel based on this, *Suicide Wall* by Alexander Paul (1996), has inspired an effort to create a second Vietnam Memorial on the Mall, one with white marble, to display the names of postwar suicides. A home page, suicidewall.com, is devoted to that effort.

5. The deliberate ambiguity of the wall is underlined by the presence nearby of two other memorials, both realist images that challenge Lin's sense of memory and memorializing. One is a bronze statue of three armed American soldiers in battle fatigues, appropriately multiracial, staring at the wall from the edge of the monument's grassy slope. The parade of visitors mostly passes them by, their isolation exceeded only by the Vietnam Women's Memorial even farther back in the trees. Both are monuments to authorized versions of the war and to strategic forgetting, forgetting the South Vietnamese troops who were reputed allies and the civilian population against whom the atrocities of the war were directed by all sides. In a moving and poetic depiction of the site, MacCannell remarks on the incongruous presence of these metallic combat soldiers: "They appear to be coming out of some bushes, looking at the memorial. They appeared to me as if they have just paused to gather enough strength and courage to go over to the memorial to find their own names" (1992: 282).

6. How different is one contemporary American example. Mani women formalize grieving and memory making, performed in the public sphere through exhumation but also in a dramatic tradition of communal laments. The grief work of Joan Didion following the unexpected death of her husband was hardly that (2005). Her mourning was rumination and inward looking: mental rehearsals and re-rehearsals of the hours of his dying, a "surface rationality" she says, afloat on an unstable fluidity; perplexed questions about what is "normal" and what not; sensations of vulnerability and isolation; searching for anchor points in poetry, novels, medical texts, religion. In her telling, grief is privatized, even claustrophobic. The title of her book is revealing: *The Year of Magical Thinking*. In the American view, the rational and reasonable sits in opposition to the magical, two realms that should not intersect and do so only in our confusion and dismay. Mani woman likely would think otherwise.

7. I recognize that I am not describing everybody in this characterization. Those I have in mind are white middle-class North Americans, since they set the religious, political, and economic agenda for everyone else. Nor are they homogeneous, as there are important regional and intraclass differences. Whether the cult of memory notion would be useful for describing death practices and beliefs among African Americans or those whose traditions derive from Iberian Catholicism is an open question. But it seems certain that the practices I describe in this chapter will spill over into many communities beyond those of middle-class whites. The expression "cult of memory" is used by Ariès to describe changing sensibilities toward death beginning early in the nineteenth century (1974: 73).

8. On matters of "selection, emphasis, and presentation" in the assertion of community values and the details of an individual life, the obituary/news story of the Prohibition-era gangster Alphonsus "Al" Capone is instructive, to put it mildly. Published in the *New York Times* of January 26, 1947, he is described as "fat" four times, including "the fat boy from Brooklyn" and "the fat man from Chicago." He is

labeled a cruel "cutthroat" and a "rod" (hired killer) who "delivered three neat homicides" as "gifts" on Christmas day. When finally sentenced to federal prison, says the Associated Press writer, "the fat man's face went dark and the ugly scar went white." Very much a contrast, and reflecting a more recent temperament, is the February 21, 1998, obituary of another criminal, appearing in *The Boston Globe*. The headline: "Theodore 'Teddy' Green, 82; his job: 'I rob banks,' he said." Green's full life of bank robbery, including serving hard time at Alcatraz just like Capone, is described as though lifted from a job résumé, sans the colorful insights. "Just the facts," Sgt. Joe Friday might have said.

9. Personal communication with the author.

10. Men are still more likely to have an obituary than women, and in contemporary newspapers, women's tend to be shorter unless they are the wives or daughters of famous people, or celebrities themselves. Career choice also makes a difference. Longer obituaries are written for those in the arts, entertainment, and science. Shorter notices appear for people in blue-collar, technical, and business occupations. Newspaper writers sometimes have working relationships with funeral directors, the latter recommending who should be written up and supplying much of the information the writer uses. Funeral directors are overwhelmingly men, and that may or may not suggest intentional bias. What it does show, however, is that the content of the obituary page is influenced by factors not evident to the casual newspaper reader.

11. The *Post's* style sheet is available at http://www.postnewsads.com/legacy/write-memorial.html (as of 2/17/04). Indicative of the working relationship between newspapers and funeral companies is the paper's statement: "This guide is intended primarily as an aide [sic] for funeral directors in helping families assemble obituary information and for Denver Newspaper Agency employees in editing the obituary for publication." Increasingly, however, family members are writing obituaries themselves and e-mailing them to newspapers, sometimes with a scanned photo. The two newspapers where I live offer these additional services: an online guest book for condolences, e-mail notification when a guest signs in, and links to funeral homes and charities. They promote as well a "partnership" with legacy.com. "We can also help you build a Life Story page, featuring a full bibliography, photo gallery, guest book and customized charity links—all of which will stay online as a lasting tribute." I thank my brother Stephen Green, formerly of the *Sacramento Bee*, for leading me to information on newspaper obituaries, who writes them, and industry policies on format.

12. My source for the Singer article is http://newyorker.com/fact/content/020708fa_fact, accessed April 9, 2007.

13. Starck's article, the source of the quotations here, is at http://www.griffith.edu.au/school/art/text/oct01/starck.htm.

14. A witty travelogue of obituary history and practices is Marilyn Johnson's *The Dead Beat* (2006). Generous with her coverage of both sides of the Atlantic, the writing in the British papers is still the best.

15. One area where flamboyant memorializing has always been de rigueur is hagiography, idolization of the saintly dead. But was any saint ever venerated more grandiloquently than NASCAR driver Dale Earnhardt, killed in a last lap crash at

Daytona and eulogized in a *USA Today* column by Sandy Grady (February 21, 2001, 15A)? At his death, says Grady, "it seemed as if a hand switched off all the racing engines in the world." Earnhardt "was an artifact from tougher times," and if you ever stared down a statue of a Confederate soldier—"lanky, brooding, a glint of menace in his eyes"—then you have met him. You and I go flabby with our 401(k)s and stock options, he says, but not Earnhardt. "He was real." The writer complains that given how this demigod of the raceway died, unnamed do-gooders will be demanding new safety rules, the kinds of harnesses and helmets that might have saved him, even calling for an end to NASCAR itself. But they do not count. Earnhardt "was a ghost from another age . . . a ruthless, slash and burn destroyer—an image richly earned in a hundred spinouts . . . part of the American élan for living on the edge that sent paratroopers into D-Day darkness and John Glenn into space." There will not be another like him, for "Dale Earnhardt was the real thing—a lost piece of America. Maybe that explains the tears from hard men who do not easily shed them."

16. There is a large literature on cemetery design and memorial iconography. For prehistory, see Mike Parker Pearson, *The Archaeology of Death and Burial* (1999). Richard Morris, *Sinners, Lovers, and Heroes* (1997) is good on the nineteenth century. Two essential works are Gary Laderman, *The Sacred Remains* (1996) and David Charles Sloane, *The Last Great Necessity* (1991).

17. Much is written in the popular press about celebrities when they die unexpectedly, maybe too much. They had, after all, more than their fifteen minutes of fame, but fans are determined they should have that and more. Several good critical studies of the postmortem "celeb phenom" are Tony Walter, ed., *The Mourning for Diana* (1999b); Adrian Kear and Deborah Lynn Steinberg, eds., *Mourning Diana* (1999); and Anthony Elliott, *The Mourning of John Lennon* (1999). Elvis, of course, never died. He simply left the building.

18. It is hard not to appreciate the humor these gentlemen bring to their business. Their T-shirts come with a choice of slogans, including "we put the fun back in funeral" and "think INside the box." There are posters as well. "Live a Little, You Only Die Once, A funeral is your only chance to leave an enduring impression and possibly an emotional scar or two." "The Earthworms Will Be Speechless. On your final day, make sure your loved ones are gathered together in utter shock and disbelief." "Why Should You Care What People Think? You're Dead. You only get one shot at this death thing. Don't let your friends and family screw it up." The Batesville site is at http://biz.batesville.com/LogoStore/default.asp. Online shoppers looking for death related knickknacks should click over to the gift shop of the National Museum of Funeral History (www.nmfh.org/#) in Houston. Who could not use a pair of silver coffin earrings, a syringe pen, or a casket paperweight? And for evening reading, there is a book of 182 celebrity death certificates, including those for Marilyn Monroe, John Belushi, and Truman Capote. The Museum's motto, "Any Day Above Ground Is a Good One," is available on a T-shirt.

19. As I write, word is out that Microsoft has filed a patent application for what their engineers call "immortal computing," digital information stored in such a way that it will be available to future generations and even future civilizations. "People could store messages to descendants, information about their lives or interactive holograms of themselves for access by visitors at their tombstones and urns. . . . the

artifacts could be symbolic representations of people, reflecting elements of their personalities. The systems might be set up to take action—e-mailing birthday greetings to people identified as grandchildren, for example." See http://seattlepi. nwsource.com/business/300636_msftimmortal22.html, accessed January 25, 2007. What next, a digital chess game with your uncle under the sod while family members tidy up his grave?

20. There is no space here to list all the relevant cybersources, but fortunately a good start has already been made by Abbott & Hast Publications at their impressive "death care" Web site (www.abbottandhast.com/links.html). It is intended for the funeral services industry but goes well beyond buying and selling. They have information on "criticism/consumer-advocate groups," organizations such as the Indian Burial Association Project directed by a Minneapolis pastor who is Lakota, death humor, and a category for "automotive enthusiasts." Curious about the latter, I found a number of vintage and refurbished hearse clubs with photos of their sparkling old machines, obviously much loved by the owners. Is there still a use for them? Absolutely. The Denver Hearse Club sponsors an evening of hearse drag racing; $25 if you want to drive, $10 "to watch and gawk." It is worth noting that electronic technology is being used to promote the use of undisturbed natural sites as cemeteries as well. Plans are underway in Marin County, California, for burials in woodlands and in abandoned cemeteries allowed to return to nature. This is an American adaptation of England's highly successful ecoburial movement. The promoter, Tyler Cassity, wants to create cemeteries without markers, but with specific plots located electronically and displayed on the Internet. "You would walk through [the woods] with a handheld device, like a Palm Pilot, and, as you walked through, the device would be triggered by GPS (Global Positioning Satellite) points. It's the perfect marriage of the completely natural and the completely virtual so that the memorial aspect is invisible unless you choose to see it." Standing in a dense stand of trees, Cassity says, "This is what the cemetery will look like, like nature." *San Francisco Chronicle*, August 22, 2004, A1, 12.

21. "Professional" advice on writing heartfelt messages is not something that came in with the Internet. It began with valentines. In 1783 one Thomas Sabine, a London printer, issued a chapbook entitled *The Complete Valentine Writer; or, The Young Men and Maidens Best Assistant.* Almost immediately it was imitated in this country by printers anxious to cash in on Sabine's discovery that there was a large market among less-than-literate young men who wanted a valentine that would catch a maiden's attention. Imagine how this example of prepackaged sentiment must have appealed to a teenager barely able to write his name: "Oh, come my love, my own delight, My joy by day, my dream by night, And both our hearts shall close entwine, A blessing from St. Valentine." Such was part of the run up to the modern greeting card industry, another venue for merging commercial and private experience. See Schmidt (1995) for a history of American holidays, including Christmas, Easter, and Mother's Day. The Valentine poem quoted is on page 60 of his fascinating book.

22. Some of this material is from an interview with Sharon Mnich (August 19, 2004). Her dedication and energy is impressive—I have no idea if that is typical of other virtual cemetery webmasters—and she is clear in her hope that online memorials will someday replace those in newspapers.

23. Dogs, cats, turtles and even horses are buried, more often in the ground than online. Most larger cities have pet cemeteries listed in the phone book, some well maintained and others not. Gary Collison (2004) describes the long history of horse burial, not just of pets but military and race horses too. Two notables got a special send off. Chief, the U.S. Army's last official cavalry mount, died in 1968. He was buried standing up, with full military honors. Little Sorrel, Stonewall Jackson's horse, or what could be found of him, was finally put to rest in 1997. More than 500 people attended the burial, some tossing carrots and oats onto the grave. And that is not the end of it. There are pet caskets, urns, and personalized storage containers for the dearly departed's cremains. Enter "Pets to Rest" as a search term to find a few. Finally, a quick look on Amazon.com generated the following titles, evidence of conviction by some pet owners that they will see Fido again: *There is Eternal Life for Animals*, by Niki Behrikis Shanahan; *Cold Noses at the Pearly Gates*, by Gary Kurz; and *The Soul of Your Pet: Evidence for the Survival of Animals After Death*, by Scott S. Smith.

24. Grierson describes her interests as, among other things, globalization and the politics of knowledge and representation. The most convenient way to access her paper is to use the title "From Cemeteries to Cyberspace" as a search term (accessed 2004). Her thinking is rooted in the theorizing of Michel Foucault and his concept of *heterotopia,* any space where the self seems to occupy multiple positions at once. The endless regression of one's image in an arrangement of mirrors is an example. Foucault argues that in a globalized, digitized world, traditional history and the uniqueness of individual places are superceded by simultaneity, by juxtaposition, and by conflation of near and far. The dead are present in virtual memorials if we want them to be, literally in our face. And yet they are not. As if in the mirrors of a cosmic fun house, they are there yet absent, a bit of electronic slight of hand we lovingly accept. Our keyboard-launched thoughts "go with them," or "to them," but really there is no "place" to which they go at all.

25. Personal messages and memorabilia left at graves are not new, but the practice has spread into cyberspace. A prominent example is the Ohel, or grave, of Rabbi Menachem M. Schneerson, the Lubavitcher Rebbe, who was buried at Cambria Heights, New York, in 1994. He received many letters from followers during his lifetime, and people continue to send mail, faxes, and e-mail. Access the Ohel at http://www.chabad.org/generic.aspAID=36247, where there are instructions for sending e-mail. For a discussion of the uses of the Internet within the Jewish Diaspora, see Kirshenblatt-Gimblett (1996).

26. I have removed the identification of the writer, but the message in its entirety is included here because it reveals the intensity of so many of these postings. One can doubt the literal truth of what the writer hopes for but still acknowledge the desire to offer comfort. That person writes: "I don't mean for this to sound cruel in any way, but I thought that this might somehow ease your pain as it has helped me. Our neighbor boy [Ben, apparently] recently was killed by a hit-and-run driver while walking across a street, and my son was good friends with him. To help with our grieving, someone had suggested my son create a Virtual Memorial, and Kelly's was the second one I happened to read. One of the things that comforted me the day Ben died was learning that a coworker had given birth to a baby at approximately the same time that Ben was pronounced brain dead. I've heard it said that God

brings another life into the world when one leaves, and I felt a certain peace in knowing that Ben was now with God and this little one would spend some time on earth. I just wanted to share with you that when your Kelly left this earth as an angel on June 12, 1986, my son, Ben's friend, entered the world. It's all part of a plan that we just cannot understand, but we can be assured that God is in control. I have explained to my son that our lives on earth are so short, but heaven is for eternity. We will see Ben again and be with him forever someday, and all of you who loved Kelly will be reunited someday to live with her forevermore. May God grant you peace and strength until that day arrives."

27. The use of the Internet for religious purposes is discussed in Dawson and Cowan (2004). Topics include cyberheaven, praying on line, virtual spiritual communities, virtual pilgrimage, seeking out the apocalypse, and warnings of the end times sent to us through cyberspace. On the latter, Paolo Apolito's *The Internet and the Madonna* (2005) is an exceptional and imaginative piece of online ethnography, a model of how that kind of research can be done. Subtitled *Religious Visionary Experience on the Web*, it explores religious apparitions both on and offline, and the complex relationships between science, cybertechnology, and religious sightings. Apolito shows why the interaction of religion and science is more complex and interesting than the overheated science vs. religion debates suggests.

28. Not everyone is convinced that cyberspace and mourning are a good combination, especially not funeral company operator Thomas Lynch. He e-mailed his thoughts about that to newspaper columnist Shelby Gilje, and, always a voice of reason on matters terminal, what Lynch said is worth noting. "And to the extent that we are pushed in that direction, both by marketing of funerals and the marketing of immediate burials and cremations, to regard a death in the family as a 'virtual' experience instead of a hands-on one, we are doing ourselves no great favors. Better to bear the fire from our own houses to light the pyres for the dead, or bring our shovels and our wonderments along to the grave than enter this Disney World of Death Care that is now emerging".

CHAPTER 7. THE FUTURE OF DEATH

1. In the tradition of Durkheim, Hertz saw the body as a "collective representation," a physical object as proxy for human relationships, and so the starting point for discussion of a society's death practices as a (somewhat) organized whole. In Borneo, the fate of the body determined that of the soul and the soul's subsequent relations with those still living. "As the corpse is formless and repulsive during the intermediary period [between death and disposal], so the soul of the dead is homeless and the object of dread. Unable to enter the society of the dead, it must lead a pitiful existence on the fringes of human habitation. In its discomfort, the soul is liable spitefully to inflict illness upon the living. Elaborate observances are required to divert its hostility. The 'great feast' terminates this miserable period by honoring the now dry bones of the deceased, confirming the soul's arrival in the land of the ancestors, and marking the reestablishment of normal relations among the survivors" (Metcalf and Huntington 1991: 34).

2. There is another implication worth noting. De Certeau's understanding of belief as behavioral and contractual undermines, it seems to me, the "spiritual but not religious" cliché of contemporary speech. I understand why some make that

distinction, privileging their own "journeying" over what they perceive (probably rightly) as the rigidity and staleness of an older creedal view. So too, some highly vocal religionists in the so-called culture wars of public life have contributed to the spread of the fanciful spirituality they dislike. That is not accidental; I am sure they need their devils. But in either case, belief is still a matter of contracting with divine agencies. The debate is not who is a believer and who is not, because all are. The difference between spirituality and religiosity, as that is popularly construed, is just a matter of taste in expectational practices.

3. From Thoreau to John Muir, the Boy Scouts, the Sierra Club, and the current interest in ecoburials, the proposition that nature is the truest manifestation of God's handiwork has long been a fixture of American piety, making nature a preferred locale for engagement with the inner self. Belden Lane, a sensitive, theologically inspired interpreter of this tradition, suggests that we do not just find the sacred in the natural world; it finds us. Yet as visitors to sacred sites, we often enter in without discerning what is fully there. "We aren't accustomed to attributing intent or cognizance to inanimate locations in the environment" (2002: 21). He makes a useful point, one that returns us to the contrarian impulse of the vernacular. Certain geographical sites—Lourdes, the Grand Canyon, the grounds of the Twin Towers—seem to emanate such power on their own that state and ecclesiastical authorities feel compelled to promulgate "official" interpretations of their significance, if only to reign in the exuberance.

4. A counterpoint to this post-Protestant discussion is forcefully made by Father Andrew Greeley, a prominent sociologist of religion, novelist, and public intellectual. He argues that for Catholics the mundane world has always been sacramental and "enchanted." Catholics tend to have an "analogical imagination" and see in ordinary things—sexuality, mother love, or community, for example—the "lurking," as he says, of an incarnate God. "Put more simply, the Catholic imagination loves metaphors; Catholicism is a verdant rainforest of metaphors. The Protestant imagination distrusts metaphors; it tends to be a desert of metaphors" (2000: 9). Where Catholics are analogical, with hints of God appearing all around them, Protestants are dialectical, imagining God at a great, transcendent distance. In art, music, architecture, and statuary, the Holy for Catholics is a near presence; in Protestant thought, enthusiasm for that kind of holiness risks idolatry and superstition. As a good sociologist, Greeley marshals real numbers from the National Opinion Research Center at the University of Chicago to support his distinction. If he is correct, then it is one of the great ironies of recent American history that the post-Protestant world Porterfield describes is in inspiration a very Catholic one.

5. Paul's comment is at 1Corinthians 15: 26. My borrowing from his line is to intentionally contrast a visionary's insight with the more mundane, legalistic, and technological practices that define death for most Americans now. I would guess that in Paul's time he saw far more of physical death, as everyone living in the Roman world must have, than those of us living now. Perhaps death as an everyday, even casual presence necessitates a longer view, the only escape imaginable under such conditions. Its relative sequestration in the present, by contrast, opens space for fantasies about technological fixes.

6. There are many books on hospice care with guidelines for "dying well." Physician Timothy Quill's *Caring for Patients at the End of Life* (2001) is one of the

good ones. He addresses the underlying assumptions of hospice care, the quality of doctor-patient communication, and current clinical issues such as "double effect" and "options of last resort" (including self-starvation, physician-assisted suicide) and safeguards against their misuse. The clarity he brings to these matters is not just medical. The concluding chapter, on his brother's death, gives the book a dimension unlike many others of the genre.

7. Joan Cassell has written extensively on attitudes toward death in the ICU. A trauma surgeon she interviewed "noted that surgeons talk about foiling the Grim Reaper. The important thing was defeating death and getting the patient out of the hospital, even if to a nursing home. . . . When a patient's death is discussed at the M & M conference, the surgeon is asked if he or she did everything possible to save that patient. The surgeon is *not* asked about the patient's subsequent fate" (2005: 74). Nor are M and M conferences always decorous. Chen describes her experience as a painful but necessary one. Cassell discovered it could also inflame professional egos. "Screaming scenes are not unknown among surgeons, many of whom have the reputation of being prima donnas and who are often described by OR nurses as being 'high strung'" (2005: 75). Given that life and death are on the line every day, high anxiety seems understandable, even if unhelpful.

8. Culturally congruent care can be provided only when patient beliefs and practices are known and appropriately integrated into professional service. A model for that is found in transcultural communication skills, and they have been the focus of much subsequent research (Muñoz and Luckmann 2005). The idea is that nurses, social workers, and chaplains can be effective as transcultural communicators, since in their routine duties they sometimes function as cultural brokers between patients, families, and the various subcultures of the health care institution where they work.

9. Prominent among those reasons are the Tuskegee syphilis experiments, which began in the early 1930s and were ended (with a formal apology from the president and multimillion payouts to survivors) in the 1970s. And like other American institutions before the mid twentieth century, hospitals were generally segregated. While most whites have little or no memory of this, many blacks do. Barrett adds, with considerable emphasis, that the diversity of the African American community is as great as any other and that part of the skill of cross-cultural care is going to the trouble to understand, quite literally, where a patient "is coming from." Variables of class, income, education, religious affiliation, and rural or urban orientation are all relevant and necessary information, as important as a case history of symptoms.

10. One group of researchers suggests a simpler approach. Steinhauser et al. (2006), in their survey of a sample of cancer patients, concluded that gently asking the patient if he or she is "at peace" is better than asking, "What are your religious or spiritual beliefs?" Some patients perceived the latter as a threat to privacy and appropriate boundaries. The authors put it this way: "Physician: I'm wondering how you're doing living with your illness. I sometimes hear people talk about whether or not they're at peace. Do you feel you are at peace in your life right now?" This usually comes when treatment is advanced and the end may be in sight; it avoids unnecessary theological issues, and seems less like a formalized inquiry demanding a reply than an act of relationship building between physician and patient.

11. The study was that of Unruh, Versnel, and Kerr (2002). They use the term "unplugged" to describe this uniquely postmodern way of thinking about spirituality.

Sociologist Peter Berger recognized this years ago in what he called the "homeless mind," and Wade Roof (1993) developed the theme in describing modern church affiliations as stopping off points of spiritual "journeying" rather than "homes" where one lives embedded in a community. So too the more recent works of Cimino and Lattin (1998) and Beaudoin (2003), where choice of faith is much like any other "shopping experience." And in the current fashion, the journeying can be done on one's laptop. Brasher's *Give Me That Online Religion* (2001) calls cyberspace the "Ultimate Diaspora."

12. Harvey Chochinov, a physician, and Beverley Cann, a nurse, compiled an extensive list of styles of spiritual care (2005). They included group and meaning-centered psychotherapy, insight therapy, art, music, visualization, dream interpretation, meditation, life review, forgiveness, reconciliation, and religious expression. Specific interventions included "ongoing dialogue regarding spiritual concerns, however broadly patients may frame or define them" (S-110), including therapeutic touch, aromatherapy, biofeedback, guided imagery, and acupuncture. Trying to simplify this, they developed what they call "Dignity Therapy." They pose "questions that offer an opportunity for patients to address aspects of life that they feel most proud of or that were most meaningful; the personal history that they most want remembered. . . . These sessions are tape recorded, transcribed and edited, and then returned to the patient. This creates a tangible product, a legacy, or generativity document, which in effect allows the patient to leave behind something that will transcend death" (S-111). They say Dignity Therapy is brief, can be practiced at the bedside, and can have useful affects for all concerned.

BIBLIOGRAPHY

Albom, Mitch
    1997   *Tuesdays with Morrie: An Old Man, a Young Man, and Life's Greatest Lesson.*
          New York: Doubleday.

Allen, Thomas B.
    1995   *Offerings at the Wall: Artifacts from the Vietnam Veterans Memorial
          Collection.* Atlanta: Turner Publications.

Alvarado, Carlos S.
    2000   Out-of-Body Experiences. In *Varieties of Anomalous Experience*, ed. Etzel
          Cardena, Stephen Jay Lynn, and Stanley Krippner. Washington, D.C.:
          American Psychological Association.

American Geriatrics Society
    1997   Measuring the Quality of Care at the End of Life: A Statement of
          Principles. *Journal of the American Geriatrics Society* 45: 526–27.

Ammerman, Nancy T.
    1997   Golden Rule Christianity: Lived Religion in the American Mainstream. In
          Lived Religion in America: Toward a History of Practice, ed. David D. Hall.
          Princeton, N.J.: Princeton University Press.

Anderson, Benedict
    1991   *Imagined Communities: Reflections on the Origin and Spread of Nationalism.*
          Rev. ed. London: Verso.

Annas, George
    2005   "Culture of Life" at the Bedside – The Case of Terri Schiavo. *New England
          Journal of Medicine* 352: 1710–15.

Antze, Paul and Michael Lambek
    1996   *Tense Past: Cutural Essays in Trauma and Memory.* New York: Routledge.

Apolito, Paolo
    2005   *The Internet and the Madonna: Religious Visionary Experience on the Web.*
          Chicago: University of Chicago Press.

Appadurai, Arjun
    2002   Disjuncture and Difference in the Global Cultural Economy. In *The
          Anthropology of Globalization: A Reader*, ed. Jonathan Xavier Inda and
          Renato Rosaldo. Oxford: Blackwell.

Ariès, Philippe
    1962   *Centuries of Childhood: A Social History of Family Life.* New York: Vintage.
    1974   *Western Attitudes Toward Death from the Middle Ages to the Present.*
          Baltimore: Johns Hopkins University Press, 1981.
    1981   *The Hour of Our Death.* New York: Vintage.

Arnold, Robert M., Stuart J. Youngner, Renie Schapiro, and Carol Mason Spicer, eds.
    1995   *Procuring Organs for Transplant: The Debate over Non-Heart-Beating
          Cadaver Protocols.* Baltimore: Johns Hopkins University Press.

Atkins, Jeannine
    1999   *A Name on the Quilt: A Story of Remembrance.* New York: Simon and
          Schuster.

Atkinson, David William
  1992 *The English Ars Moriende.* New York: Peter Lang.
Attig, Thomas
  1996 *HowWe Grieve: Relearning the World.* New York: Oxford University Press.
Atwater, P. M. H.
  1994 *Beyond the Light: What Isn't Being Said About Near-Death Experience.* New York: Carol Publication Group.
  1999 *Children of the New Millennium.* New York: Three Rivers Press.
  2003 *The New Children and Near-Death Experiences.* Rochester, Vt.: Bear & Company.
Baldridge, Steven W.
  1992 Granite Mountain Record Vault. *Encyclopedia of Mormonism*, ed. Daniel H. Ludlow. Vol. 2. New York: Macmillan.
Barrett, Ronald K.
  2001 Death and Dying in the Black Experience: An Interview with Ronald K. Barrett, Ph.D. *Innovations in End of Life Care 3*, 5; www.edc.org/lastacts
  2005 Dialogues in Diversity: An Invited Series of Papers, Advance Directives, DNRs, and End of Life Care for African Americans. *Omega 52*, 3: 249–61.
Beaudoin, Tom
  2003 *Consuming Faith, Integrating Who We Are With What We Buy.* Lanham, Md.: Sheed and Ward.
Becker, Ernest
  1973 *The Denial of Death.* New York: Free Press.
Behar, Ruth
  1996 *The Vulnerable Observer: Anthropology That Breaks Your Heart.* Boston: Beacon Press.
Bell, Catherine
  1997 *Ritual: Perspectives and Dimensions.* New York: Oxford University Press.
Bellah, Robert N., Richard Madsen, William M. Sullivan, Ann Swidler, and Steven M. Tipton
  1985 *Habits of the Heart: Individualism and Commitment in American Life.* Berkeley: University of California Press.
Ben-Amos, Dan and Liliane Weissberg, eds.
  1999 *Cultural Memory and the Construction of Identity.* Detroit: Wayne State University Press.
Bennett, Gillian
  1987 *Traditions of Belief: Women, Folklore and the Supernatural Today.* London: Penguin.
  1999 *Alas, Poor Ghost! Traditions of Belief in Story and Discourse.* Logan: Utah State University Press.
Bernardin, Joseph
  1997 *The Gift of Peace.* Chicago: Loyola Press.
Bernstein, Joanne E.
  1983 *Books to Help Children Cope with Separation and Loss.* New York: Bowker.
Bloom, Harold.
  1992 *The American Religion: The Emergence of a Post-Christian Nation.* New York: Touchstone.

Bluebond-Langner, Myra
   1978   *The Private Worlds of Dying Children*. Princeton, N.J.: Princeton University
          Press.
Bodnar, John
   1992   *Remaking America: Public Memory, Commemoration, and Patriotism in the
          Twentieth Century*. Princeton, N.J.: Princeton University Press.
Bostrom, Kathleen Long
   2000   *What About Heaven?* Wheaton, Ill.: Tyndale House.
Bowker, John
   1991   *The Meanings of Death*. Cambridge: Cambridge University Press.
Brasher, Brenda E.
   2001   *Give Me That Online Religion*. San Francisco: Jossey-Bass.
Bregman, Lucy
   2003   *Death and Dying, Spirituality and Religions: A Study of the Death Awareness
          Movement*. New York: Peter Lang.
   2006   Spirituality: A Glowing and Useful Term in Search of a Meaning. *Omega*
          53, 1: 5–26.
Breier-Mackie, Sarah J.
   2005   PEGS and Ethics Revisited: A Timely Reflection in the Wake of the Terri
          Schiavo Case. *Gastroenterological Nursing* 28: 292–97.
Bremmer, Jan N.
   2002   *The Rise and Fall of the Afterlife*. New York: Routledge.
Brooke, John L.
   1994   *The Refiner's Fire: The Making of Mormon Cosmology, 1644–1844*. New
          York: Cambridge University Press.
Brooks, Patricia
   2002   *Where the Bodies Are: Final Visits to the Rich, Famous, and Interesting*.
          Guilford, Conn.: Globe Pequot Press.
Brown, John Gary
   1994   *Soul in the Stone: Cemetery Art From America's Heartland*. Lawrence:
          University Press of Kansas.
Brown, Laurie Krasney and Marc Brown
   1996   *When Dinosaurs Die*. Boston: Little, Brown.
Brown, Peter
   1981   *The Cult of the Saints: Its Rise and Function in Latin Christianity*. Chicago:
          University of Chicago Press.
Brown, Warren S.
   1998   Cognitive Contributions to Soul. In *Whatever Happened to the Soul?* ed.
          Warren S. Brown, Nancy Murphy, and H. Newton Malony. Minneapolis:
          Fortress Press.
Buscaglia, Leo
   1982   *The Fall of Freddie the Leaf: A Story of Life for All Ages*. Thorofare, N.J.:
          C.B. Slack.
Bynum, Caroline Walker
   1992   *Fragmentation and Redemption: Essays on Gender and the Human Body in
          Medieval Religion*. New York: Zone Books.
   1995   *The Resurrection of the Body in Western Christianity, 200–1336*. New York:
          Columbia University Press.

Byock, Ira
  1997   *Dying Well: The Prospect for Growth at the End of Life.* New York: Riverhead
         Books.
Caplan, Arthur L., ed.
  2006   *The Case of Terri Schiavo: Ethics at the End of Life.* Amherst, New York:
         Prometheus Books.
Carlson, Lisa
  1998   *Caring for the Dead: Your Final Act of Love.* Hinsburg, Vt.: Upper Access
         Books.
Cassell, Joan
  2005   *Life and Death in Intensive Care.* Philadelphia: Temple University Press.
Cerminara, Kathy L.
  2006   Theresa Marie Schiavo's Long Road to Peace. *Death Studies* 30: 101–12.
Certeau, Michel de
  1985   What We Do When We Believe. In *On Signs*, ed. Marshall Blonsky.
         Baltimore: Johns Hopkins University Press.
Chen, Pauline W.
  2007   *Final Exam: A Surgeon's Reflections on Mortality.* New York: Knopf.
Cherry, Christopher
  1995   Are Near-Death Experiences Really Suggestive of Life After Death? In
         Beyond Death: Theological and Philosophical Reflections on Life After Death,
         ed. Dan Cohn-Sherbok and Christopher Lewis. New York: St. Martin's.
         145–63.
Chiong, Winston
  2005   Brain Death Without Definitions. *Hastings Center Report* 35: 20–30.
Chochinov, Harvey Max and Beverley J. Cann
  2005   Interventions to Enhance the Spiritual Aspects of Dying. *Journal of
         Palliative Care* 8 (Supplement) 1: S103–5.
Cimino, Richard and Don Lattin
  1998   *Shopping for Faith: American Religion in the New Millennium.* San
         Francisco: Jossey-Bass.
Clark, Emma Chichester
  2003   *Up in Heaven.* New York: Random House.
Clifton, Lucille
  1983   *Everett Anderson's Goodbye.* New York: Henry Holt.
Collison, Gary
  2004   They Bury Horses, Don't They? Unpublished manuscript.
Conkin, Paul K.
  1997   *American Originals: Homemade Varieties of Christianity.* Chapel Hill:
         University of North Carolina Press.
Conniff, Richard
  2003   Dead Lines. *Smithsonian Magazine* 34, 7 (October): 84–90.
Cooey, Paula M.
  1994   *Religious Imagination and the Body: Feminist Analysis.* New York: Oxford
         University Press.
Corcoran, Kevin, ed.
  2001   *Soul, Body, and Survival: Essays on the Metaphysics of Human Persons.*
         Ithaca, N.Y.: Cornell University Press.

Crossan, John Dominic and Jonathan L. Reed
  2004 *In Search of Paul*. San Francisco: Harper.
Cruz, Joan Carroll
  1977 *The Incorruptibles: A Study of the Incorruption of the Bodies of Various Catholic Saints and Beati*. Rockford, Ill.: Tan Books.
Csordas, Thomas
  1994 *Embodiment and Experience: The Existential Ground of Culture and Self*. New York: Cambridge University Press.
D'Andrade, Roy G. and Claudia Strauss
  1992 *Human Motives and Cultural Models*. Cambridge: Cambridge University Press.
Danforth, Loring M.
  1982 *The Death Rituals of Rural Greece*. Princeton, N.J.: Princeton University Press.
Davies, Douglas J.
  2000 *The Mormon Culture of Salvation*. Aldershot: Ashgate.
Dawson, Lorne L. and Douglas E. Cowan
  2004 *Religion Online: Finding Faith on the Internet*. New York: Routledge.
Deetz, James and Edwin N. Dethlefsen
  1967 Death's Head, Cherub, Urn and Willow. *Natural History* 76: 28–37.
Deloria, Vine
  1973 *God Is Red*. New York: Dell.
Desjarlais, Robert R.
  1992 *Body and Emotion: The Aesthetics of Illness and Healing in the Nepal Himalayas*. Philadelphia: University of Pennsylvania Press.
Didion, Joan
  2005 *The Year of Magical Thinking*. New York: Knopf.
Ditto, Peter H.
  2006 What Would Terri Want? On the Psychological Challenges of Surrogate Decision Making. *Death Studies* 30: 135–48.
Durkheim, Émile
  1915 *The Elementary Forms of Religious Life*. London: Allen and Unwin.
Duke, James T.
  1992 Eternal Marriage, *Encyclopedia of Mormonism*, ed. Daniel H. Ludlow. Vol. 2. New York: Macmillan.
Eadie, Betty J.
  1992 *Embraced by the Light*. Placerville, Calif.: Gold Leaf Press.
Eck, Diana L.
  1982 *Banaras, City of Light*. New York: Knopf.
Eliason, Eric A.
  2001 *Mormons and Mormonism: An Introduction to an American World Religion*. Urbana: University of Illinois Press.
Ellis, Jon B. and Jamie E. Stump
  2000 Parents' Perceptions of Their Children's Death Concept. *Death Studies* 24: 65–70.
Ellott, Anthony
  1999 *The Mourning of John Lennon*. Berkeley: University of California Press.

Epstein, Lawrence
    1990   A Comparative View of Tibetan and Western Near-Death Experiences. In *Reflections on Tibetan Culture*, ed. Lawrence Epstein and Richard F. Sherburne. Lewiston, N.Y.: Edwin Mellen Press.

Everett, Holly
    2002   *Roadside Crosses in Contemporary Memorial Culture*. Denton: University of North Texas Press.

Fox, Renée C. and Judith P. Swazey
    1992   *Spare Parts: Organ Replacement in American Society*. New York: Oxford University Press.

Francis, Doris, Leonie Kellaher, and Georgina Neophytou
    2005   *The Secret Cemetery*. Oxford: Berg.

Froggatt, Katherine
    2001   Life and Death in English Nursing Homes: Sequestration or Transition? *Aging and Society* 21: 319–32.

Furnish, Victor Paul
    1999   *The Theology of the First Letter to the Corinthians*. New York: Cambridge University Press.

Furst, Jill and Leslie McKeever
    1995   *The Natural History of the Soul in Ancient Mexico*. New Haven, Conn.: Yale University Press.

Gallup, George, Jr. and D. Michael Lindsay
    1999   *Surveying the Religious Landscape: Trends in U.S. Beliefs*. Harrisburg, Pa.: Morehouse.

Garber, Benjamin
    1995   The Child and Adolescent Literature About the Death of a Parent. *Adolescent Psychiatry* 20: 217–36.

Geertz, Clifford
    1973   *The Interpretation of Cultures*. New York: Basic Books.
    1983   *Local Knowledge: Further Essays in Interpretive Anthropology*. New York: Basic Books.

Gennep, Arnold van
    1960   *Rites of Passage*. Chicago: University of Chicago Press.

Giddens, Anthony
    1992   *Modernity and Self-Identity: Self and Society in the Late Modern Age*. Stanford, Calif.: Stanford University Press.

Gill, T. M. and A. R. Feinstein
    1994   A Critical Appraisal of the Quality of Quality of Life Measurements. *Journal of the American Medical Association* 272: 619–26.

Gillis, John R., ed.
    1994   *Commemorations: The Politics of National Identity*. Princeton, N.J.: Princeton University Press.

Gillman, Neil
    2000   *The Death of Death: Resurrection and Immortality in Jewish Thought*. Woodstock, Vt.: Jewish Lights.

Girgis, Afaf and Rob W. Sanson-Fisher
    1995   Breaking Bad News: Consensus Guidelines for Medical Practitioners. *Journal of Clinical Oncology* 13, 9: 2449–56.

Glaser, Barney G. and Anselm L. Strauss
  1965 *Awareness of Dying.* Chicago: Aldine.
  1968 *A Time for Dying.* Chicago: Aldine.
Goss, Robert E. and Dennis Klass
  2005 *Dead But Not Lost, Grief Narratives in Religious Traditions.* Walnut Creek, Calif.: AltaMira Press.
Gordon, Avery
  1997 *Ghostly Matters: Haunting and the Sociological Imagination.* Minneapolis: University of Minnesota Press.
Gordon, Bruce
  2000 Malevolent Ghosts and Ministering Angels: Apparitions and Pastoral Care in the Swiss Reformation. In *The Place of the Dead: Death and Remembrance in Late Medieval and Early Modern Europe*, ed. Bruce Gordon and Peter Marshall. Cambridge: Cambridge University Press.
Gorer, Geoffrey
  1965 *Death, Grief, and Mourning in Contemporary Britain.* Garden City, N.Y.: Doubleday.
Greeley, Andrew
  2000 *The Catholic Imagination.* Berkeley: University of California Press.
Greeley, Andrew M. and Michael Hout
  1999 Americans' Increasing Belief in Life After Death: Religious Competition and Acculturation. *American Sociological Review* 64: 813–35.
Greenberg, Judith E. and Helen H. Carey
  1986 *Sunny, the Death of a Pet.* New York: Franklin Watts.
Greyson, Bruce
  1983 The Near-Death Experience Scale: Construction, Reliability, and Validity. *Journal of Nervous and Mental Disease* 171: 369–75.
  1997 The Near-Death Experience as a Focus of Clinical Attention. *Journal of Nervous and Mental Disease* 185: 327–34.
  1998 Biological Aspects of Near-Death Experiences. *Perspectives in Biology and Medicine* 42: 14–32.
  2001 Posttraumatic Stress Symptoms Following Near-Death Experiences. *American Journal of Orthopsychiatry* 71: 368–73.
Guroian, Vigen
  1998 *Tending the Heart of Virtue: How Classic Stories Awaken a Child's Moral Imagination.* New York: Oxford University Press.
Guy, Thurman
  1993 Exploratory Study of Elementary-Aged Children's Conceptions of Death Through the Use of Story. *Death Studies* 17: 27–54.
Hacking, Ian
  1990 *The Taming of Chance.* Cambridge: Cambridge University Press.
Hafferty, Frederic W.
  1991 *Into the Valley: Death and the Socialization of Medical Students.* New Haven, Conn.: Yale University Press.
Halbwachs, Maurice
  1992 *On Collective Memory.* Chicago: University of Chicago Press.
Hallam, Elizabeth and Jenny Hockey
  2001 *Death, Memory and Material Culture.* Oxford: Berg.

Hallam, Elizabeth, Jenny Hockey, and Glennys Howarth
   1999   *Beyond the Body: Death and Social Identity*. London: Routledge.
Hansen, Klaus
   1981   *Mormonism and the American Experience*. Chicago: University of Chicago Press.
Harding, Susan
   1987   Convicted by the Holy Spirit: The Rhetoric of Fundamentalist Baptist Conversion. *American Ethnologist* 14: 167–81.
Harley, Brian and Glenn Firebaugh
   1993   Americans' Belief in an Afterlife: Trends over the Past Two Decades. *Journal for the Scientific Study of Religion* 32: 269–78.
Hart, Bethne, Peter Sainsbury, and Stephanie Short
   1998   Whose Dying? A Sociological Critique of the "Good Death." *Mortality* 3: 65–77.
Hecht, Jennifer Michael
   2003   *The End of the Soul: Scientific Modernity, Atheism, and Anthropology in France*. New York: Columbia University Press.
Heilman, Samuel C.
   2001   *When a Jew Dies: The Ethnography of a Bereaved Son*. Berkeley: University of California Press.
Henig, Robin Marantz
   2005   Will We Ever Arrive at the Good Death? *New York Times Magazine*, August 7, 26–68.
Hertz, Robert
   1960   *Death and the Right Hand*. Glencoe, Ill.: Free Press.
Hobsbawm, Eric and Terence Ranger
   1983   *The Invention of Tradition*. Cambridge: Cambridge University Press.
Hockey, Jenny
   1996   Encountering The "Reality of Death" Through Professional Discourses: The Matter of Materiality. *Mortality* 1: 45–60.
Holden, Dwight
   1989   *Gran-Gran's Best Trick: A Story for Children Who Have Lost Someone They Love*. New York: Magination Press.
Holloway, Karla F. C.
   2002   *Passed On: African American Mourning Stories*. Durham, N.C.: Duke University Press.
Hook, C. Christopher and Paul S. Mueller
   2005   The Terri Schiavo Saga: The Making of a Tragedy and the Lessons Learned. *Mayo Clinic Proceedings* 80: 1411–13.
Howe, James and Catherine Stock
   2004   *Kaddish for Grandpa: In Jesus' Name Amen*. New York: Atheneum.
Hughes, Richard T.
   2001   Soaring with the Gods: Early Mormons and the Eclipse of Religious Pluralism. In *Mormons and Mormonism: An Introduction to an American World Religion*, ed. Eric A. Eliason. Urbana: University of Illinois Press.
Hume, Janice
   2000   *Obituaries in American Culture*. Jackson: University Press of Mississippi.

Introvigne, Massimo
  1996   Embraced by the Church? Betty Eadie, Near Death Experiences, and
          Mormonism. *Dialogue: A Journal of Mormon Thought* 29: 99–119.
Iserson, Kenneth V.
  2001   *Death to Dust: What Happens to Dead Bodies?* Tucson, Ariz.: Galen Press.
James, William
  1929   *The Varieties of Religion Experience: A Study in Human Nature.* New York:
          Modern Library.
Jankowiak, William R.
  1993   *Sex, Death, and Hierarchy in a Chinese City.* New York: Columbia
          University Press.
Jocham, H. R., T. Dassen, G. Widdershoven, and R. Halfens
  2006   Quality of Life in Palliative Care Patients: A Literature Review. *Journal of
          Clinical Nursing* 15, 9: 1188–95.
Johnson, Marilyn
  2006   *The Dead Beat. Lost Souls, Lucky Stiffs, and the Perverse Pleasures of
          Obituaries.* New York: HarperCollins.
Johnson, Mary
  2006   Terri Schiavo: A Disability Rights Case. *Death Studies* 30:
          163–76.
Jonsen, Albert R.
  1997   The Birth of Bioethics: The Origins of a Demi-Discipline. *Medical
          Humanities Review* 2: 9–21.
  1998   *The Birth of Bioethics.* New York: Oxford University Press.
Jordan, MaryKate
  1989   *Losing Uncle Tim.* Morton Grove, Ill.: Albert Whitman.
Joslin, Mary
  1998   *The Goodbye Boat.* Grand Rapids, Mich.: Eerdmans.
Judd, Naomi
  2000   *Guardian Angels.* New York: HarperCollins.
Justice, Christopher
  1997   *Dying the Good Death: The Pilgrimage to Die in India's Holy City.* Albany:
          State University of New York Press.
Kaufman, Sharon R.
  2000a   In the Shadow Of "Death with Dignity": Medicine and Cultural Quandaries
          of the Vegetative State. *American Anthropologist* 102: 69–83.
  2000b   Talking Back to The "Culture of Life." *Anthropology News* 46, 5: 34.
  2005   *And a Time to Die: How American Hospitals Shape the End of Life.* New York:
          Scribner.
Kaufman, Sharon R. and Lynn M. Morgan
  2005   The Anthropology of the Beginnings and Ends of Life. *Annual Review of
          Anthropology* 34: 317–42.
Kastenbaum, Robert
  2004   *On Our Way: The Final Passage Through Life and Death.* Berkeley:
          University of California Press.
Kear, Adrian and Deborah Lynn Steinberg, eds.
  1999   *Mourning Diana.* London: Routledge.

Keesing, Roger M.
  1982 *Kwaio Religion: The Living and the Dead in a Solomon Island Society*. New York: Columbia University Press.
Kellehear, Allan
  1993 Culture, Biology, and the Near-Death Experience: A Reappraisal. *Journal of Nervous and Mental Disease* 181: 148–56.
  1996 *Experiences Near Death*. New York: Oxford University Press.
Keller, Holly
  1987 *Goodbye, Max*. New York: William Morrow.
Keyes, Charles F.
  1987 From Birth to Death: Ritual Process and Buddhist Meanings in Northern Thailand. *Folk* 29: 181–206.
Kirshenblatt-Gimblett, Barbara
  1996 The Electronic Vernacular. In *Connected: Engagement with Media*, ed. George E. Marcus. Chicago: University of Chicago Press.
Klass, Dennis, Phyllis R. Silverman and Steven L. Nickman, eds.
  1996 *Continuing Bonds, New Understandings of Grief*. Philadelphia: Taylor and Francis.
Kleespies, Phillip M.
  2004 *Life and Death Decisions, Psychological and Ethical Considerations in End-of-Life Care*. Washington, D.C.: American Psychological Association.
Kleinman, Arthur, Veena Das, and Margaret Lock, eds.
  1997 *Social Suffering*. Berkeley: University of California Press.
Kline, Stephen
  1998 The Making of Children's Culture. In *The Children's Culture Reader*, ed. Henry Jenkins. New York: New York University Press. 95–109.
Knipe, David M.
  2003 When a Wife Dies First: The *Musivayanam* and a Female Brahman Ritualist in Coastal Andhra. In *The Living and the Dead: Social Dimensions of Death in South Asian Religions*, ed. Liz Wilson. Albany: State University of New York Press.
Kübler-Ross, Elisabeth
  1969 *On Death and Dying*. New York: Touchstone.
  1975 *Death: The Final Stage of Growth*. New York: Simon and Schuster.
  1983 *On Children and Death*. New York: Macmillan.
Kugel, James L.
  1997 *The Bible as It Was*. Cambridge, Mass.: Harvard University Press.
Kuper, Adam
  1999 *Culture: The Anthropologists' Account*. Cambridge, Mass.: Harvard University Press.
Lachman, Gary
  2004 Heavens and Hells: The Inner Worlds of Emanuel Swedenborg. In *The Inner West: An Introduction to the Hidden Wisdom of the West*, ed. Jay Kinney. New York: Tarcher/Penguin.
Laderman, Gary
  1996 *The Sacred Remains: American Attitudes Toward Death, 1799–1883*. New Haven, Conn.: Yale University Press.
  2003 *Rest in Peace: A Cultural History of Death and the Funeral Home in Twentieth-Century America*. Oxford: Oxford University Press.

Lamars, Elisabeth P.
   1995   Children, Death, and Fairy Tales. *Omega* 31, 2: 151–67.
Lambek, Michael
   1996   The Past Imperfect: Remembering as a Moral Practice. In *Tense Past: Cultural Essays in Trauma and Memory*, ed. Paul Antze and Michael Lambek. New York: Routledge.
   2000   The Anthropology of Religion and the Quarrel Between Poetry and Philosophy. *Current Anthropology* 41, 3: 309–20.
   2002   *The Weight of the Past: Living with History in Mahajanga, Madagascar*. New York: Palgrave.
Lane, Belden C.
   2001   *Landscapes of the Sacred, Geography and Narrative in American Spirituality*. Baltimore: Johns Hopkins University Press.
Lawton, Julia
   2000   *The Dying Process: Patients' Experiences with Palliative Care*. New York: Routledge.
Lesy, Michael
   1973   *Wisconsin Death Trip*. Albuquerque: University of New Mexico Press.
Lewis, C. S.
   1961   *A Grief Observed*. New York: Bantam Books.
Libby, Larry
   1993   *Someday Heaven*. Sisters, Ore.: Questar.
Lincoln, Bruce
   1999   *Theorizing Myth: Narrative, Ideology, and Scholarship*. Chicago: University of Chicago Press.
   2003   *Holy Terrors: Thinking About Religion After September 11*. Chicago: University of Chicago Press.
Lock, Margaret M.
   1993   Cultivating the Body: Anthropology and Epistemologies of Bodily Practice and Knowledge. *Annual Review of Anthropology* 22 (ed. W. H. Durham): Palo Alto, Calif., Annual Reviews. 133–55.
   1996   Organ Recovery: Making Death Useful. *Medical Humanities Review* 10, 1: 51–55.
   1999   The Problem of Brain Death: Japanese Disputes About Bodies and Modernity. In *The Definition of Death: Contemporary Controversies*, ed. Stuart J. Youngner, Robert M. Arnold, and Renie Schapiro. Baltimore: Johns Hopkins University Press. 239–36
   2002   *Twice Dead: Organ Transplants and the Reinvention of Death*. Berkeley: University of California Press.
Lofland, Lyn H.
   1978   *The Craft of Dying: The Modern Face of Death*. London: Sage.
Ludlow, Daniel, ed.
   1992   *Encyclopedia of Mormonism*. New York: Macmillan.
Lutz, Katherine
   1988   *Unnatural Emotions: Everyday Sentiments on a Micronesian Atoll and Their Challenge to Western Theory*. Chicago: University of Chicago Press.
Lynch, Thomas
   1997   *The Undertaking: Life Studies from the Dismal Trade*. New York: W.W. Norton.
   2000   *Bodies in Motion and at Rest: Essays*. New York: W.W. Norton.

Lyon, David
    2000   *Jesus in Disneyland.* Oxford: Polity Press/Blackwell.

MacCannell, Dean
    1992   *Empty Meeting Grounds: The Tourist Papers.* London: Routledge.

Macpherson, Catriona and Cathy Cooke
    2003   Pilot of a Workbook for Children Visiting a Loved One in a Hospice. *International Journal of Palliative Nursing* 9: 397–403.

Martin, Dale B.
    1995   *The Corinthian Body.* New Haven, Conn.: Yale University Press.

Mauss, Marcel
    1967   *The Gift: Forms and Functions of Exchange in Archaic Societies.* New York: W.W. Norton.

McConkie, Bruce R.
    1958   *Mormon Doctrine.* Salt Lake City: Bookcraft.

McDannell, Colleen and Bernhard Lang
    1988   *Heaven, a History.* New Haven, Conn.: Yale University Press.

McGrath, Alister
    2004   *The Twilight of Atheism.* New York: Doubleday.

Meier, John P.
    2000   The Debate on the Resurrection of the Dead: An Incident from the Ministry of the Historical Jesus? *Journal for the Study of the New Testament* 77: 3–24.

Mejia, Rodrigo and Murray M. Pollack
    1995   Variability in Brain Death Determination Practices in Children. *Journal of the American Medical Association* 274, 7: 550–53.

Metcalf, Peter and Richard Huntington
    1991   *Celebrations of Death: The Anthropology of Mortuary Ritual.* Cambridge: Cambridge University Press.

Meyer, Richard E.
    1992   *Cemeteries and Gravemarkers: Voices of American Culture.* Logan: Utah State University Press.

Michaelowski, Raymond and Jill Dubisch
    2001   *Run for the Wall: Remembering Vietnam on a Motorcycle Pilgrimage.* New Brunswick, N.J.: Rutgers University Press.

Mills, Joyce C.
    1993   *Gentle Willow: A Story for Children About Dying.* Washington, D.C.: Magination Press.

Mims, Cedric
    1999   *When We Die: The Science, Culture, and Rituals of Death.* New York: St. Martin's Press.

Mitchell, D. L., M. J. Bennett, and L. Manfrin-Ledet
    2006   Spiritual Development of Nursing Students: Developing Competence to Provide Spiritual Care to Patients at the End of Life. *Journal of Nursing Education* 45, 9: 365–70.

Mitford, Jessica
    1963   *The American Way of Death.* New York: Simon and Schuster
    1998   *The American Way of Death Revisited.* New York: Knopf.

Moody, Raymond
    2001   *Life After Life: The Investigation of a Phenomenon—Survival of Bodily Death.*
        New York: HarperCollins.

Moore, Timothy E. and Reet Mae
    1987   Who Dies and Who Cries: Death and Bereavement in Children's
        Literature. *Journal of Communications* 37, 4: 52–64.

Morgan, David
    1998   *Visual Piety: A History and Theory of Popular Religious Images.* Berkeley:
        University of California Press.

Morris, Richard
    1997   *Sinners, Lovers, and Heroes: An Essay on Memorializing in Three American
        Cultures.* Albany: State University of New York Press.

Morse, Melvin L.
    1994   Near-Death Experiences and Death-Related Visions in Children:
        Implications for the Clinician. *Current Problems in Pediatrics* 24: 55–83.
    2000   *Where God Lives.* New York: HarperCollins.

Muñoz, Cora and Joan Luckmann
    2005   *Transcultural Communication in Nursing.* Clifton Park, N.Y.: Thomson.

Narayanasamy, Aru
    2002   The ACCESS Model: a Transcultural Nursing Practice Framework. *British
        Journal of Nursing* 11:643–50.
    2006   The Impact of Empirical Studies of Spirituality and Culture on Nurse
        Education. *Journal of Clinical Nursing* 15, 7: 840–51.

Narayanasamy, Aru and Jan Owens
    2001   A Critical Incident Study of Nurses' Responses to the Spiritual Needs of
        Their Patients. *Journal of Advanced Nursing* 33: 446–55.

Newman, Lesléa
    1995   *Too Far Away to Touch.* New York: Houghton Mifflin.

Nickel, Dawn Dorothy
    2005   Dying in the West: Health Care Policies and Caregiving Practices in
        Montana and Alberta, 1880–1950. Ph.D. dissertation, Department of
        History, University of Alberta.

Nuland, Sherwin B.
    1993   *How We Die: Reflections on Life's Final Chapter.* New York: Knopf.

Orsi, Robert A.
    1997   Everyday Miracles: The Study of Lived Religion. In *Lived Religion in
        America: Toward a History of Practice,* ed. David D. Hall. Princeton, N.J.:
        Princeton University Press.
    2005   *Between Heaven and Earth: The Religious Worlds People Make and the
        Scholars Who Study Them.* Princeton, N.J.: Princeton University Press.

Osmond, Rosalie
    2003   *Imagining the Soul: A History.* Phoenix Mill, UK: Sutton.

Owens, Lance S.
    1994   Joseph Smith and Kabbalah: The Occult Connection. *Dialogue, a Journal
        of Mormon Thought* 27: 117–94.

Pagels, Elaine
    1988   *Adam, Eve, and the Serpent.* New York: Random House.
    2003   *Beyond Belief: The Secret Gospel of Thomas.* New York: Random House.

Panourgiá, Neni
  1995   *Fragments of Death, Fables of Identity: An Athenian Anthropography*.
          Madison: University of Wisconsin Press.
Parry, Jonathan P.
  1994   *Death in Banaras*. Cambridge: Cambridge University Press.
  2004   Sacrificial Death and the Necrophagous Ascetic. In *Death, Mourning, and
          Burial: A Cross-Cultural Reader*, ed. Antonius C. G.M. Robben. Oxford:
          Blackwell.
Parry, Joshua E., Larry R. Churchill, and Howard S. Kirshner
  2005   The Terri Schiavo Case: Legal, Ethical, and Medical Perspectives. *Annals of
          Internal Medicine* 143: 744–48.
Paterson, Katherine
  2000   Why Do You Write for Children? *Theology Today* 56: 569–76.
Paul, Alexander
  1996   *Suicide Wall*. Portland, Ore.: PakDonald Publishing.
Paul, Erich Robert
  1992   *Science, Religion, and Mormon Cosmology*. Urbana: University of Illinois
          Press.
Pearson, Mike Parker
  1999   *The Archaeology of Death and Burial*. College Station: Texas A&M
          University Press.
Pellegrino, Marjorie White
  1999   *I Don't Have an Uncle Phil Anymore*. Washington, D.C.: Magination Press.
Porterfield, Amanda
  2001   *The Transformation of American Religion: The Story of a Late-Twentieth-
          Century Awakening*. Oxford: Oxford University Press.
Power, Dale
  1997   *Do-It-Yourself Coffins for Pets and People*. Atglen, Pa.: Schiffer.
Powner, David J., Bruce M. Ackerman, and Ake Grenvik
  1996   Medical Diagnosis of Death in Adults: Historical Contributions to Current
          Controversies. *The Lancet* 348, 9036: 1219–24.
President's Commission for the Study of Ethical Problems in Medicine and
          Biomedical and Behavioral Research
  1981   *Defining Death: A Report on the Medical, Legal, and Ethical Issues in the
          Definition of Death*. Washington, D.C.: U.S. Government Printing Office.
Preston, Tom and Michael Kelly
  2006   A Medical Ethics Assessment of the Case of Terri Schiavo. *Death Studies*
          30: 121–33.
Prior, Lindsay
  1989   *The Social Organization of Death: Medical Practice and Social Practices in
          Belfast*. New York: St. Martin's Press.
Prothero, Stephen
  1997   Lived Religion and the Dead: The Cremation Movement in Gilded Age
          America. In *Lived Religion in America: Toward a History of Practice*, ed.
          David D. Hall. Princeton, N.J.: Princeton University Press. 92–115.
  2001   *Purified by Fire: A History of Cremation in America*. Berkeley: University of
          California Press.

Pyszcznski, T., J. Greenberg, and S. Solomon
    1999   A Dual-Process Model of Defense Against Conscious and Unconscious Death-Related Thoughts: An Extension of Terror Management Theory. *Psychological Review* 106: 835–45.

Quill, Timothy E.
    1996   *A Midwife Through the Dying Process: Stories of Healing and Hard Choices at the End of Life.* Baltimore: Johns Hopkins University Press.
    2001   *Caring for Patients at the End of Life: Facing an Uncertain Future Together.* New York: Oxford University Press.
    2005   Terri Schiavo—A Tragedy Compounded. *New England Journal of Medicine* 352: 1630–133.

Raspberry, Salli and Carole Rae Watanabe
    2001   *The Art of Dying: Honoring and Celebrating Life's Passages.* Berkeley, Calif.: Celestialarts.

Reynolds, Frank E. and Earle H. Waugh, eds.
    1977   *Religious Encounters with Death: Insights from the History and Anthropology of Religions.* University Park: Pennsylvania State University Press.

Roach, Mary
    2003   *Stiff: The Curious Lives of Human Cadavers.* New York: W.W. Norton.

Rogers, Fred
    1988   *When a Pet Dies.* New York: Putnam.

Romanowski, William D.
    2000   Evangelicals and Popular Music. In *Religion and Popular Culture in America*, ed. Bruce David Forbes and Jeffrey H. Mahan. Berkeley: University of California Press.

Roof, Wade Clark
    1993   *A Generation of Seekers: The Spiritual Journeys of the Baby Boom Generation.* San Francisco: Harper.

Roscoe, Lori A., Hana Osman, and William E. Haley
    2006   Implications of the Schiavo Case for Understanding Family Caregiving Issues at the End of Life. *Death Studies* 30: 149–61.

Ruby, Jay
    1995   *Secure the Shadow: Death and Photography in America.* Cambridge, Mass.: MIT Press.

Sacks, Jonathan
    2003   *The Dignity of Difference: How to Avoid the Clash of Civilizations.* London: Continuum.

Sahlins, Marshall
    1996   The Sadness of Sweetness: The Native Anthropology of Western Cosmology. *Current Anthropology* 37, 3: 395–414.

Sanford, Doris and Graci Evans
    1986   *It Must Hurt a Lot.* Hong Kong: Questar.

Sasso, Sandy Eisenberg
    1999   *For Heaven's Sake.* Woodstock, Vt.: Jewish Lights.

Scheper-Hughes, Nancy and Margaret M. Lock
    1987   The Mindful Body: A Prolegomenon to Future Work in Medical Anthropology. *Medical Anthropology Quarterly* 1, 1: 6–41.

Scheper-Hughes, Nancy and Carolyn Sargent
    1998   *Small Wars: The Cultural Politics of Childhood*. Berkeley: University of California Press.

Schmidt, Leigh Eric
    1995   *Consumer Rites: The Buying and Selling of American Holidays*. Princeton, N.J.: Princeton University Press.
    1997   Practices of Exchange: From Market Culture to Gift Economy in the Interpretation of American Religion. In *Lived Religion in America: Toward a History of Practice*, ed. David D. Hall. Princeton, N.J.: Princeton University Press.

Schmitt, Jean-Claude
    1998   *Ghosts in the Middle Ages, the Living and the Dead in Medieval Society*. Chicago: University of Chicago Press.

Seale, Clive
    1998 *Constructing Death: The Sociology of Dying and Bereavement*. New York: Cambridge University Press.

Seremetakis, C. Nadia
    1991   *The Last Word: Women, Death and Divination in Inner Mani*. Chicago: University of Chicago Press.

Sharp, Leslie A.
    1995   Organ Transplantation as a Transformative Experience: Anthropological Insights into the Restructuring of the Self. *Medical Anthropology Quarterly* 9: 357–89.

Siegel, Marvin, ed.
    1997   *The Last Word: The New York Times Book of Obituaries and Farewells: A Celebration of Unusual Lives*. New York: William Morrow.

Silverman, Phyllis Rolfe
    2000   *Never too Young to Know: Death in Children's Lives*. Oxford: Oxford University Press.

Silverman, Phyllis R. and Dennis Klass
    1996   Introduction: What's the Problem? In *Continuing Bonds: New Understandings of Grief*, ed. Dennis Klass, Phyllis R. Silverman, and Steven L. Nickman. Washington, D.C.: Taylor and Francis. 3–27.

Singer, Mark
    2002   The Death Beat. *New Yorker* (August 7, 2002).

Sloane, David Charles
    1991   *The Last Great Necessity: Cemeteries in American History*. Baltimore: Johns Hopkins University Press.

Smith, Joseph Fielding
    1965   *Man: His Origin and Destiny*. Salt Lake City: Deseret Books.

Sproul, Barbara C.
    1979   *Primal Myths: Creating the World*. New York: HarperCollins.

Sque, Magi, Sheila Payne, and Jill Macleod Clark.
    2006   Gift of Life or Sacrifice? Key Discourses to Understanding Donor Families' Decision-Making. *Mortality* 11: 117–32.

Stanton, Scott
    1998   *The Tombstone Tourist: Musicians*. Portland, Ore.: 3T Publishing.

Starck, Nigel
  2001 Capturing Life—Not Death: A Case for Burying the Posthumous Parallax. *Text* 5 (October).
  2005 Posthumous Parallel and Parallax: The Obituary Revival on Three Continents. *Journalism Studies* 6: 267–83.
Stark, Rodney and William Sims Bainbridge
  1985 *The Future of Religion: Secularization, Revival, and Cult Formation.* Berkeley: University of California Press.
Stark, Rodney and Roger Finke
  2000 *Acts of Faith: Explaining the Human Side of Religion.* Berkeley: University of California Press.
Steinhauser, K. E., C. I. Voils, E. C. Clipp, H. B. Bosworth, and N. A. Christakis
  2006 "Are You at Peace?" One Item to Probe Spiritual Concerns at the End of Life. *Archives of Internal Medicine* 166, 1: 101–5.
Stern, Julian and Sarah James
  2006 Every Person Matters: Enabling Spiritual Education for Nurses. *Journal of Clinical Nursing* 15, 7: 897–904.
Sturkin, Marita
  1997 *Tangled Memories: The Vietnam War, the AIDS Epidemic, and the Politics of Remembering.* Berkeley: University of California Press.
  2004 The Aesthetics of Absence: Rebuilding Ground Zero. *American Ethnologist* 31, 3: 311–25.
Sudnow, David
  1967 *On Passing: The Social Organization of Dying.* Englewood Cliffs, N.J.: Prentice-Hall.
Suzuki, Hikaru
  2000 *The Price of Death: The Funeral Industry in Contemporary Japan.* Stanford, Calif.: Stanford University Press.
Swedenborg, Emanuel
  1965 [1758] *Heaven and Its Wonders and Hell.* New York: Citadel Press.
Thomas, Jane Resh
  1988 *Saying Good-Bye to Grandma.* New York: Houghton Mifflin.
Thomas, Robert McG., Jr.
  2001 *52 McGs: The Best Obituaries from Legendary New York Times Writer Robert McG. Thomas, Jr.* New York: Citadel Press.
Thompson, Becky W.
  1994 *A Hunger So Wide and So Deep: American Women Speak Out on Eating Problems.* Minneapolis: University of Minnesota Press.
Thoreau, Henry David
  1937 *Walden and Other Writings of Henry David Thoreau,* Brooks Atkinson, ed. New York: Modern Library.
Townsend, Maryann and Ronnie Stern
  1980 *Pop's Secret.* Reading, Mass.: Addison-Wesley.
Traube, Elizabeth G.
  1996 "The Popular" In American Culture. *Annual Review of Anthropology* 25: 127–51.
Troyer, John
  2007 Embalmed Vision. *Mortality* 12: 22–47.

Turner, Victor
    1968   *The Drums of Affliction: A Study of Ritual Processes Among the Ndembu of Zambia*. Oxford: Clarendon Press.
    1969   *The Ritual Process*. Chicago: Aldine.
Unruh, Anita M., Joan Versnel, and Natasha Kerr
    2002   Spirituality Unplugged: A Review of Commonalities and Contentions, and a Resolution. *Canadian Journal of Occupational Therapy* 69: 5–19.
Van den Berg, Marinus
    1994   *The Three Birds: A Story for Children About the Loss of a Loved One*. New York: Magination Press.
Van Der Zee, James, Owen Dodson, and Camille Billops
    1978   *The Harlem Book of the Dead*. Dobbs Ferry, N.Y.: Morgan and Morgan.
Van Lommel, Pim, Ruud Van Wees, Vincent Meyers, and Ingrid Elfferich
    2001   Near Death Experience in Survivors of Cardiac Arrest: A Prospective Study in the Netherlands. *The Lancet* 358: 2039–45.
Varley, Susan
    1984   *Badger's Parting Gifts*. New York: William Morrow.
Veatch, Robert M.
    1999   The Conscience Clause: How Much Individual Choice in Defining Death Can Our Society Tolerate? In *The Definition of Death: Contemporary Controversies*, ed. Stuart J. Younger. Baltimore: Johns Hopkins University Press.
    2005   Terri Schiavo, Son Hudson and "Nonbeneficial" Medical Treatments. *Health Affairs* 24: 976–79.
Veatch, Robert M. and Tom L. Beauchamp
    1996   *Ethical Issues in Death and Dying*. Upper Saddle River, N.J.: Prentice-Hall.
Verdery, Katherine
    1999   *The Political Lives of Dead Bodies: Reburial and Postsocialist Changes*. New York: Columbia University Press.
Vigna, Judith
    1991   *Saying Goodbye to Daddy*. Morton Grove, Ill.: Albert Whitman.
Viorst, Judith
    1971   *The Tenth Good Thing About Barney*. New York: Simon and Schuster.
Vitebsky, Piers
    1992   *Dialogues with the Dead: The Discussion of Mortality Among the Sora of Eastern India*. New Delhi: Cambridge University Press.
Waldman, Diane
    2006   Schiavo Videos: Context and Reception, Timely Triage. *Jump Cut: A Review of Contemporary Media* 48: 1–6.
Walter, Tony
    1996   *The Eclipse of Eternity, A Sociology of the Afterlife*. New York: St. Martin's Press.
    1999a   *On Bereavement: The Culture of Grief*. Buckingham: Open University Press.
    1999b   (ed.). *The Mourning for Diana*. Oxford: Berg.
    2002   Spirituality in Palliative Care: Opportunity or Burden? *Palliative Medicine* 16: 133–39.

Webb, Marilyn
  1997   *The Good Death: The New American Search to Reshape the End of Life.* New
         York: Bantam Books.
Welker, Michael
  2000   Resurrection and Eternal Life. In *The End of the World and the Ends of God:
         Science and Theology on Eschatology*, ed. John Polkinghorne and Michael
         Welker. Harrisburg, Pa.: Trinity Press International.
White, David Gordon
  2003   Ashes to Nectar: Death and Regeneration Among the *Rasa Siddhas* and
         Nath Siddhas. In *The Living and the Dead: Social Dimensions of Death in
         South Asian Religions*, ed. Liz Wilson. Albany: State University of New
         York Press.
White, Stephen
  1997   Hindu Cremations in Britain. In *The Changing Face of Death: Historical
         Accounts of Death and Disposal*, ed. Peter C. Jupp and Glennys Howarth.
         New York: St. Martin's Press.
Williams, A. L.
  2006   Perspectives on Spirituality at the End of Life: A Meta-Summary. *Palliative
         Support Care* 4, 4: 407–17.
Wills, Garry
  1992   *Lincoln at Gettysburg: The Words That Remade America.* New York: Simon
         and Schuster.
Wright, Roberta Hughes and Wilber B. Hughes, III
  1996   *Lay Body Down: Living History in African American Cemeteries.* Detroit:
         Visible Ink Press.
Wuthnow, Robert
  1998   *After Heaven: Spirituality in America Since the 1950s.* Berkeley: University
         of California Press.
Youngner, Stuart J., Robert M. Arnold, and Renie Schapiro
  1999   *The Definition of Death: Contemporary Controversies.* Baltimore: Johns
         Hopkins University Press.
Youngner, Stuart J., C. Seth Landefeld, Claudia J. Coulton, Barbara W. Juknialis, and
     Mark Leary
  1989   "Brain Death" and Organ Retrieval. *Journal of the American Medical
         Association* 261, 15: 2205–10.
Zaleski, Carol
  1986   *Otherworld Journeys: Accounts of Near-Death Experience in Medieval and
         Modern Times.* New York: Oxford University Press.
Zaleski, Carol and Philip Zaleski, eds.
  2000   *The Book of Heaven: An Anthology of Writings from Ancient to Modern Times.*
         New York: Oxford University Press.
Zelizer, Viviana
  1985   *Pricing the Priceless Child: The Changing Social Value of Children.*
         Princeton, N.J.: Princeton University Press.

INDEX

ACKNOWLEDGMENTS

This book was inspired by a 1998 National Endowment for the Humanities Summer Seminar hosted by David and Sheila Rothman at Columbia University. In addition, a grant from the Walter Chapin Simpson Center for the Humanities at the University of Washington helped get the project started. For the feedback every writer needs, my thanks to those who read portions of the manuscript and gave advice on what to say and how to say it better. They include Erik Seeman at SUNY Buffalo; Dawn Nickel, then at the University of Alberta; and Tom Murphy, Edmonds Community College near Seattle. Sharon L. Mnich of Virtual-Memorials.com explained what goes on behind the home-pages of online memorials. June Carswell, Director of the Carlisle, UK, cemetery where ecologically friendly burial practices began, generously and literally walked me through the history of that fascinating place. Denise Glover created the index in her always competent way and I am grateful to her, as well as to John Mericle and Carol Green who patiently helped with the proof reading. Jacob Fisher provided critical help with computerizing the bibliography. Paysha Stockton was heroic, reading most of the manuscript and correcting my lapses with great tact. Every writer should have a former student, now a professional journalist, as enthusiastic and helpful as she. My thanks too to editors Peter Agree who welcomed the manuscript despite its delayed arrival, to Alison Anderson who saw it through production, and to the anonymous reader whose helpful comments were generously given.

I am most appreciative that David Linn volunteered his painting, Similitude #2, for the book cover. Raman Frey of the Frey Norris Gallery in San Francisco kindly got us together. Mr. Linn's impressive work is at http://www.davidlinn.com.

As is true of anyone who teaches, I have met a lot of exceptional students who filled my classes on the comparative study of death, and they helped make it my favorite course. Just as important, I was very lucky to have two outstanding mentors, although they may wonder how their student came to write a book on a topic like this. I have great affection for Harold P. Simonson, University of Puget Sound, and Erika Bourguignon, Ohio State University. Finally, a very special thank you to Carol, who for years cheerfully shared with me this admittedly peculiar fascination. Fish and chips late on a summer night in the Keswick, Cumbria, church cemetery is our idea of fun.

If you have comments write me at jwgreen@u.washington.edu. I would be pleased to hear from you.